TRAVELS
INTO
POLAND

William Coxe

ARNO PRESS & THE NEW YORK TIMES
New York · 1971

Reprint Edition 1971 by Arno Press Inc.

Reprinted from a copy in
The New York Public Library

LC# 76-135802

ISBN 0-405-02744-3

The Eastern Europe Collection

ISBN for complete set: 0-405-02730-3

Manufactured in the United States of America

Publisher's Note: Travels into Poland was the only section reprinted from the original three volume edition of Travels into
Poland, Russia, Sweden and Denmark.

TRAVELS

INTO

POLAND, RUSSIA, SWEDEN,

AND

DENMARK.

INTERSPERSED WITH HISTORICAL RELATIONS
AND POLITICAL INQUIRIES.

ILLUSTRATED WITH CHARTS AND ENGRAVINGS.

By WILLIAM COXE, A. M. F. R. S.

FELLOW OF KING'S COLLEGE, CAMBRIDGE; AND CHAPLAIN TO
HIS GRACE THE DUKE OF MARLBOROUGH.

IN TWO VOLUMES.

THE SECOND EDITION.

VOLUME THE FIRST.

LONDON:

PRINTED FOR T. CADELL, IN THE STRAND.
MDCCLXXXV.

Right Honourable Lord HERBERT.

MY LORD,

AS the advantages which I enjoyed from accompanying your Lordfhip upon your travels enabled me to collect the materials for the following work, it cannot be infcribed to any other perfon with fo much propriety as to your Lordfhip. You, I flatter myfelf, will recollect with pleafure the refult of thofe inquiries to which you were particularly attentive; and I am happy in this publick opportunity of expreffing the grateful fenfe which I entertain of being honoured with your Lordfhip's friendfhip; and of declaring the fincere regard and attachment with which I am,

MY LORD,

Your Lordfhip's moft faithful

And obedient fervant,

WILLIAM COXE.

King's College, Cambridge,
April 2, 1784.

P R E F A C E.

THE following pages contain the refult of that intelligence which I collected, and thofe obfervations which occurred, during my travels through the Northern kingdoms of Europe; and it is neceffary to apprize the reader upon what foundation the principal facts are fupported.

In regard to Poland, I was honoured with information from perfons of the higheft rank and authority; and fortunately obtained poffeffion of fome original letters written from Warfaw, before and during the Partition, which have enabled me to throw a confiderable light over that interefting period. I prefume, therefore, that the account of Poland comprehends many particulars which have not been hitherto prefented to the publick.

With refpect to Ruffia, as the Emprefs herfelf deigned to anfwer fome queries relative to the ftate of the publick prifons *; this gracious condefcenfion in fo great a fovereign could not but facilitate my further inquiries.

To this I muft add, that the late celebrated hiftorian †, Mr. Muller, favoured me with various communications on fome of the moft important and intricate parts of the Ruffian annals, and pointed out to me the moft approved writers on this empire.

The nature of the Swedifh government rendered the fources of information eafy of accefs; and, fince my return to England, feveral

---

* See Vol. II. p. 76.

† Mr. Muller died in the latter end of 1783. The Emprefs, who, in confideration of his great merit, had honoured him with the order of St. Vladimir, has, in refpect to his memory, conferred a penfion on his widow, and ennobled his fon.

2

Swedifh

Swedifh gentlemen, well verfed in the conftitution of their country, have fupplied much additional intelligence.

As the materials which I acquired in Denmark were lefs extenfive than thofe collected in the other parts, the account of that kingdom is confined to thofe circumftances which I was able to afcertain, it having been my invariable refolution never to adopt uncertain accounts, but to adhere folely to thofe facts which appeared to me to be derived from the moft unqueftionable authorities.

In the hiftorical relations I have had recourfe to many Englifh and foreign authors, and particularly feveral German writers of unimpeached veracity, who were refident for a confiderable time in fome of the Northern kingdoms, and from whom I have drawn many anecdotes not known to the Englifh reader.

Throughout this work I have fcrupuloufly cited the authors whom I have confulted, and have fubjoined in the Appendix to the firft volume a lift of the principal books employed on this occafion, with an explanation of the references by which they are diftinguifhed.

I cannot clofe this preface without expreffing my obligations to Mr. Wraxall, Mr. Pennant, and Dr. Pulteney, for their refpective affiftance, acknowledged in the courfe of the work. Colonel Floyd alfo claims my fincereft thanks for communicating his accurate Journal of our Tour, to whofe obfervations and defcriptions, befide the extracts in the following pages, I gratefully confefs myfelf indebted for many interefting particulars.

CON-

CONTENTS of VOLUME I.

CONTENTS.

BOOK III.

TRAVELS into RUSSIA.

BOOK

T R A V E L S

I N T O

P O L A N D.

HISTORY AND GOVERNMENT OF POLAND.

B O O K I.

C H A P. I.

Researches into the origin and progress of the Polish *government.
—An inquiry into the causes of the gradual diminution of royal
prerogative, and establishment of a monarchy wholly elective.—
Licentious power and conduct of the nobles.—Bad effects of aris-
tocratical authority.*

IT is a matter of extreme difficulty to investigate in any country the origin and progress of its constitution ; as well because the beginning of all histories is involved in obscurity and
fable ; as because that body of laws and usages, which forms
the essence of every government, is not created at once, in any
particular period, or by a single event, but generally results
from a series of circumstances, many of them scarce separately

· B discernible.

discernible. In Poland, however, the political observer has this singular advantage, that a succession of accurate historians * (some of whom flourished soon after the æra when the most important branches of the Polish constitution were ascertained) have developed with uncommon precision and care the various occurrences and institutions, from which the extraordinary form of government, at present subsisting in that kingdom, was gradually derived. By means of their authentic narratives we are enabled to trace, in what manner, and from what concurrence of circumstances, a monarchy nearly absolute, sunk in the course of a few centuries, without any deposition of the prince or violent convulsion, into a state of almost total aristocracy.

A brief inquiry into the principal incidents which produced this remarkable constitution, accompanied by such political reflexions as the progress of the detail suggests, will not, I flatter myself, prove uninteresting; and will properly introduce a view of Poland in its present state.

The sovereigns of Poland are usually ranged into four classes. I. Of the house of Lesko. II. Of Piast. III. Of Jaghellon. IV. Of different families. These classes divide the history of Poland into four corresponding periods.

I. The first † period is allowed by the best Polish historians to be entirely fabulous; they therefore generally commence their narratives at the second æra.

II. The earliest part even of this second epoch has an air of

---

* Dlugossius, the father of Polish history, was born in 1415, only 45 years after the demise of Casimir the Great, from whose reign Poland dates her written laws. He begins his history from the earliest period of the Polish annals, and carries it down to the year 1480.

† Quæ de Lecho ejusque successoribus ad Piastum usque et ultra memorantur, sunt obscura, fabulosa, et falsa, quare silentio transmittimur, ne variis narrationibus immoremur; are the words of Lengnich, Hist. Polon. p. 2. The fabulous story of Lesko is as follows: Upon the death of Lesko I. duke of Poland, a race was appointed on horseback, and the victor was to be nominated sovereign. Lefzec, one of the candidates, in order to secure the victory, strewed part of the course with nails, leaving a clear passage for his own horse. This stratagem was discovered by another of the candidates, and made known to the people; the latter rose, massacred Lefzec, and proclaimed the other duke, who assumed the name of Lesko II. The æra in which this Lesko reigned is so uncertain, that some historians refer it to the 6th, others the 7th, and even the 8th century.

romance;

romance; and the account of Piaſt, who gave his name to a line of kings, and from whom all the natives of Poland who have aſcended the throne are to this day called Piaſt, is little elſe than a ſeries of fictions. By ſome he is ſaid to have been a wheelwright, by others a common peaſant, and by all to have gained the crown through the viſible interpoſition of two angels. Nor indeed can we expect any faithful accounts of a people buried in barbariſm, wholly without letters, and immerſed in Pagan ſuperſtition. We cannot therefore date the authenticity of the Poliſh annals earlier than the acceſſion of Miciſlaus II. the fourth ſovereign of the line of Piaſt: from his reign Poland began to be connected with Germany, the hiſtorians of which country, as well as thoſe of Sweden and Denmark, throw a conſiderable light upon Poliſh affairs prior to the exiſtence of native hiſtorians.

Some writers have obſerved, that during the whole of the ſecond period the monarchy was always elective, and the ſovereign limited in his power; others, on the contrary, have affirmed, that the crown was hereditary, and its authority abſolute: but this controverſy may be eaſily reconciled; the crown ſeemed hereditary from its continuance in the ſame family, and had at the ſame time an elective appearance, becauſe, upon the death of the king, his ſucceſſor was formally * nominated and recognized in an aſſembly of the nobility and clergy of the realm. With reſpect to the extent of the king's authority, his power, as in the generality of feudal governments when exerciſed by an able and enterpriſing prince, triumphed over all controul; but, in the hands of an incapable ſovereign, was eaſily depreſſed by the privileges of a licentious and warlike nobility.

---

* Memorati ergo principes, non per ejuſmodi electionem, qualis hodie celebratur, ad regnum pervenerunt, ſed electio quam paſſim nominant ſcriptores, revera erat declaratio procerum & nobilium, quæ præcedebat, antequam regimen novi principes ingrederentur. Lengnich, Jus Publicum Regni Poloniæ, v. I. p. 58.

Towards

Towards the clofe of this fecond period, Cafimir the Great. retrenched the turbulent and oppreffive authority of the principal barons ; and granted certain immunities to the nobles and gentry. This great monarch. was aware, that no other expedient could introduce order into this kingdom, except a limitation of the vaft influence poffeffed by the * Palatines or principal nobility : if he had been fucceeded by a line of hereditary monarchs, it is probable that the barons would never have recovered their former afcendancy ; and that the feudal fyftem would have been gradually annihilated in Poland as in other parts of Europe.

But his nephew Louis, king of Hungary, who fucceeded him, being a foreigner, was obliged, in order to enfure the poffeffion of the throne, to fubfcribe certain conditions, which infringed the power of the fovereign, and gave frefh vigour to that of the barons and inferior nobles. The principal conceffions made by Louis were, not to impofe any additional taxes by his mere regal authority without the confent of the nation ; and that in cafe of his demife without male heirs, the privilege of appointing a fovereign fhould revert to the nobles at large †. In confequence of this agreement, Louis was allowed to afcend the throne without oppofition ; and having no fons, he, with a view of infuring the fucceffion to his fon-in-law the Emperor Sigifmund married to his eldeft daughter Maria, promifed, in addition to all the former grants, to diminifh, the taxes, to repair the fortreffes at his own expence, and to confer no dignities or offices upon foreigners ‡.

III. The third period begins upon the death of Louis, when the Poles very politically fet afide Sigifmund, who would have been formidable to their newly acquired immunities ; and elected for their king Ladiflaus Jaghellon duke of Lithuania,

---

* Palatinorum et judicum infinita poteftas coercita eft, &c. Sarnicius, p. 1141.
† Dlugoffius. Lib. IX. p. 1102, &c.

‡ See Lengnich, Pac. Con. Aug. III. Pref. p. 5.

in

in confequence of his fully confirming all the ftipulations of Louis, and efpoufing Hedwige youngeft daughter of the deceafed monarch.

As, by the renunciation of Louis, the kings of Poland were divefted of the right to impofe taxes without confent of the nation, Ladiflaus affembled the nobles * in their refpective provinces in order to obtain an additional tribute. Thefe provincial affemblies gave birth to the dietines ; which, however, no longer retain the power of raifing money in their feveral diftricts, but only elect the nuntios or reprefentatives for the general diet.

Ladiflaus III. fon of Ladiflaus Jaghellon purchafed his nomination to the fucceffion, during the life of his father, by a confirmation of all the privileges above enumerated, which he folemnly ratified at his acceffion.

Under Cafimir III. † brother and fucceffor to Ladiflaus III. feveral further innovations were introduced into the original conftitution, all unfavourable to regal prerogative. One of the principal changes which took place in this reign, and which laid the foundation of ftill more important revolutions in the Polifh government, was the convention of a national diet invefted with the fole power of granting fupplies. Each Palatinate or province was permitted to fend to this general diet, befide the Palatines and other principal barons, a certain number of nuntios or reprefentatives, chofen by the nobles and burghers ‡. This reign is therefore confidered by the popular party as the æra, at which the freedom of the conftitution was permanently eftablifhed. Cafimir was engaged in feveral unfuccefsful wars, which exhaufted the royal treafures ; and as he could not impofe any taxes without the confent of the nation, he was under the neceffity of applying repeatedly to the

* Prelatorum, Baronum et Militarium. Lengnich, Jus Pub. vol. II. p. 35.
† Sometimes called Cafimir IV.

‡ See Chap. VIII. for proof that the burghers were permitted to fend reprefentatives.

diet:

BOOK diet for fubfidies : almoft every fupply was accompanied with
I. a lift of grievances, and produced a diminution of prerogative.
In Poland, as in all feudal governments, the barons, at the head
of their vaſſals, are bound to fight in defence of the kingdom:
before the reign of Cafimir III. the king could require ſuch
military, or, as they were called, feudal fervices ; but this monarch, in compenſation for fome pecuniary aid, gave up that
privilege, and renounced * the power of fummoning the nobles to his ſtandard ; he likewife agreed not to enact any laws
without the concurrence of the national diet.

John Albert, fecond fon of Cafimir, being elected in preference to his elder brother Ladiſlaus, king of Hungary and
Bohemia, aſſented without heſitation, as the price of this partiality, to all the immunities extorted from his predeceſſors ;
and fwore to their obfervance in a general † diet held at Petri-
kau, 1469.

Alexander, brother and fucceſſor of John Albert, declared,
in 1505, the following limitations of fovereign authority to be
fundamental laws of the kingdom.   1. The king cannot impofe taxes.   2. He cannot require the feudal fervices ; 3. nor
alienate the royal domains ; 4. nor enact laws ; 5. nor coin
money ; 6. nor alter the procefs in the courts of juftice.

Sigifmond I. fucceeded Alexander : one ‡ of the Poliſh hiftorians, fpeaking of his reign, exclaims with much indigna-
tion, " The king is almoft wholly deſtitute of power ; he can-
" not procure any fubfidy on the moſt prefling emergency, for
" carrying on war, or for the portion of his daughters, with-
" out increafing the privileges of the nobility." Notwithſtanding, however, this exclamation, we cannot forbear to remark, that the power of levying taxes at diſcretion is the moſt

---

* Quod nullas conſtitutiones faceret, neque   † Præclarorum Baronum ac nuntiorum de
terrigenas ad bellum moveri mandaret, abfque   fingulis terris hic congreſſorum univerſorum
conventione communi in finguiis terris inſti-   confilio ac voluntate, &c. Conſt. Pol. v. I.
tuendâ.   p. 294.
  Conſt. Pol. v. I. p. 186.   ‡ Orichovius.

                                                                              dangerous

dangerous prerogative that can be lodged in the hands of a sovereign, and the moſt formidable engine of deſpotic authority : the acquiſition of it by the monarchs of France finally ſubverted the liberties of that kingdom ; and it was made the firſt object of reſiſtance by the aſſertors of freedom in our own country. If indeed we were inclined to point out any particular period, at which the Poliſh conſtitution attained its moſt perfect ſtate, we ſhould perhaps fix on the reign of Sigiſmond I. when the perſon and property of the ſubject were ſecured by ample proviſions; and the crown ſtill retained conſiderable influence. But the time was arrived, when an inordinate paſſion for liberty led the nobles to render the throne wholly elective ; and at each election to continue their encroachments upon the regal authority, until the king was reduced to a mere pageant. The firſt public attempt towards eſtabliſhing this favourite object of the Poles, a free election of the king, was brought forward in the reign of Sigiſmond Auguſtus, ſon and ſucceſſor of Sigiſmond I. who was conſtrained in 1550 to agree, that no future monarch ſhould ſucceed to the throne, unleſs he was freely elected by the nation.

The death of Sigiſmond Auguſtus without iſſue gave efficacy to this conceſſion, which might otherwiſe have been counteracted by the popularity and influence attendant on a claimant by hereditary ſucceſſion. For it may not be improper to remark, that, during the Jaghellon line, the ſovereigns upon their acceſſion, or election, although formally raiſed to the throne by the conſent of the nation, ſtill reſted their pretenſions upon hereditary right, as well as upon this conſent ; always ſtyling themſelves *heirs* of the kingdom of Poland. Sigiſmond Auguſtus, in whom the male line of the Jaghellon family became extinct, was the laſt who bore that title [*].

IV. The fourth period begins upon the demiſe of Sigiſmond

[*] Lengnich, Jus Pub. v. I. p. 59.

Auguſtus,

Auguſtus, in 1572, when all title to the crown from hereditary right was formally abrogated, and the moſt abſolute
freedom of election eſtabliſhed upon the moſt permanent baſis. '
At this æra a charter of immunities was drawn up at a general
diet, a ratification of which it was determined to exact from
the new ſovereign, prior to his election. The ground-work
of this charter, termed in the Poliſh law *Pacta Conventa*, was
the whole body of privileges obtained from Louis and his ſuc-
ceſſors, with the following additions : 1. That the king ſhould
be elective, and that his ſucceſſor ſhould never be appointed
during his life. 2. That the diets, the holding of which depended ſolely upon the will of the kings, ſhould be aſſembled
every two years. 3. That every * noble or gentleman in the
whole realm ſhould have a vote in the diet of election. 4.
That, in caſe the king ſhould infringe the laws and privileges
of the nation, his ſubjects ſhould be abſolved from their oaths
of allegiance. From this period the *Pacta Conventa*, occaſionally enlarged, have been confirmed by every ſovereign at
his coronation.

Henry of Valois, duke of Anjou and brother of Charles IX.
King of France, was the firſt ſovereign who aſcended the throne
after the conſtitution had been thus new-modelled. He ſecured his election, as well by private bribes to the nobles, as
by a ſtipulation to pay an annual penſion to the Republic from
the revenues of France. His example has been neceſſarily
followed by each ſucceeding ſovereign, who, beſide an unconditional ratification of the *Pacta Conventa*, has been always
conſtrained to purchaſe the crown by a public largeſs and by
private corruption ; circumſtances which endear to the Poles
an elective monarchy.

Under Stephen Bathori, the regal power was ſtill further
abridged by the appointment of ſixteen reſident ſenators,

* See the Definition of a Noble. Ch. VIII.

chofen

chofen at each diet, to attend the king, and to give their opinion in all matters of importance, fo that he could not iffue any decree without their confent *.   Another fatal blow was alfo given to his prerogative in 1578, by taking from him the fupreme jurifdiction, or the power of judging in the laft refort the caufes of the nobles, excepting fuch as arife within a fmall diftance † of the fovereign's place of refidence : it was enacted, that without the concurrence of the king each palatinate or province fhould elect in their dietines their own judges, who fhould form fupreme courts of juftice, called *Tribunalia Regni* ‡; and that in thefe courts the caufes of the nobles fhould be decided finally and without appeal; a mode of judicature which prevails to this day.

The turbulent reign of John Cafimir was marked by the introduction of the *Liberum Veto* ‖, or the power which each nuntio claims and exercifes of interpofing a negative, and in confequence of that interpofition of breaking up the diet; a privilege which the fovereign himfelf does not poffefs, and which has contributed more than any other innovation to deftroy the due balance of the Polifh conftitution.

But the king was ftill the fountain of honour : he conferred the principal dignities and great offices of the republic; and beftowed the Starofties, or Royal fiefs, which are held during the life-time of the poffeffor.   Hence he ftill maintained great influence in the councils of the nation; but this laft folitary branch of royal prerogative was wrefted from his prefent Majefty at the eftablifhment of the Permanent Council §.

* This appointment was made, in 1573, under Henry, but did not abfolutely take place till the reign of Stephen. Lengnich, Jus Pub. v. I. p. 344. ll. 44.

† The courts exercifing juftice in the king's name within the diftrict are called Afefforia Regni. Until the death of John Sobiefki, the kings judged frequently in perfon, but this ceafed to be the cuftom from the time of

Auguftus II. and the Great Chancellor now exercifes, in his Majefty's name, that branch of royal prerogative.

‡ Lengnich, Jus Pub. v. II. p. 536.

‖ For an account of the Liberum Veto, fee Chap. VI.

§ A delineation of the Permanent Council, in the words of the edict which eftablifhed it, is given in Chapter V.

Thus it appears, that, from the time of Louis to the prefent period, the nobles have continued without interruption to diminifh the regal authority, and to augment their own privileges. Many of the conceffions which they obtained from the fovereigns of the Jaghellon line, were juft and reafonable, and aimed only at an equitable degree of freedom. When, however, an abfolute right to difpofe of fo tempting an object as the crown gave them repeated opportunities of prefcribing unconditional terms to every candidate for the throne, they were no longer content with that equal diftribution of power, which is the excellence of a limited monarchy; but afpired to and nearly attained a direct ariftocracy under a regal title and form.

From this general review of the revolutions in the conftitution of Poland, we may eafily infer, that, notwithftanding their fo much boafted liberty, the Poles are by no means equally free. Indeed their hiftorians, however they may differ in other points, unanimoufly agree in reprobating their affectation of liberty, the fhadow rather than the reality of freedom; which is in fact merely a turbulent fyftem of Ariftocratic licentioufnefs, where a few members of the community are above the controul of law, while the majority are excluded from its protection. We fhould fuppofe, that, if in any inftance they were free, it would be in the election of a king, one of their moft vaunted privileges; and yet Sarnifki addreffes the Poles with great truth in the following words: " Turn over your annals, and you will fcarcely find a fingle " example of a free election *." Another Polifh hiftorian of great note, the celebrated Staniflaus Lubienfki bifhop of Plotfko, juftly contends that the Poles, free as they pretend to be, are abfolutely in a ftate of flavery, to which they have been

---

* Revolvite annales veftros, vix ullum exemplum liberæ electionis invenietis.

reduced

reduced by an inconfiderate paffion for liberty *. In a word, it is evident beyond the poffibility of doubt, from the hiftory of this country, that the Poles were more free at home, and more independent and flourifhing abroad, when the fovereign had more authority, when the nobles affifted at the diets without the privilege of diffolving them; and when they fubmitted themfelves and their peafants to the jurifdiction of the king. The proof of this affertion is founded on the following facts.

1. The prefent wretched ftate of the towns compared with their former flourifhing condition, during the reigns of the Jaghellon family, when the burghers even poffeffed a right of fending nuntios to the diets †, forms a ftrong contraft to their former profperity; and attefts the melancholy effects of ariftocratical defpotifm. 2. The wretched condition and poverty of the peafants, whofe increafe of oppreffion has kept pace in an equal proportion with the increafe of the power of the nobles; for when the king loft his weight in the conftitution, this moft numerous and ufeful order of fociety loft a patron and protector. 3. A total confufion introduced into the adminiftration of public affairs; and a ftate of anarchy, which prevents deliberation, and delays the adoption of neceffary meafures even in times of the moft preffing emergency. 4. The declenfion of the importance, and contraction of the territories of the republic. During the reigns of the kings of the Jaghellon family, before the nobles had acquired a decided preponderancy in the ftate, the kingdom of Poland was far more powerful and extenfive than it is at prefent: fince the changes in the conftitution, and the introduction of anarchy,

---

* Expendamus paululum ftatum reipublicæ: inconfultus libertatis amor dum iidem leges ferunt, qui pœnis obnoxii funt, et impunitatis defiderio, juris, quo tot fæculis patria ftetit, convellunt fundamenta, nos eo redegit *ut liberi peffimo cuique ferviamus.* Nulla legum reverentia, nulla poteftatis verecundia: tantum quifque audet, quantum habet virium. Dudum jam agricolas miferos afpero fervitutis jugo preffimus, &c. p. 194.
† See Chap. VIII.

C 2

falfely

BOOK
I.
falsely called liberty, the Poles have not only made no conquest except what they have been forced to relinquish; but
have seen even their original territories gradually mouldering
away, and at last considerably reduced by the late partition.
A kingdom with more than twelve millions of inhabitants, if
well regulated, would never have fallen so easy a prey to the
ambition of its neighbours: its internal strength, assisted by
its natural alliances, would have been sufficient to have protracted, if not prevented, its dismemberment. Nor are the
fatal effects of the evils inherent in the constitution yet fully
exhausted: the same incapacity of resisting the encroachments of neighbouring powers, which made the Poles so
tamely accede to the late division, will render them equally
submissive, whenever any future claims shall be urged by a
combination of the neighbouring states; and compel them to
acquiesce under any pretensions, however chimerical, or however unjust.

Anarchy, in short, and confusion are not only tolerated,
but are even supposed by the nobles, who reap the benefit of
those evils, to be absolutely necessary for the support of the
constitution; so that there is a proverb, which implies that
Poland subsists by anarchy. In opposition to this absurd idea,
an historian, whom I have before mentioned, advises his
countrymen no longer to suffer the republic to be governed
by chance, or to submit to the cast of the die the administration of affairs, on which their very existence as a nation
depends *.

King Stanislaus Letzinski and the Abbé Konarski are the
most celebrated of the modern Polish authors, who have exposed in the strongest colours the disorders of the government,

---

* Non condemnetis (says Sarniski, in the
striking passage to which I allude, and of
which it was impossible to preserve the spirit
in a translation) quæso prudentissimorum vi-
rorum consilia; nec sinatis amplius *casu* rempublicam regi, nec permittatis *dubiæ aleæ* res,
in quibus vita et mors, salus et interitus, ad
limen sedent.

                                        and

and the exorbitancy of the privileges poffeffed by the nobles; but what avail the reprefentations of hiftorians againft factions, againft a tumultuous nobility, or againft the cabals of neigh-bouring powers? It is hardly poffible to fuppofe that Poland, without an army, without money, without fortreffes, without re-fources, and without good government the fource of all the other calamities, will ever emerge from her prefent fituation: her misfortunes will not only continue, but will gradually increafe, notwithftanding the remonftrances of a few real patriots; until by flow progrefs, or fome violent revolution, Poland either fubfides into an hereditary monarchy, or a well-ordered republic; or, which is more probable, is totally fwallowed up by the neighbouring powers.

Ladiflaus

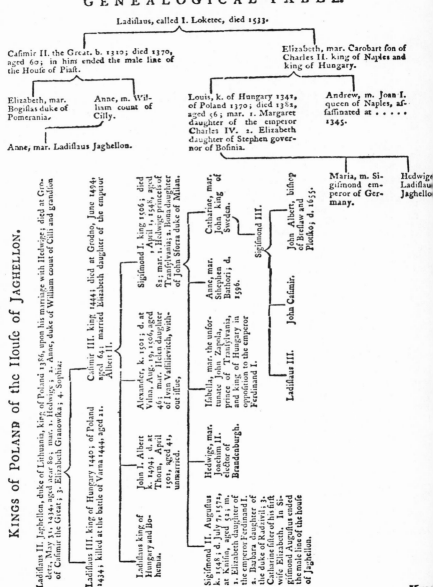

Ladiſlaus, called I. Loketec, died 1533.

Caſimir II. the Great. b. 1310; died 1370, aged 60; in him ended the male line of the Houſe of Piaſt.

Elizabeth, mar. Carobart ſon of Charles II. king of Naples and king of Hungary.

Elizabeth, mar. Bogiſlas duke of Pomerania.

Anne, m. William count of Cilly.

Anne, mar. Ladiſlaus Jaghellon.

Louis, k. of Hungary 1342, of Poland 1370; died 1382, aged 56; mar. 1. Margaret daughter of the emperor Charles IV. 2. Elizabeth daughter of Stephen governor of Boſnia.

Andrew, m. Joan I. queen of Naples, aſſaſſinated at . . . . . 1345.

Maria, m. Sigiſmond emperor of Germany.

Hedwige Ladiſlau Jaghello

KINGS OF POLAND of the Houſe of JAGHELLON.

Ladiſlaus II. Jaghellon, duke of Lithuania, king of Poland 1386, upon his marriage with Hedwige; died at Grodetz, May 31, 1434, aged near 80; mar. 1. Hedwige; 2. Anne, duke of William count of Cilli and grandſon of Caſimir the Great; 3. Elizabeth Gianowſka; 4. Sophia.

Caſimir III. king 1444; died at Grodno, June 1494, aged 64; married Elizabeth daughter of the emperor Albert II.

Sigiſmond I. king 1506; died , April 1, 1548, aged 82; mar. 1. Hedwige princeſs of Tranſylvania; 2. Bona daughter of John Sforza duke of Milan.

Anne, mar. Stephen Bathori, d. 1596.

Catharine, mar. John king of Sweden.

Sigiſmond III.

John Albert, biſhop of Breſlau and Plotſko; d. 1655.

Ladiſlaus III. king of Hungary 1440; of Poland 1434; killed at the battle of Varna 1444; aged 21.

John I. Albert k. 1494; d. at Thorn, April 1501, aged 41, unmarried.

Alexander, k. 1501; d. at Vilna, Aug. 19, 1506, aged 46; mar. Helen daughter of Ivan Vaſilievitch, without iſſue,

Iſabella, mar. the unfortunate John Zapola, prince of Tranſylvania, and king of Hungary in oppoſition to the emperor Ferdinand I.

Sigiſmond III.

John Caſimir.

Ladiſlaus king of Hungary and Bohemia.

Hedwige, mar. Joachim II. elector of Brandenburgh.

Sigiſmond II. Auguſtus k. 1548; d. July 7, 1572, at Kniſin, aged 52; m. 1. Elizabeth daughter of the emperor Ferdinand I. 2. Barbara daughter of the duke of Radzivil; 3. Catharine ſiſter of his firſt wife Elizabeth. In Sigiſmond Auguſtus ended the male line of the houſe of Jaghellon.

Kings of Poland of different Families.

Henry of Va-lois duke of Anjou, after-wards king of France, king of Poland, May 1573, ab-dicated June 1574.	Stephen Ba-thori, king of Poland Dec. 14, 1575, upon his marriage with Anne Jaghellon; d. at Grodno Dec. 12, 1586, aged 54.	Sigismond III. son of Sigif-mir, k. Nov. 1587; k. Aug. 19, 1587; saw April 30, 1632; d. at Meretz, May 20, 1648. See the former table Marr. 1. with Anne daught. of Charles archduke of Austria; 2. Constantia sister of Anne.	Ladislaus IV. k. Nov. 1632; dicated Sept. 19, 1668; at Nevers in France, Dec. aged 35; m. 1. Louisa daughter of the emperor Ferdinand II. his brother's widow. 2. Louisa Ma-ria princess of Nevers.	John II. Casi-mir, k. Nov. 20, 1648; ab-16, 1668; d. Nov. 10, 1673; 52; m. 1 France, Dec 64; m. Louisa daughter of the emperor Ferdinand III.	Michael Ko-ribut Wieino-wiski, k. June 19, 1668; d. at Leopold, 16, 1672, aged Marie de la Grange d'Ar-quien,	John III. So-bieski, k. June 21, 1674; d. at Villanow, June 17, 1696, aged 66; m. Christina Maria daughter of Ar-quien,	Augustus II. elector of Sax-ony, k. June 27, 1697; died at 1733; died at Warsaw, Jan. 1733, aged 63; margrave of Brandenburgh Bareith. Christian daughter of Joseph I.

Augustus III. elector of Sax-ony, k. Oct. 5; died at Dresden, Oct. 1763; mar. Maria Josephina daughter of the emperor Joseph I.

Stanislaus Augustus, k. Sept. 1764.

Stanislaus Let-zinski, chol-en in opposition to Augustus II. July 12, 1704; driven from Poland; again elected by a party upon the death of Au-gustus II. again obliged to retire; re-tained the title of king; d. at Luneville, Feb. 23, 1766. His daughter Marie mar. Louis XV.

CHAP.

C H A P.   II.

Election of Staniſlaus Auguſtus.—*His excellent regulations op-*
poſed by the neighbouring powers.—*Hiſtory of the Diſſidents—*
their privileges aboliſhed by the diet of 1766.—*Confederacies*
in their favour ſupported by the Empreſs of Ruſſia.—*Reſtored*
to their rights by the diet of 1768.—*Proceedings of that diet.*
—*Riſe of the civil commotions.*

BOOK
I.

UPON the demiſe of Auguſtus II. Staniſlaus Auguſtus, ſon
of Count Poniatowſki the friend and companion of
Charles XII. was ſupported in his pretenſions to the crown by
the Empreſs of Ruſſia, and the King of Pruſſia ; their aſſiſtance,
joined to that of a ſtrong party among the nobles who had declared in his favour, and aided by his great perſonal accom-
pliſhments, raiſed him to the throne of Poland. Five thouſand
Ruſſian troops ſtationed at a ſmall diſtance from the plain of
Vola, wherein the diet of election was aſſembled, ſecured good
order, and overawed the violence of the oppoſite party. The
practice of cantoning a body of ſoldiers near the plain where
the Poliſh kings are elected, has been adopted by different foreign powers for near a century ; a mode of proceeding, which,
however galling it may appear to the licentious nobility, prevents the effuſion of blood that formerly deluged theſe popular
aſſemblies.

Staniſlaus was in the 32d year of his age when he aſcended
the throne in 1764, and ſeemed calculated by his virtues and
abilities to raiſe Poland from its deplorable ſtate ; if the defects
of the conſtitution had not fettered his exertions for the public
good. The faireſt hopes were conceived of his future reign ;
but theſe flattering preſages at firſt realized, were ſoon diſap-
pointed by the factions of a turbulent people, fomented by the

3   intrigues

intrigues of the neighbouring powers : thus the reign of the most amiable among the Polish sovereigns was doomed to experience the dreadful effects of that exceſſive liberty, which is almoſt inconſiſtent with the exiſtence of government. The firſt acts of his Majeſty's reign were highly adapted to introduce order and regularity into the interior adminiſtration, and to reſcue his country from her dependence upon foreign powers. The tendency of theſe excellent regulations to increaſe the power and conſequence of Poland gave umbrage to the adjacent ſtates ; and were likewiſe vigorouſly oppoſed by a ſtrong party within the kingdom : at this criſis too, religious diſputes blending themſelves with political cabals, the flame of civil diſcord burſt forth with a violence which had not hitherto raged even in Poland.

The body of Poliſh religioniſts, termed Diſſidents, make a principal figure in the ſubſequent commotions ; their concerns being the real or pretended object of attention in every material tranſaction. The hiſtory of this party is thus ſketched by the Poliſh hiſtorians.

The reformation made its way into Poland under Sigiſmond I. who perſecuted its followers : their number however gaining ground, his ſon Sigiſmond Auguſtus * not only indulged them in the moſt liberal exerciſe of their worſhip ; but admitted them together with the Greeks, and all other ſects then ſubſiſting in Poland, to a ſeat in the diet, and to all the honours and privileges before excluſively confined to the catholics. Theſe maxims of unlimited toleration were ſo generally adopted by the nation at large, that the members of the diet, which aſſembled upon the deceaſe of Sigiſmond Auguſtus, being of different perſuaſions, determined on a reciprocal indulgence of their reſpective tenets. In order to avoid any hate-

* Sigiſmond Auguſtus gave ſuch evident marks of favour to the proteſtant confeſſion, that he was even ſuſpected of being inclined to change his religion, " ut etiam de ipſo " rumor eſſet ac ſi avita ſacra renuntiare " vellet." Lengnich, Jus Publ. II. p. 554.

ful

BOOK I.

ful diftinctions, they called themfelves indifcriminately "dif- "fidents in religion *," a phrafe intimating, not, according to our notions, feparatifts from an eftablifhed church, but fimply perfons holding a diverfity of opinions in religious matters. It was at the fame time enacted, that this difference of religious fentiments fhould create no difference in civil rights; and accordingly in the *Pacta Conventa* formed by the diet, the following claufe was inferted as part of the coronation oath to be tendered to the new fovereign. " I will keep peace among " the diffidents †." This claufe Henry of Anjou fwore to obferve, before he was permitted to afcend the throne

In procefs of time, however, the Roman catholics, having, under the protection and influence of fucceffive fovereigns, acquired a confiderable afcendency, ventured to appropriate the expreffion of diffidents to all thofe who diffented from the catholic religion. This alteration in the ufe of the title was attended at firft with no incroachments on the privileges of the other fects; and the term diffidents, though now conveying the idea of a feparation from the eftablifhed worfhip, was not

---

* This remarkable decree is as follows: " Et quoniam, aiunt ordines, in noftrâ Re- " publ. non parum eft diffidium in caufâ Re- " ligionis Chriftianæ, occurrendo ne ex hâc " caufâ inter homines damnofa quædam fedi- " tio oriatur, uti in aliis Regnis clare vide- " mus, fpondemus hoc nobis invicem, pro " nobis & fuccefforibus noftris in perpe- " tuum, fub vinculo juramenti, fide, honore " & confcientiis noftris, quod, *qui fumus* " *diffidentes de religione*, pacem inter nos " confervare, & propter diverfam fidem, & " mutationes in ecclefiis, fanguinem non ef- " fundere, neque multare pecuniâ, infamiâ, " carceribus & exilio, & fuperioritati alicui " aut officio ad ejufmodi proceffum nullo mo- " do auxilium dare: quin imo, fi quis fan- " guinem effundere voluerit, ex iftâ cauffâ " opponere nos omnes erimus obftricti, licet " etiam id alioquin fub prætextu decreti, aut " alicujus proceffus judiciarii facere voluerit " a Pacta Conventa Augufti III." p. 20.
We need not be furprized at this general

fenfe of the diet, fo contrary to the general principles of the catholics, when we confider that the catholic nuntios were inferior in number to thofe of the other perfuafions, fo that the former were well fatisfied to obtain an equality with the others. The proteftant party in the nation was at this period fo ftrong, that it was even taken into confideration to elect for their king a Polifh nobleman, who had embraced the reformed religion. " Cum in fenatu fi non majorem, parem ta- " men catholicis partem efficerent, inter " equites autem prævalerent." Lengnich, Jus Pub. v. II. p. 555. See alfo Lind's Letters on the State of Poland, p. 82.

† " Pacem inter diffidentes fervabo." Henry, who objected to this univerfal toleration, tried to withhold his confent; upon which one of the Polifh envoys cried out, " Unlefs your Majefty confirms this article, " you cannot be king of Poland," nifi eam conditionem approbaveris, Rex Poloniæ non eris. Pac. Con. Aug. III. p. 19.

yet

yet regarded in an obnoxious light. The diffidents indeed ſtill continued in ſuch unqueſtioned poſſeſſion of all rights civil and religious, that, when it was agreed by both catholics and proteſtants to perſecute the arians, it was thought neceſſary, prior to their perſecution, to expel them from the body of diſſidents. In conſequence of this excluſion, the arians, in the reign of John Caſimir, were firſt rendered incapable of being elected nuntios, afterwards deprived of their places of worſhip, and finally baniſhed from Poland *.

This perſecution of the arians, inadvertently aſſented to by the proteſtants and Greeks, was only a prelude to that which they in their turn ſuffered from the catholics: for, as the catholic party became the moſt powerful, the term diſſidents, now confined only to perſons profeſſing the proteſtant † and Greek religions, began to grow of a leſs inoffenſive import, and to convey an idea of non-conformity. The ſectaries diſtinguiſhed by that appellation, perceiving the intention of the catholics to undermine their privileges, ſtipulated and obtained, that they ſhould not be blended with the arians, or fall under the penal laws enacted againſt that ſect. But theſe promiſes were inſenſibly eluded, their privileges were gradually diminiſhed; in the courſe of a few years they were ſubjected to a variety of diſqualifications, and at length, in 1733, formally incapacitated from ſitting in the diet ‡. An old law of Ladiſlaus II.

* The following quotations from Lengnich prove the truth of theſe facts:
" Credebant ariani ſe ad diſſidentes perti-
" nere, verum neque diſſidentes illos in eorum
" numero eſſe voluerunt.
" Poſt mortem Uladiſlai IV. catholici de-
" clarabant, non eſſe diſſidentes niſi qui tri-
" unum Deum colerent.
" In comitiis 1658, rex nuntium, quia ſectæ
" arianorum erat, ad manûs oſculum admit-
" tere nolebat; et nuntii inter ſe conſtitue-
" bant, ne ipſorum conclavi arianis locus
" eſſet." Jus Pub. II. 567 & ſeq.

For the extirpation of the arian ſect, John Caſimir was dignified by the pope with the title of orthodox, as if orthodoxy conſiſted in perſecution.
Tantærnæ animis cæleſtibus iræ!
† Namely, the Lutherans and Calviniſts; all other proteſtant ſects, the Mennonites, anabaptiſts, and quakers, being not included among the diſſidents: and the perſecuting laws enacted againſt the arians are in full force againſt them. Pac. Con. Aug. III. p. 28, 29.
‡ Lengnich, Hiſt. Pol. p. 376.

againſt

againſt hereticks, as well as the penalties levelled againſt the arians, were revived, and occaſionally put in force againſt the diſſidents.

Theſe continued perſecutions greatly diminiſhed their number, and rendered of courſe their remonſtrances ineffectual. The catholics, who now took the lead in the diet, went ſo far as to declare it high treaſon in the diſſidents to ſeek the reſtoration of their immunities by the interceſſion of foreign powers; although many of theſe foreign powers were guarantees to the treaty of Oliva, in which it was ſtipulated, that the rights of the diſſidents ſhould be maintained in their full latitude *.

Such was the ſituation of the diſſidents at the acceſſion of his preſent majeſty; who, though himſelf ſtrongly inclined to toleration, was yet obliged to concur with the general ſenſe of the diet; and to confirm in their full extent all the laws which had been promulgated againſt them. The diſſidents applied to the courts of London, Peterſburg, Berlin, and Copenhagen, as the mediating powers in the treaty of Oliva; who warmly ſupported their cauſe, and preſented memorials to the enſuing diet, demanding a reſtoration not only of their religious eſtabliſhments, but alſo of all their ancient privileges ſecured to them by the abovementioned treaty. The diet of 1766, however, was not of a temper to accede to theſe propoſals.

The enemies of toleration contended, that the privileges alluded to were become obſolete, having been repeatedly aboliſhed in various diets; and that the diſſidents had no well-founded claim either to the reſtitution of their civil immunities, or to the toleration of their worſhip: the biſhop of Cracow, the moſt bigotted of the catholics, even propoſed a law againſt all who ſhould abet the oppoſite party. Violent alter-

---

* For the account of the diſſidents, ſee Lengnich, Pac. Con. Aug. III. 16—30. and Jus Publ. ſparſim.

cations

cations arose in the affembly, when the Pruffian and Ruffian memorials were read ; and as an immediate tumult was appre-hended, the king retired from the diet without proroguing it, as ufual, to the following day. The primate likewife refufed to continue the fitting, and the members feparated in great diforder. On the fubfequent day the fpirit of intolerance was in no degree abated ; the moderate party was over-ruled, and the acts againft the diffidents were confirmed without referve. But, in order to conciliate the mediating powers, the bench of bifhops, by command of the diet, drew up nine articles in fa-vour of the diffidents, relative to the free exercife of their worfhip. Thefe conceffions not being thought fufficiently fa-vourable, while the exceptionable laws remained unrepealed, the Emprefs of Ruffia remonftrated againft the proceedings of the diet ; and the diffidents began to form confederacies in dif-ferent parts of the kingdom. They were joined by many dif-contented catholics, and affifted by a large body of Ruffian troops, who entered Thorn, where the firft and principal con-federacy took its rife. All the mediating powers, Great-Bri-tain, Denmark, Pruffia, and Sweden, teftified their approbation of thefe confederacies. The difputes foon began to embrace other objects befide religion ; political grievances were likewife brought forward ; and feveral confederacies ftarted up in dif-ferent parts of the kingdom among the catholic nobles ; all of whom affected to be advocates for toleration, and declared their intentions of fupporting the caufe of the diffidents. Prince Radzivil, who had fignalized himfelf in oppofing the king's election, was appointed marfhal to all the catholic con-federacies, united in one formidable affociation under the ap-pellation of malecontents. The coalition of this catholic con-federacy, with that of the diffidents, foon after took place in the palace of prince Radzivil at Warfaw. Mean while the king convoked an extraordinary diet, as the only probable means to
prevent

prevent a civil war, and to appeafe the Emprefs of Ruffia, whofe troops were advanced within a fmall diftance of Warfaw. The diet, however, which was fummoned for the purpofe of reconciling the oppofite parties, failed in producing the intended effect: the bifhop of Cracow and his partifans inveighed with fuch bitternefs againft the pretenfions of the diffidents and againft the interference of foreign powers; that he, together with the bifhop of Kiof and a few others, the moft violent of their party, were arrefted in the night by a corps of Ruffian troops, and fent, without further trial, to Ruffia, where they experienced a rigorous imprifonment *.

---

* The bifhop of Cracow and his affociates were arrefted on the 15th of October, 1767; they were detained in prifon above five years, not being releafed before the beginning of 1773. They were firft confined at Smolenfko, and afterwards at Kaluga. The following extracts from fome manufcript letters in my poffeffion give fome account of their imprifonment, and of the bifhop's return:

"At firft their confinement was very rigorous, and particularly in their journey to Smolenfko; for although they were conducted together, and then imprifoned at the fame place, yet they were never permitted to fee each other during the firft fix months. Afterwards they were lefs rigoroufly treated. They were removed from Smolenfko on fufpicion of a correfpondence between the bifhop of Cracow and his partifans in Lithuania; and although this fufpicion was not founded, yet it occafioned the refolution adopted by the court of Peterfburg to tranfport them to Kaluga." Warfaw, 15 February, 1773.

"The bifhop of Cracow is already arrived: he had difpatched an exprefs from Minfk to the Great Chancellor of the crown to announce his return on the 14th. The exprefs came on Thurfday afternoon, and was followed by another the next day with the news, that the bifhop himfelf was on his route; and in effect he arrived at five in the afternoon. In the fuburbs of Praga, being met by the pope's nuntio, together with the bifhops of Cujavia and Pofnania,

"he quitted his own carriage, and got into that of the bifhop of Pofnania, into whofe palace he alighted at Warfaw. He was accompanied by perfons of the firft diftinction, and followed by a crowd of people, huzzaing as he paffed the ftreets; fome out of affection, others from imitation, or excited by fecret emiffaries. The doors of the palace being open to all who chofe to enter, the apartments were immediately filled with perfons of all ranks, bifhops, fenators, minifters and officers of ftate, nobles, priefts, citizens, together with the loweft of the populace, and even beggars, all huddled together pell-mell, eager to behold, liften to, and applaud the bifhop, who had fo unexpectedly made his appearance. He fpoke for a confiderable time, and related the hiftory of his imprifonment, which he affured them had not made any alteration in his fentiments of religion and liberty. 'I have been twice,' added he, 'arrefted by the Ruffians, the firft time with the primate Potofki, the fecond at my late confinement, and perhaps I may yet be caft into prifon a third time.'

"He propofes to retire in a fhort time to his diocefe, and it is reported that he intends to forbid the priefts from wearing wigs and ruffles: he himfelf wears neither. His hair is grown grey fince his confinement, and he looks confiderably older; he covers his head with a red cap which he made himfelf.

"Yefterday he had an audience of the "king,

The diet, intimidated by the fate of their leading members, and being no longer inflamed by their eloquence, appointed, though not without fome altercation and tumult, a grand committee to adjuft the affairs of the diffidents in conjunction with the mediating powers, and then broke up. This grand committee expreffed the moft favourable difpofition towards the diffidents, and propofed that all the laws enacted againft them fhould be repealed, and their antient privileges reftored. Thefe refolutions being laid before the extraordinary diet, which was convened the beginning of the following year, 1768, were ratified almoft without oppofition. This ready and unanimous acquiefcence of the diet in regulations, totally repugnant to the fentiments of the majority, can only be accounted for by the dread of the Ruffian troops quartered in Warfaw, and the influence of bribes judicioufly diftributed by the Ruffian minifter. The operation of the fame caufes rendered the diet equally compliant in other particulars : and induced them to eftablifh feveral * civil regulations, tending to perpetuate the defects of the conftitution, and which had no

"king, with whom he remained a full hour,
"namely, from eleven to twelve. He ad-
"dreffed his majefty with great decency and
"refpect; and, among other things, begged
"pardon, if, before his arreft, he had ex-
"preffed himfelf either in a manner or in
"terms which were difpleafing, affuring him
"at the fame time of his attachment, fide-
"lity, and zeal for the fervice of his king,
"and the good of his country. After the
"audience, he attended mafs, and prefented
"his majefty with the New Teftament, ac-
"quitting himfelf of that ceremony with
"propriety and decorum.

"The bifhop of Kiof, having feparated
"from the bifhop of Cracow on the other
"fide of Minfk, will not be here for fome
"time. The palatine of Cracow and his fon
"continue between Smolenfko and Kaluga,
"the place of their confinement, in order to
"attend upon Colonel Bachmatou, their con-

"ductor, who was taken ill upon their jour-
"ney. The palatine, willing to repay with
"gratitude and humanity the attention
"which he received from the colonel during
"his confinement, could not be prevailed
"upon to quit him in his illnefs; and as he
"has fome knowledge of phyfic, he is in-
"hopes of completing his cure."

* Thefe regulations, which refpect chiefly the eftablifhing in perpetuity of the elective monarchy, of the Liberum Veto, and of unanimity in all matters of ftate, are all detailed in the articles of the diet of 1768, publifhed at Warfaw : the principal claufes are the fame as are mentioned in the fourth chapter of this book relative to the changes made in the conftitution in 1775; the reader will find them amply mentioned and accompanied with fome judicious remarks, in Lind's Prefent State of Poland, Letter III.

other

other recommendation except their fubferviency to the Ruffian defigns upon Poland.

The nation at large feemed at this juncture to have caught the fubmiffive fpirit of the diet; and received the new edicts with every fymptom of cordiality. Poland feemed to enjoy for a moment an univerfal tranquillity ; but it was that fullen tranquillity which precedes a tempeft, and announces to the intelligent obferver the moft violent commotions.

During thefe tranfactions, the king, without influence, and confequently without a fhadow of authority, was one while hurried down the popular current ; and the next moment forced by the mediating powers to accede to all the conditions which they laid before him : a wretched fituation for a prince of his fpirit and magnanimity, and below which it is fcarcely poffible for any fovereign to be reduced. But more grievous fcenes yet awaited the unfortunate monarch ; he was doomed to behold his country torn to pieces by the moft dreadful of all calamities, a religious war ; to be frequently deprived almoft of common neceffaries ; and to be indebted for his very fubfiftence to the voluntary contributions of his friends : to be little better than a ftate prifoner in his capital ; to be carried off and nearly affaffinated : to fee his faireft provinces wrefted from him ; and, finally, to depend, for his own fecurity and that of his fubjects, upon the protection of thofe very powers, who had difmembered his empire.

The Polifh malecontents could certainly alledge fome very plaufible caufes of diffatisfaction. The laws paffed at the laft diet bore a greater refemblance to the abfolute mandates of a Ruffian viceroy, than to the refolutions of a free affembly. The outrage committed upon the bifhop of Cracow and his adherents entirely fubverted all liberty of debate ; while the authoritative manner, in which the mediating powers of Berlin and Peterfburg ftill continued to interfere in the affairs of
Poland,

Poland, threatened a more grievous fubjection. Thefe fpecious grounds of difguft, joined to an ill-timed fpirit of difcontent which had gone forth throughout the nation againft the king, occafioned the inteftine commotions that foon reduced Poland to the moft dreadful ftate of defolation.

The diet had not long been diffolved, before the indulgences granted to the diffidents firft excited a general difcontent among the Roman catholic party : feveral confederacies made their appearance towards the frontiers of the Turkifh empire in defence of the facred catholic faith ; they carried ftandards before them highly calculated to inflame the zeal of the populace ; upon fome of thefe ftandards images of the Virgin Mary and the infant Jefus were delineated ; upon others the fpread eagle of Poland, with the mottos " Conqueft or Death," " For religion and liberty *." Some banners bore as a device a red crofs, under which was infcribed " the fymbol of vic- " tory." The private foldiers of the confederacy, like the crufaders of old, wore a crofs interwoven in their clothes. One party of thefe infurgents feized upon the fortrefs of Bar in Podolia, and another got poffeffion of Cracow. The royal troops, who were fent againft them, were either routed or prevailed upon to join them. In this dreadful crifis of affairs the fenate petitioned the embaffador from the court of Peterfburg not to withdraw the Ruffian troops from the kingdom, as they, afforded the only fecurity againft the confederates : the requeft was readily complied with, and Poland became a fcene of bloodfhed and devaftation. In the various conflicts between the two parties, the fuperiority of Ruffian difcipline generally prevailed. The confederates, however, at firft fecretly encouraged by the houfe of Auftria, affifted by the Turks, and fupplied with money and officers by the French, were able to protract hoftilities from the diffolution of the diet in 1768,

* Aut vincere aut mori.—Pro religione et libertate.

to the divifion of Poland in 1772. To enter into a detail of military operations falls not within the defign of this work. From the various acts of cruelty and revenge which diftinguifh and difgrace this part of the Polifh hiftory, I fhall felect only one event too remarkable to be omitted; the attempt made by the confederates to affaffinate the king.

The following circumftantial account of this fingular occurrence was communicated to me by my ingenious friend Nathaniel Wraxall, Efq; whofe name is well known in the literary world; and who, during his refidence at Warfaw, obtained the moft authentic information upon fo interefting a tranfaction: as he has obligingly permitted me to enrich my work with this narration, I am happy to lay it before the reader in his own words.

C H A P.   III.

Attempt to affaffinate the king of Poland.——*His majefty attacked by the confpirators in the ftreets of* Warfaw, *wounded, and carried off.*——*His adventures and miraculous efcape.*——*Return to* Warfaw.——*Account and fate of the principal confpirators.*

" IN the midft of thefe turbulent and difaftrous fcenes, the
" confederates (who ever confidered the king as unlaw-
" fully elected, and who imputed to his fatal elevation and
" direction, or approbation, all the various ills under which the
" kingdom groaned from the Ruffian oppreffion) planned and
" executed one of the moft daring enterprizes of which mo-
" dern hiftory makes mention. I mean the attempt to affaf-
" finate the king. It is fomewhat remarkable, that in an age
" fo

" fo humanifed, fo free from the enormous and flagitious
" crimes common in barbarous centuries, fo enlightened as is
" the prefent, this is the third attempt on a crowned head in
" my remembrance. Louis XV. Jofeph I. of Portugal, and
" Staniflaus Auguftus, all narrowly efcaped affaffination. As
" the attempt on his Polifh majefty was perhaps the moft atro-
" cious, and his efcape certainly the moft extraordinary and
" incredible of the three, I fhall be as minute as poffible in
" the enumeration of all the principal circumftances which led
" to, and which attended this remarkable event.

" A Polifh nobleman, named Pulafki, a general in the army
" of the confederates, was the perfon who planned the atroci-
" ous enterprize; and the confpirators who carried it into ex-
" ecution were about forty in number, and were headed by
" three chiefs, named Lukawfki, Strawenfki, and Kofinfki.
" Thefe three chiefs had been engaged and hired to that pur-
" pofe by Pulafki, who in the town of Czetfchokow in Great
" Poland obliged them to fwear in the moft folemn manner,
" by placing their hands between his, either to deliver the king
" alive into his hands, or, in cafe that was impoffible, to put
" him to death. The three chiefs chofe thirty-feven perfons
" to accompany them. On the 2d of November, about a
" month after they had quitted Czetfchokow, they obtained ad-
" miffion into Warfaw unfufpected or undifcovered by the
" following ftratagem. They difguifed themfelves as peafants
" who came to fell hay, and artfully concealed their faddles,
" arms, and cloaths under the loads of hay which they brought
" in waggons, the more effectually to efcape detection.

" On Sunday night, the 3d of September, 1771, a few of
" thefe confpirators remained in the fkirts of the town; and
" the others repaired to the place of rendezvous, the ftreet of
" the Capuchins, where his majefty was expected to pafs by
" about his ufual hour of returning to the palace. The king

E 2. " had

" had been to vifit his uncle prince Zartorifki, grand chancel-
" lor of Lithuania, and was on his return from thence to the
" palace between nine and ten o'clock.   He was in a coach,
" accompanied by at leaft fifteen or fixteen attendants, befide
" an aid-de-camp in the carriage : fcarce was he at the dif-
" tance of two hundred paces from prince Czartorifki's palace,
" when he was attacked by the confpirators, who commanded
" the coachman to ftop on pain of inftant death.   They fired
" feveral fhot into the carriage, one of which paffed through
" the body of a heyduc, who endeavoured to defend his mafter
" from the violence of the affaffins.   Almoft all the other per-
" fons * who preceded and accompanied his majefty were dif-
" perfed ; the aid-de-camp abandoned him, and attempted to
" conceal himfelf by flight.   Mean while the king had opened
" the door of his carriage with the defign of effecting his
" efcape under fhelter of the night, which was extremely dark.
" He had even alighted, when the affaffins feized him by the
" hair, exclaiming in Polifh with horrible execrations, ' We
" have thee now ; thy hour is come.'   One of them difcharged
" a piftol at him fo very near, that he felt the heat of the
" flafh ; while another cut him acrofs the head with his fabre,
" which penetrated to the bone.   They then laid hold of his
" majefty by the collar, and, mounting on horfeback, dragged
" him along the ground between their horfes at full gallop for
" near five hundred paces through the ftreets of Warfaw †.

" All

---

* " It is incredible that fuch a number of
" perfons as were with his Polifh majefty on
" that memorable night, fhould all fo bafely
" abandon him, except the fingle heyduc
" who was killed, and who fo bravely de-
" fended his mafter.   This man was a pro-
" teftant ; he was not killed on the fpot, but
" expired next morning of his wounds.   The
" king allows a penfion to his widow and
" children."

† " It is aftonifhing, that, in the number

" of balls which paffed through the carriage,
" not one fhould hurt or wound the king.
" Several went through his *pelijfe*, or fur
" great-coat.   I have feen this cloak, and
" the holes made in it by the piftol bullets.
" Every part of the cloaths which his majefty
" wore on that night are carefully preferved.
" It is no lefs wonderful, that when the af-
" faffins had feized on the king, they fhould
" carry him through fuch a number of ftreets
" without being ftopped.   A Ruffian centinel
" did

" All was confusion and disorder during this time at the
" palace, where the attendants who had deserted their master
" had spread the alarm. The foot-guards ran immediately to
" the spot from whence the king had been conveyed, but they
" found only his hat all bloody, and his bag: this increased
" their apprehensions for his life. The whole city was in an
" uproar. The assassins profited of the universal confusion,
" terror and consternation, to bear away their prize. Finding,
" however, that he was incapable of following them on foot,
" and that he had already almost lost his respiration from the
" violence with which they had dragged him, they set him
" on horseback; and then redoubled their speed for fear of
" being overtaken. When they came to the ditch which
" surrounds Warsaw, they obliged him to leap his horse over.
" In the attempt the horse fell twice, and at the second fall
" broke its leg. They then mounted his majesty upon an-
" other, all covered as he was with dirt.

" The conspirators had no sooner crossed the ditch, than
" they began to rifle the king, tearing off the order * of the
" Black Eagle of Prussia which he wore round his neck, and
" the diamond cross hanging to it. He requested them to
" leave his handkerchief, which they consented to: his tablets
" escaped their rapacity. A great number of the assassins re-
" tired after having thus plundered him, probably with intent
" to notify to their respective leaders the success of their en-
" terprise; and the king's arrival as a prisoner. Only seven

" did hail them; but, as they answered in
" Russian, he allowed them to pass, imagining
" them to be a patrole of his nation. This
" happened at some distance from the place
" where they had carried off the king. The
" night was besides exceedingly dark, and
" Warsaw has no lamps. All these circum-
" stances contribute to account for this ex-
" traordinary event."

* " It was Lukawski, one of the three

" chiefs of the band, who tore off the rib-
" bon of the Black Eagle, which his Prussian
" majesty had conferred on the king when
" he was Count Poniatowski. One of his
" motives for doing this, was by shewing the
" order of the Black Eagle to Pulaski and
" the confederates, to prove to them incon-
" testibly that the king was in their hands,
" and on his way. Lukawski was afterwards
" executed."

" remained

BOOK
I.

" remained with him, of whom Kofinfki was the chief. The
" night was exceedingly dark ; they were abfolutely ignorant
" of the way ; and, as the horfes could not keep their legs,
" they obliged his majefty to follow them on foot, with only
" one fhoe, the other being loft in the dirt.

" They continued to wander through the open meadows,
" without following any certain path, and without getting to
" any diftance from Warfaw. They again mounted the king
" on horfeback, two of them holding him on each fide by the
" hand, and a third leading his horfe by the bridle. In this
" manner they were proceeding, when his majefty, finding
" they had taken the road which led to a village called Bura-
" kow, warned them not to enter it, becaufe there were fome
" Ruffians ftationed in that place who might probably attempt
" to refcue him *. Finding himfelf, however, incapable of
" accompanying the affaffins in the painful pofture in which
" they held him kept down on the faddle, he requefted them,
" fince they were determined to oblige him to proceed, at leaft
" to give him another horfe and a boot †. This requeft they
" complied with ; and continuing their progrefs through al-
" moft impaffable lands, without any road, and ignorant of
" their way, they at length found themfelves in the wood of
" Bielany, only a league diftant from Warfaw. From the

* " This intimation, which the king gave
" to his affaffins, may at firft fight appear
" extraordinary and unaccountable, but was
" really dictated by the greateft addrefs and
" judgment. He apprehended with reafon
" that, on the fight of a Ruffian guard, they
" would inftantly put him to death with their
" fabres, and fly ; whereas by informing
" them of the danger they incurred, he in
" fome meafure gained their confidence : in
" effect, this behaviour of the king feemed to
" foften them a little, and made them believe
" he did not mean to efcape from them."

† The king in his fpeech to the diet on the
trial of the confpirators, interceded ftrongly
for Kofinfki, or John Kutfma, to whom he

gratefully expreffes himfelf indebted for thefe
favours in the following words :

" As I was in the hands of the affaffins, I
" heard them repeatedly afk John Kutfma, if
" they fhould not affaffinate me, but he al-
" ways prevented them. He was the firft who
" perfuaded them to behave to me with greater
" gentlenefs ; and obliged them to confer
" upon me fome fervices which I then greatly
" wanted ; namely, one to give me a cap,
" and a fecond a boot, which at that time
" were no trifling prefents : for the cold air
" greatly affected the wound in my head ; and
" my foot, which was covered with blood,
" gave me inexpreffible torture, which conti-
" nued every moment increafing."

" time

" time they had paffed the ditch they repeatedly demanded of
" Kofinfki their chief, if it was not yet time to put the king
" to death ; and thefe demands were reiterated in proportion
" to the obftacles and difficulties they encountered.

" Meanwhile the confufion and confternation increafed at
" Warfaw. The guards were afraid to purfue the confpira-
" tors, left terror of being overtaken fhould prompt them in
" the darknefs to maffacre the king ; and on the other hand,
" by not purfuing they might give them time to efcape with
" their prize, beyond the poffibility of affiftance. Several of
" the firft nobility at length mounted on horfeback, and fol-
" lowing the track of the affaffins, arrived at the place where
" his majefty had paffed the ditch. There they found his
" *peliffe*, which he had loft in the precipitation with which he
" was hurried away : it was bloody, and pierced with holes
" made by the balls or fabres. This convinced them that he
" was no more.

" The king was ftill in the hands of the feven remaining
" affaffins, who advanced with him into the wood of Bielany,
" when they were fuddenly alarmed by a Ruffian patrole or
" detachment. Inftantly holding council, four of them dif-
" appeared, leaving him with the other three, who compelled
" him to walk on. Scarce a quarter of an hour after, a fecond
" Ruffian guard challenged them anew. Two of the affaf-
" fins then fled, and the king remained alone with Kofinfki
" the chief, both on foot. His majefty, exhaufted with all
" the fatigue which he had undergone, implored his conductor
" to ftop, and fuffer him to take a moment's repofe. Kofinfki
" refufed it, menacing him with his naked fabre ; and at the
" fame time informed him, that beyond the wood they fhould
" find a carriage. They continued their walk, till they came
" to the door of the convent of Bielany. Kofinfki appeared
" loft in thought, and fo much agitated by his reflections, that
" the

4.

" the king perceiving his diforder, and obferving that he wan-
" dered without knowing the road, faid to him, ' I fee you are
" at a lofs which way to proceed.   Let me enter the convent
" of Bielany, and do you provide for your own fafety.' ' No,'
" replied Kofinfki, ' I have fworn.'

" They proceeded till they came to Mariemont, a fmall pa-
" lace belonging to the houfe of Saxony, not above half a
" league from Warfaw : here Kofinfki betrayed fome fatis-
" faction at finding where he was, and the king ftill demand-
" ing an inftant's repofe, he confented at length.   They fat
" down together on the ground, and the king employed thefe
" moments in endeavouring to foften his conductor, and in-
" duce him to favour or permit his efcape.   His majefty re-
" prefented the atrocity of the crime he had committed in at-
" tempting to murder his fovereign, and the invalidity of an
" oath taken to perpetrate fo heinous an action : Kofinfki lent
" attention to this difcourfe, and began to betray fome marks of
" remorfe. ' But,' faid he, ' if I fhould confent and reconduct
" you to Warfaw, what will be the confequence ?——I fhall be
" taken and executed !'

" This reflection plunged him into new uncertainty and
" embarrafsment.   ' I give you my word,' anfwered his ma-
" jefty, ' that you fhall fuffer no harm ; but if you doubt my
" promife, efcape while there is yet time.   I can find my way
" to fome place of fecurity ; and I will certainly direct your
" purfuers to take the contrary road to that which you have
" chofen.'   Kofinfki could not any longer contain himfelf,
" but, throwing himfelf at the king's feet, implored forgive-
" nefs for the crime he had committed ; and fwore to protect
" him againft every enemy, relying totally on his generofity
" for pardon and prefervation.   His majefty reiterated to him
" his affurances of fafety.   Judging, however, that it was pru-
" dent to gain fome afylum without delay, and recollecting that
                                                      " .there

" there was a mill at fome confiderable diftance, he immedi-
" ately made towards it.   Kofinfki knocked, but in vain ; no
" anfwer was given : he then broke a pane of glafs in the
" window, and intreated for fhelter to a nobleman who had
" been plundered by robbers.   The miller refufed, fuppofing
" them to be banditti, and continued for more than half an
" hour to perfift in his denial.   At length the king approached,
" and fpeaking through the broken pane, endeavoured to per-
" fuade him to admit them under his roof, adding, ' If we
" were robbers, as you fuppofe, it would be very eafy for us to
" break the whole window, inftead of one pane of glafs.'   This
" argument prevailed.   They at length opened the door, and
" admitted his majefty.   He immediately wrote a note to
" General Coccei, colonel of the foot-guards.   It was literally
" as follows : ' Par une efpece de miracle je fuis fauvé des
" mains des affaffins. Je fuis ici au petit moulin de Marie-
" mont. Venez au plutôt me tirer d'ici. Je fuis bleffé,
" mais pas fort *.'   It was with the greateft difficulty, how-
" ever, that the king could perfuade any one to carry this
" note to Warfaw, as the people of the mill, imagining that
" he was a nobleman who had juft been plundered by rob-
" bers, were afraid of falling in with the troop.   Kofinfki
" then offered to reftore every thing he had taken ; but his
" majefty left him all, except the blue ribbon of the White
" Eagle.

" When the meffenger arrived with the note, the aftonifh-
" ment and joy was incredible.   Coccei inftantly rode to the
" mill, followed by a detachment of the guards. He met Ko-
" finfki at the door with his fabre drawn, who admitted him
" as foon as he knew him.   The king had funk into a fleep,

---

* " By a kind of miracle I am efcaped   " poffible, and take me from hence. I am
" from the hands of affaffins. I am now at   " wounded, but not dangeroufly."
" the mill of Mariemont. Come as foon as

" caufed by his fatigue; and was ftretched on the ground,
" covered with the miller's cloak.   Coccei immediately threw
" himfelf at his majefty's feet, calling him his fovereign, and
" kiffing his hand.   It is not eafy to paint or defcribe the
" aftonifhment of the miller and his family, who inftantly
" imitated Coccei's example,   by throwing themfelves on
" their knees *.   The king returned to Warfaw in General
" Coccei's carriage, and reached the palace about five in the
" morning. His wound was found not to be dangerous; and
" he foon recovered the bruifes and injuries, which he had
" fuffered during this memorable night.

" So extraordinary an efcape is fcarce to be paralleled in
" hiftory, and affords ample matter of wonder and furprife.
" Scarce could the nobility or people at Warfaw credit the
" evidence of their fenfes, when they faw him return.   Cer-
" tainly neither the efcape of the king of France from Damien,
" or of the king of Portugal from the confpiracy of the Duke
" d'Aveiro, were equally amazing or improbable, as that of
" the king of Poland.   I have related it very minutely, and
" from authorities the higheft and moft inconteftible.

" It is natural to inquire what is become of Kofinfki, the
" man who faved his majefty's life, and the other confpirators.
" He was born in the palatinate of Cracow, and of mean ex-
" traction: having affumed the name of Kofinfki †, which is
" that of a noble family, to give himfelf credit. He had been
" created an officer in the troops of the confederates under
" Pulafki. It would feem as if Kofinfki began to entertain the
" idea of preferving the king's life from the time when Lu-
" kawfki and Strawenfki abandoned him ; yet he had great
" ftruggles with himfelf before he could refolve on this con-

---

* " I have been at this mill, rendered   " miller to the extent of his wifhes in build-
" memorable by fo fingular an event.   It is   " ing him a mill upon the Viftula, and allow-
" a wretched Polifh hovel, at a diftance from   " ing him a fmall penfion."
" any houfe.   The king has rewarded the   † His real name was John Kutfma.

" duct,

" duct, after the solemn engagements into which he had en-
" tered.   Even after he had conducted the king back to War-
" saw, he expressed more than once his doubts of the propriety
" of what he had done, and some remorse for having deceived
" his employers.

" Lukawski and Strawenski were both taken, and several
" of the other affassins.   At his majesty's peculiar request and
" intreaty, the diet remitted the capital punishment of the in-
" ferior conspirators, and condemned them to work for life on
" the fortifications of Kaminiec, where they now are.   By his
" his interceffion likewise with the diet, the horrible punish-
" ment and various modes of torture, which the laws of Po-
" land decree and inflict on regicides, were mitigated; and
" both Lukawski and Strawenski were only simply beheaded.
" Kosinski was detained under a very strict confinement, and
" obliged to give evidence against his two companions.   A
" person of distinction, who saw them both die, has affured
" me, that nothing could be more noble and manly than all
" Lukawski's conduct previous to his death.   When he was
" carried to the place of execution, although his body was al-
" most extenuated by the severity of his confinement, diet,
" and treatment, his spirit unsubdued raised him above the
" terrors of an infamous and public execution.   He had not
" been permitted to shave his beard while in prison, and his
" drefs was squalid to the greatest degree; yet none of thefe
" humiliations could deprefs his mind.   With a grandeur of
" soul worthy of a better caufe, but which it was impoffible
" not to admire, he refufed to see or embrace the traitor Ko-
" sinfki.   When conducted to the scene of execution, which
" was about a mile from Warfaw, he betrayed no emotions of
" terror or unmanly fear.   He made a short harangue to the
" multitude affembled upon the occafion, in which he by no
" means expreffed any forrow for his paft conduct, or contri-

" tion

" tion for his attempt on the king, which he probably regarded
" as meritorious and patriotic. His head was fevered from his
" body.

" Strawenſki was beheaded at .... ſame time, but he neither
" harangued the people, nor ſhewed any ſigns of contrition.
" Pulaſki, who commanded one of the many corps of confede-
" rate Poles then in arms, and who was the great agent and
" promoter of the aſſaſſination, is ſtill alive *, though an out-
" law and an exile. He is ſaid, even by the Ruſſians his ene-
" mies, to poſſeſs military talents of a very ſuperior nature ;
" nor were they ever able to take him priſoner during the ci-
" vil war.

" To return to Koſinſki, the man who ſaved the king's life.
" About a week after Lukawſki and Strawenſki's execution,
" he was ſent by his majeſty out of Poland. He now reſides
" at Semigallia in the papal territories, where he enjoys an an-
" nual penſion from the king.

" A circumſtance almoſt incredible, and which ſeems to
" breathe all the ſanguinary bigotry of the 16th century, I
" cannot omit. It is that the papal nuntio in Poland, inſpired
" with a furious zeal againſt the diſſidents, whom he believed
" to be protected by the king, not only approved the ſcheme
" for aſſaſſinating his majeſty, but bleſſed the weapons of the
" conſpirators at Czetſchokow, previous to their ſetting out
" on their expedition. This is a trait indiſputably true, and
" ſcarcely to be exceeded by any thing under the reign of
" Charles IX. of France, and of his mother Catharine of
" Medicis."

In addition to Mr. Wraxall's account I am enabled to add
the following circumſtances :

Upon General Coccei's arrival at the mill, the firſt queſtion

---

* After the concluſion of theſe troubles, American ſervice, and was killed in the at-
Pulaſki eſcaped from Poland, and repaired to tempt to force the Britiſh Lines at the ſiege
America : he diſtinguiſhed himſelf in the of Savannah in 1779.

which

which his majefty afked was, whether any of his attendants had fuffered from the affaffins ; and upon being informed that one of the heyducs was killed upon the fpot, and another dangeroufly wounded, his mind, naturally feeling, now rendered more fufceptible by his late danger, was greatly affected ; and his joy at his own efcape was confiderably diminifhed.

Upon his return to Warfaw, the ftreets through which he paffed were illuminated with torches, and crouded by an immenfe concourfe of people, who followed him to the palace, crying out inceffantly " The king is alive." Upon his entering the palace, the doors were flung open, and perfons of all ranks were admitted to approach his perfon, and to felicitate him upon his efcape. The fcene, as I have been informed by feveral of the nobility who were prefent, was affecting beyond defcription. Every one ftruggled to get near him, to kifs his hand, or even to touch his cloaths : all were fo tranfported with joy, that they even loaded Kofinfki with careffes, and called him the faviour of their king. His majefty was fo affected with thefe figns of zeal and affection, that he expreffed in the moft feeling manner his ftong fenfe of thefe proofs of their attachment, and declared it was the happieft hour of his whole life. In this moment of rapture he forgot the dangers he had avoided, and the wounds he had received ; and as every one feemed anxious to learn the circumftances of his efcape, he would not fuffer his wounds to be infpected and dreffed before he had himfelf fatisfied their impatience, by relating the difficulties and dangers he had undergone. During the recital, a perfon unacquainted with the language might have difcovered the various events of the ftory from the changes of expreffion in the countenances of the byftanders, which difplayed the moft fudden alterations from terror to compaffion, from compaffion to aftonifhment, and from aftonifhment to rapture ; while the univerfal filence was only broken by fighs and tears of joy.

The

The king having finished the account, again repeated his assurances of gratitude and affection for the unfeigned proofs they had given of their love and attachment; and dismissed them, by adding, that he hoped he had been thus miraculously preserved by Divine Providence, for no other purpose than to pursue with additional zeal the good of his country, which had ever been the great object of his attention.

Being now left alone, his majesty permitted the surgeons to examine the wound in his head. Upon cutting away the skin, it appeared that the bone was hurt, but not dangerously; from the quantity of clotted blood, the operation of dressing was tedious and painful, and was submitted to by the king with great patience and magnanimity. The surgeons proposed at first to bleed him in the foot; but they laid aside this intention upon finding both his feet swollen considerably, and covered with blisters and bruises.

The family of the heyduc, who had saved the king's life by the loss of his own, was amply provided for: his body was buried with great pomp; and his majesty erected an handsome monument to his memory, with an elegant inscription expressive of the man's fidelity and of his own gratitude.

I saw the monument: it is a pyramid standing upon a sarcophagus, with a Latin and Polish inscription; the former I copied, and it is as follows.

" Hic jacet Georgius Henricus Butzau, qui regem Stanislaum " Augustum nefariis parricidarum telis impetitum, die III Nov. " 1771, proprii pectoris clypeo defendens, geminatis ictibus " confossus, gloriose occubuit. Fidelis subditi necem lugens, Rex " posuit hocce monumentum illius in laudem, aliis exemplo*."

---

* " Here lies George Henry Butzau, who, " on the 3d of November, 1771, opposing " his own breast to shield Stanislaus Augustus " from the weapons of nefarious parricides, " was pierced with repeated wounds, and " gloriously expired. The king, lamenting " the death of a faithful subject, erected this " monument, as a tribute to him, and an " incentive to others."

CHAP.

[39]

C H A P.   IV.

Account of the plan and progress of the partition of Poland.—
Projected by the king of Pruffia.—*Adopted by the emperor of*
Germany, *and finally acceded to by the emprefs of* Ruffia.—
The confent of the king and diet of Poland *extorted after great*
oppofition.——*Changes in the government introduced by the par-*
titioning powers.——*Spirited, but fruitlefs, refiftance of the* Polifh *delegates.*——*Fate of the diffidents.*

W E are now arrived at that remarkable event of the prefent reign, the partition of Poland ; which was planned
with fuch profound fecrecy, tnat it was fcarcely fufpected before it was carried into execution.   Poland had long derived
its principal fecurity from its peculiar fituation between three
great powers, each equally interefted to prevent the others
from acquiring any increafe of ftrength, or addition of territory : the union of thefe rival potentates was confidered as a
circumftance nearly impoffible ; and fhould fuch an unexpected union take place, it was thought incredible that the
other princes of Europe would paffively fubmit to a material
alteration in the balance of power.

Treaties upon treaties, and negotiations upon negotiations,
had guarantied to Poland the poffeffion of her territory ; and
the very three powers who difmembered her provinces, had,
at the prefent king's acceffion, folemnly renounced all right
and title to any part of the Polifh dominions.   But treaties and
guaranties are in general only adhered to until they can be
broken with fafety : the only effectual method for any ftate to
fecure its dominions, is to make itfelf refpectable by its ftrength
and unanimity, and to be prepared againft any attacks.   When

a

a powerful people impute national difasters, which a proper vigour and forefight might have prevented, to the perfidy of foreign ftates, they only bear teftimony, in more fpecious terms, to their own indolence, negligence, or weaknefs of government. Nor is that fyftematical jealoufy, which modern nations profefs to entertain for the balance of power, to be depended on as a more effectual fafeguard to any particular ftate, than the faith of treaties. This principle, though founded on the moft obvious and judicious policy, and though at times productive of the moft beneficial effects, is unluckily liable to be counteracted and defeated by an almoft innumerable variety of contingencies. Where a combination of different powers is requifite to give efficacy to this principle, thofe powers may want unanimity and concert; where again the exertion of only a fingle ftate is fufficient, that ftate may, by the temporary fituation of affairs, or the cafual interefts of its governing party, be rendered incapable of acting with proper fpirit. In a word, the anxiety of European ftates for the prefervation of the balance of power is by no means an invariable pledge of protection to any fingle nation. Venice was brought to the verge of ruin by a reliance on this principle; Poland received from it no fubftantial protection; nor did England, though ftruggling fingly againft a hoft of enemies, reap, in her late conteft, the flighteft benefit from its influence.

The natural ftrength of Poland, if properly exerted, would have formed a more certain bulwark againft the ambition of her neighbours, than the faith of treaties, or an attention, in the other European nations, to the balance of power. It is extremely worthy of remark, that of the three partitioning powers, Pruffia * was formerly in a ftate of vaffalage to the republic;

---

* In the 13th century, all Pruffia belonged to the knights of the Teutonic order. In 1454 that part, fince denominated Polifh or Weftern Pruffia, revolted to Cafimir IV. and was afterwards incorporated into the dominions of the republic; at the fame time the knights

republic ; Ruſſia * once ſaw its capital and throne poſſeſſed by the Poles ; and Auſtria, ſcarce a century ago, was indebted to a ſovereign † of this country for the preſervation of its metropolis, and almoſt for its very exiſtence.

A kingdom, ſo lately the maſter or protector of its neighbours, would never have been ſo readily overwhelmed by them, without the moſt glaring imperfections in its government. Poland, in truth, formerly more powerful than any of the ſurrounding ſtates, has, from the defects of its conſtitution, declined in the midſt of general improvements ; and, after giving law to the north, is become an eaſy prey to every invader.

The Partition of Poland was firſt projected by the king of Pruſſia. Poliſh or Weſtern Pruſſia had long been an object of his ambition : excluſive of its fertility, commerce, and population, its local ſituation rendered it highly valuable to that monarch ; it lay between his German dominions and Eaſtern Pruſſia, and while poſſeſſed by the Poles, cut off, at their will, all communication between them.   During the courſe of the laſt general war, he experienced the moſt fatal effects from this disjointed ſtate of his territories.   By the acquiſition of

knights were conſtrained to hold the remaining part, called Eaſtern Pruſſia, as a fief of the crown of Poland. In 1525 Eaſtern Pruſſia was erected into an hereditary duchy, and given to Albert of Brandenburg as a Poliſh fief. Upon his death it fell to his ſon Albert Frederick, who being impaired in his faculties, the adminiſtration was veſted firſt in Joachim Frederick elector of Brandenburg, and afterwards in Joachim's ſon John Sigiſmond, who had married Albert's daughter. Upon the demiſe of Albert without male heirs, John Sigiſmond, who ſucceeded to the duchy of Pruſſia, did homage for that duchy as a vaſſal of the republic. His grandſon Frederick William, the great Elector, was the firſt duke of Pruſſia releaſed from this badge of feudal dependence by John Caſimir ; Eaſtern

Pruſſia being declared a ſovereign, independent, and hereditary duchy.

Frederick, ſon of Frederick William the Great, aſſumed the title of King of Pruſſia, which however the Poles never acknowledged, until 1764, at the acceſſion of Staniſlaus Auguſtus. His preſent majeſty Frederick II. by the partition treaty now poſſeſſes both Weſtern and Eaſtern Pruſſia.

* Under Sigiſmond III. whoſe troops got poſſeſſion of Moſcow, and whoſe ſon Ladiſlaus was choſen great duke of Muſcovy by a party of the Ruſſian nobles.

† John Sobieſki, who compelled the Turks to raiſe the ſiege of Vienna, and delivered the houſe of Auſtria from the greateſt dangers it ever experienced.

Weſtern Pruſſia, his dominions would be rendered compact,
and his troops in time of war be able to march from Berlin to
Koningſburgh without interruption.   The period was now
arrived, when the ſituation of Poland ſeemed to promiſe the
attainment of this favourite object.   He purſued it, however,
with all the caution of an able politician.   On the commencement of the troubles, he ſhewed no eagerneſs to interfere in
the affairs of this country ; and although he had concurred
with the empreſs of Ruſſia in raiſing Staniſlaus Auguſtus to
the throne of Poland ; yet he declined taking any active part
in his favour againſt the confederates.   Afterwards, when the
whole kingdom became convulſed throughout with civil commotions, and deſolated likewiſe by the plague, he, under pretence of forming lines to prevent the ſpreading of the infec-
tion, advanced his troops into Poliſh Pruſſia, and occupied that
whole diſtrict.

Though now completely maſter of the country, and by no
means apprehenſive of any formidable reſiſtance from the diſ-
united and diſtracted Poles, yet, as he was well aware that the
ſecurity of his new acquiſition depended upon the acquieſ-
cence of Ruſſia and Auſtria, he planned the Partition of Poland.   He communicated the project to the emperor, either
upon their interview at Niefs in Sileſia, in 1769, or in that of
the following year, at Neuſtadt in Auſtria ; from whom the
overture met with a ready concurrence.   Joſeph, who had before ſecretly encouraged the confederates, and even commenced
a negociation with the Porte againſt Ruſſia, now ſuddenly altered his meaſures, and increaſed his army towards the Poliſh
frontiers.   The plague preſenting to him, as well as to the
king of Pruſſia, a ſpecious motive for ſtationing troops in the
dominions of the republic ; he gradually extended his lines,
and, in 1772, occupied the whole territory, which he has
ſince diſmembered.   But, notwithſtanding this change in his
                                                    ſentiments,

sentiments, his real views upon Poland were at first so effectually concealed, that the Polish rebels conceived that the
Austrian army was advancing to act in their favour ; not sup-
posing it possible, that the rival courts of Vienna and Berlin
could act in concert.

Nothing more remained towards completing the partition,
than the accession of the empress of Russia. That great princess was too discerning a politician not to regard with a jealous
eye the introduction of foreign powers into Poland. Possessing
an uncontrouled ascendancy over the whole country, she could
propose no material advantage from the formal acquisition of
a part ; and must purchase a moderate addition to her territory
by a considerable surrender of authority. The king of Prussia,
well acquainted with the true interests of Russia in regard to
Poland, and with the capacity of the empress to discern those
interests, forbore (it is said) opening any negotiation on the
subject of the partition, until she was involved in a Turkish
war. At that crisis he dispatched his brother Prince Henry to
Petersburg, who suggested to the empress that the house of
Austria was forming an alliance with the Porte, which, if it
took place, would create a most formidable combination against
her ; that, nevertheless, the friendship of that house was to be
purchased by acceding to the partition ; that upon this condition the emperor was willing to renounce his connection with
the Grand Signior, and would suffer the Russians to prosecute
the war without interruption. Catharine, anxious to push her
conquests against the Turks, and dreading the interposition of
the emperor in that quarter ; perceiving likewise, from the
intimate union between the courts of Vienna and Berlin, that
it would not be in her power, at the present juncture, to prevent the intended partition, closed with the proposal, and se-
lected no inconsiderable portion of the Polish territories for
herself. The treaty was signed at Petersburg in the beginning

of

BOOK I.

of February, 1772, by the Ruffian, Auftrian, and Pruffian plenipotentiaries.

As the troops of the three courts were already in poffeffion of the greateft part of Poland, the confederates, hemmed in on all fides, were foon routed and difperfed; and Europe waited in anxious expectation what would be the iffue of this unexpected union: yet fuch was the profound fecrecy with which the partitioning powers proceeded, that for fome time after the ratification of the treaty, only vague conjectures were entertained even at Warfaw * concerning their real intentions; and the late lord Cathcart, the Englifh minifter at Peterfburg, was able to obtain no authentic information of its fignature, until two months after the event.

The firft formal notification of any pretenfions to the Polifh territory was in the month of September, 1772, announced to the king and fenate affembled at Warfaw, by the Imperial embaffador; which was foon followed by the memorials of the Ruffian and Pruffian courts, fpecifying their refpective claims. It would be tedious to enter into a detail of the pleas urged by the three powers in favour of their feveral demands; it would be no lefs uninterefting to lay before the reader, the anfwers and remonftrances of the king and fenate, as well as the appeals to the other ftates which had guarantied the poffeffions of Poland. The courts of London, Paris, Stockholm, and Copen-

---

* I have a collection of MS. letters written from Warfaw before and after the partition: the following paffages from thofe letters will fhew the myfterious conduct of the three courts, and the uncertainty of the Poles concerning the difmemberment.

" On cache à Vienne les vrais motifs et le ✤ but de la prochaine entrée des troupes en " Pologne," &c. May 6, 1772.

All the letters fpeak of the apprehenfions of difmemberment; but the firft which mentions it with any certainty is dated May 19, which relates, that one of the king of Pruffia's officers, paffing through Marienburgh, even faid, that the neighbourhood of that town had fallen to the king by the partition.

May 30. " On croit de plus et plus qu'on " nous partagera, tant d'avis qui s'accordent " là deffus ne peuvent pas être fur de vaines " imaginations et conjectures," &c.

Auguft 13. " La bombe va crever, on " acheve le traité de partage," &c.

Auguft 24. " C'en eft fait, le traité ébau- " chè au mois de Fevrier vient de prendre " confiftence," &c.

hagen,

hagen, remonstrated against the usurpations; but remonstrances without assistance could be of no effect. Poland submitted to the dismemberment, not without the most violent struggles, and now, for the first time, felt and lamented the fatal effects of faction and discord.

A diet being demanded by the partitioning powers, in order to ratify the cession of the provinces, was, after some delay, convoked by the king in the following summons: " Since " there are no hopes from any quarter, and any further delays " will only tend to draw down the most dreadful calamities " upon the remainder of the dominions which are left to the " republic; the diet is convened for the 19th of April, 1773, " according to the will of the three courts: nevertheless, in " order to avoid all cause of reproach, the king, with the ad- " vice of the senate, again appeals to the guaranties of the " treaty of Oliva."

The diet met at the appointed time; and such was the spirit of the members, that, notwithstanding the deplorable situation of their country, the threats and bribes of the three powers, the partition-treaty was not carried through without much difficulty. For some time the majority of the nuntios appeared determined to oppose the dismemberment, and the king firmly persisted in the same resolution. The embassadors of the three courts enforced their requisitions by the most alarming menaces; and threatened the king with deposition and imprisonment. They also gave out by their emissaries, that in case the diet continued refractory, Warsaw should be pillaged. This report was industriously circulated, and made a sensible impression upon the inhabitants. By menaces of this sort, by corrupting the marshal of the diet, who was accompanied with a Russian guard; in a word, by bribes, promises, and threats, the members of the diet were at length prevailed on to ratify the dismemberment. In the senate, however, or upper house, there

BOOK I.

there was a majority of only fix; in the lower houfe, or af-fembly of the nuntios, of but one fingle vote in favour of the meafure *. An act was then paffed to limit the feffions of the diet to the term of a few days, and delegates were appointed, with full powers to adjuft, in concert with the embaffadors, all the terms of the difmemberment. The commiffioners, or delegates, on the breaking up of the diet in May, immediately entered upon their office; and, by the month of September, finally concluded the treaty of the partition in conformity to the dictates of the three courts. At this juncture, feveral nobles were bold enough to iffue manifeftoes and remonftrances in various parts of the kingdom, againft the ceffion of the provinces, and to reprobate the conduct of the partitioning powers; but fuch remonftrances were totally difregarded, and may be confidered only as the laft convulfions of an expiring nation.

Of the difmembered countries †, the Ruffian province is the largeft, the Auftrian the moft populous, and the Pruffian the moft commercial. The population of the whole amounts to near 5,000,000 of fouls; the firft containing 1,500,000, the fecond 2,500,000, and the third 860,000. Weftern Pruffia was the greateft lofs to Poland, as by the difmemberment of that province, the navigation of the Viftula entirely depends upon the king of Pruffia; by the lofs confequently of this diftrict a fatal blow was given to the trade of Poland; for his Pruffian majefty has laid fuch heavy duties upon the merchandize paffing to Dantzic, as greatly to diminifh the commerce of that town, and to transfer a confiderable portion of it to Memmel and Konigfburgh.

Although the limits of Poland were fettled by the treaty of

---

* By 54 againft 53.

† The reader, by confulting the map of Poland (prefixed to this work), will fee the fituation and extent of the three difmembered provinces. For an account of the Auftrian province, fee Book II Chap. I.; of the Ruffian, Book III. Chap. I.

Partition,

Partition, yet the Auſtrians and Pruſſians continually extended their frontiers: the emperor ſeized upon Caſimir, and even avowed an intention of taking poſſeſſion of Cracow and Kaminiec; while Frederick alleged theſe uſurpations as a juſtification for ſimilar incroachments on his part; urging, that he could not, conſiſtent with his own ſecurity, ſee the emperor increaſing his dominions without following his example, and aſſuming an equivalent.

Catharine was forced for a time to connive at theſe encroachments; but no ſooner was peace * eſtabliſhed with the Turks, and the rebellion of Pugatcheff cruſhed, than ſhe immediately turned her whole attention to Poland; and it is owing to her ſpirited remonſtrances, that both Auſtrians and Pruſſians have relinquiſhed their uſurpations, and confined themſelves to the limits marked by the treaty of partition.

The partitioning powers did leſs injury to the republic by diſmembering its faireſt provinces, than by perpetuating the principles of anarchy and confuſion, and eſtabliſhing on a permanent footing, that exorbitant liberty †, which is the parent of faction, and has proved the decline of the republic. Under pretence of amending the conſtitution, they have confirmed all its defects, and have taken effectual precautions to

---

* The peace between the Empreſs and the Turks was ſigned on the 21ſt of July, 1774, in Marſhal Romanzof's camp near Bulgaria; and in a letter from Warſaw, dated Auguſt 29, of the ſame year, it is ſaid, "The Emperor and King of Pruſſia continued encroaching upon the Poliſh territories, and enlarging their frontiers which were marked by the treaty of Peterſburg. But upon the concluſion of the peace, the Auſtrian and Pruſſian troops retired within their reſpective lines. Behold already the good effects of this glorious peace! What would have become of us, if the arms of the Ottoman empire had proſpered according to the wiſhes of many?"

And in another, dated Sept. 14, 1775, "The king of Pruſſia has written to the empreſs of Ruſſia a letter in a moſt enchanting ſtyle. After much praiſe, he adds, that notwithſtanding the juſtice of his claim upon thoſe parts which he has annexed to his former acquiſitions, he ſhall make no difficulty in ſacrificing them, as a proof of his readineſs to oblige her Imperial majeſty; provided the houſe of Auſtria will alſo reſtore what ſhe has taken."

† "Our liberty," ſaid a Pole, "is like a two-edged ſword in the hand of an infant, and for that very reaſon our neighbours are anxious to preſerve it entire."

render

render this unhappy country incapable of emerging from its prefent deplorable ftate.

The delegates, who ratified the treaty of partition, being alfo empowered by the diet to concert with the three courts any alterations in the conftitution which might appear benefi-cial to the kingdom, continued fitting from May 1773 to March 1775, during which period the convocation of the or-dinary diet was poftponed, until the members of the delegation had agreed to all the innovations propofed by the embaffadors; and until every part of the government was finally arranged. Notwithftanding the wretched condition of Poland, and the refiftlefs power of the three courts, yet the king and the majo-rity of the delegates long with-held their confent to the pro-pofed alterations.

Some idea of their fpirit may be formed from the following account of one of the meetings, when the propofitions relat-ing to the change of government were firft produced in Sep-tember, 1773. Prior to the appearance of the three embaf-fadors in the affembly, much was faid, and with great vehe-mence, againft the projected innovations; many reproaches were thrown out againft the authors of that plan, for facrific-ing the public advantage to their private ambition, refentment, and interefts. At the entrance of the three embaffadors, a dead filence took place for fome minutes, until the fecretary of the Ruffian embaffy began to read the plan for new-mo-delling the conftitution; then a general murmur fpread through the whole affembly, and, as he proceeded, increafed to fuch a degree as almoft to drown his voice; nor was it without frequent interruptions, that he was permitted to finifh its recital. He had fcarcely concluded, when the whole body of delegates loudly demanded the treaties of partition and al-liance: the embaffadors anfwering, that many points could not be adjufted without farther inftructions from their refpec-tive

tive courts; it was replied, that in the mean time they might introduce the treaty of commerce, which they were authorifed to conclude. At all events, it was urged, the propofal con-cerning the change of government is premature; a revolution of fuch extreme importance demands the moft deliberate exa-mination, and ought not to be hurried through, as if it was a circumftance of no concern to the nation. One of the dele-gates, who was moft violent in his oppofition, delivered his fentiments with a freedom which aftonifhed the affembly; and when the embaffadors, who did not underftand the Polifh idiom, applied to a Caftellan for an explanation of what was faid, the latter excufed himfelf, under pretence of not being qualified for the office of interpreter, as having but an imper-fect knowledge of the French language. When, at laft, one of the Palatines, who was of the embaffador's party, acquainted them with the contents of the fpeech; the orator ventured to thank him for explaining the purport of his harangue in fo able a manner; while the praifes which, in a fine tone of irony, he affected to beftow upon the Palatine for his readi-nefs to oblige, as well as for his independent fpirit, occafioned much mirth in the affembly. The undifguifed approbation given by the greateft part of the members to this orator, con-vinced the embaffadors that this was no time to obtrude their refolutions upon the delegates: they accordingly broke up the meeting, and poftponed the bufinefs to a future opportunity *. The next feffion, however, was not more favourable to their wifhes, nor did the patriotic zeal of the delegates feem to abate. Their oppofition indeed to this meafure continued fo violent, that more than a year elapfed before the embaffadors

* The following paffage in one of my MS. letters, dated to late as Nov. 13. 1774, will fhew the difficulty of fettling with the dele-gates.

" The plan for the permanent council " continues to be read; it ftill excites con-" tinual debates, and more will arife; but " all will be finifhed according to the will of " the minifters."

BOOK
I.

were able, by the influence of threats, bribery, and promifes, to obtain a majority; and before the delegates, terrified or feduced into compliance, formally acceded to the change of government. This important point being obtained, the delegation was diffolved on the 13th of April, 1775, and all the articles were confirmed by the general diet.

The following note, delivered by the three embaffadors to the delegates on the 13th of September, 1773, will give the beft general idea of the changes made in the conftitution. " The courts are fo interefted in the pacification of Poland, " that, while the treaties are getting ready to be figned and " ratified, the minifters cannot lofe any of that valuable time, " fo neceffary for the re-eftablifhment of order, and the tran- " quillity of this kingdom. We now, therefore, deliver to " the delegation a part of thofe cardinal laws, to the ratification " of which our courts will not fuffer any contradiction.

I. " The crown of Poland fhall be for ever elective, and " all order of fucceffion profcribed : any perfon who fhall " endeavour to break this law, fhall be declared an enemy to " his country, and liable to be punifhed accordingly.

II. " Foreign candidates to the throne being the frequent " caufe of troubles and divifion, fhall be excluded ; and it fhall " be enacted, that, for the future, no perfon can be chofen " king of Poland, and great duke of Lithuania, excepting a " native Pole, of noble * origin, and poffeffing land within " the kingdom. The fon, or grandfon, of a king of Poland, " cannot be elected immediately upon the death of their father " or grandfather ; and are not eligible, excepting after an in- " terval of two reigns.

III. " The government of Poland fhall be for ever free, " independent, and of a republican form.

IV. " The true principle of the faid government confifting

* That is, any gentleman.

" in

" in the ſtrict execution of its laws, and the equilibrium of
" the three eſtates, namely, the king, the ſenate, and the
" equeſtrian order, a Permanent Council ſhall be eſtabliſhed,
" in which the executive power ſhall be veſted. In this coun-
" cil the equeſtrian order, hitherto excluded from the admi-
" niſtration of affairs in the intervals of the diets, ſhall be ad-
" mitted, as ſhall be more clearly laid down in the future ar-
" rangements."

Theſe arrangements having been carried into execution, I
ſhall make a few remarks upon the ſeveral articles.

By the firſt, the houſe of Saxony, and all foreign princes,
who might be likely to give weight to Poland by their hereditary dominions, are rendered incapable of filling the throne.
By the ſecond, the excluſion of a king's ſon or grandſon, excepting after an interval of two reigns, removes the fainteſt
proſpect of an hereditary ſovereignty, and entails upon the
kingdom all the evils inſeparable from that moſt wretched
form of government, an elective monarchy. By the third
article, the *liberum veto*, and all the exorbitant privileges of
the equeſtrian order, are confirmed in their utmoſt latitude;
and by the laſt, the prerogatives of the crown, before too
greatly reduced, are ſtill farther diminiſhed, as will be more
minutely diſplayed in the enſuing chapter.

Before the concluſion of this chapter, it will be proper to
mention the fate of the diffidents. Their pretenſions were
finally ſettled between the republic and the mediating powers,
at the laſt meeting of the delegates. The catholic party oppoſed in ſo violent a manner the reſtoration of their antient
privileges, that, by the conſent of the foreign courts, they continue excluded from the diet, the ſenate, and the permanent
council. In return, however, the diffidents enjoy the free exerciſe of their religion; are permitted to have churches without bells; ſchools and ſeminaries of their own; they are ca-

pable

pable of fitting in the inferior courts of juftice ; and in the tribunal, appointed to receive appeals in matters of religion, three of their communion are admitted as affeffors.

In confequence of this toleration, the diffidents have conftructed churches in different parts of the kingdom; one built upon this occafion by the Lutherans at Warfaw, has the following infcription :

" Has ædes Deo J. O. facras
" Cœtus Varfovienfis in Auguft. Confeff. ex confenfu Sta-
" niflai Augufti Regis et Reipublicæ ftruere cœpit.
" Aprilis 24, 1777."

C H A P. V.

Government of Poland.—*Legiflative authority poffeffea oy the diet.— Executive power vefted in the permanent council.— Act for the eftablifhment of that council.—Article I. Arrangement of the permanent council.—Conftituent parts taken from the three eftates, the king, fenate, and equeftrian order. —Election of the members. —Prerogatives of the king.— Limitations of his authority.—Primate. — Marfhal of the equeftrian order.—Article II. Mode of proceeding.—Its five departments.—Foreign affairs.—Police.—War.—Juftice.— The Treafury.—Article III. Power and duties.—Article IV. Limits of its authority.—Detail of the five departments.*

THE government of Poland is with great propriety ftyled a republic, becaufe the king is fo exceedingly limited in his prerogative, that he refembles more the chief of a commonwealth, than the fovereign of a powerful monarchy.

The

The supreme legislative authority of this republic resides in the three estates of the realm, the king, senate, and equestrian order, assembled in a national diet *. The executive power, which was heretofore entrusted to the king and senate, is now, according to the new form of government, vested in the permanent council.

The act for the establishment of the permanent council, by the diet of 1775, is thus worded.

Since the former existence of the council *ad latus nostrum* in the republic is proved from the antient constitutions which mention it, and nominally from the sixth article in the confirmation of king Stephen, as well as from the constitutions † of 1576, 1590, 1607, 1641, 1669, 1677, and of 1678: We therefore establish a national council, *ad latus nostrum*, composed of the three orders, namely, of us the king, the senate, and of the equestrian order, to act in the manner prescribed as follows.

ARTICLE I. Arrangement of the Permanent Council.

I. This council shall bear the title of Supreme Permanent Council. It shall be composed of the three estates of the republic, namely, of the king, the senate, and the equestrian order, which shall be for ever inseparable, excepting during an interregnum, or in the king's absence, for which a provision is hereafter made.

The first estate, the king, as chief of the nation, is never changed; but the other two estates shall be elected, every two years, at the ordinary diet, by the majority of secret votes, in the following manner.

1. All senators and ministers are candidates of course, but the members of the equestrian order shall address themselves

---

* For an account of the diet, see the next chapter.

† The laws of Poland are called constitu- tions, and are denominated constitutions of 1576, 1590, &c. as passed in the diets which assembled in those years.

to the marſhal of the laſt diet; and, in caſe of his death or abſence, to the firſt nuntio of the province from which the marſhal was taken, three days before the diet, either in perſon, or by memorials ſigned by themſelves, and ſealed with their own coats of arms. 2. The marſhal of the diet being elected, and all the ceremonies in the chamber of the nuntios being properly performed, after the junction of the two houſes according to the conſtitution of 1768, the liſts of the candidates ſhall be read; that of the ſenators and miniſters by one of the principal ſecretaries; and that of the candidates of the equeſtrian order by the ſecretary of the diet. No perſon ſhall be excluded from being a candidate, who can prove that he poſſeſſes the neceſſary conditions and qualifications, ſuch as are hereafter deſcribed. And if any perſon ſo qualified is omitted, the great ſecretaries ſhall be anſwerable to the ſame diet for the omiſſion of ſenators and miniſters, and the marſhal of the diet for that of the members of the equeſtrian order; and if they are convicted of having deſignedly been guilty of the omiſſion, they ſhall be deprived of their charges. 3. A printed liſt of the candidates ſhall, the ſame day, be given to each member of the diet, to be taken into conſideration. 4. The enſuing day each member of the diet ſhall ſecretly mark the names of as many perſons in the printed liſt as are neceſſary to fill the permanent council. This ceremony ſhall be performed in a corner of the ſenate-houſe. The ſenators invited by the great marſhals, or, in their abſence, by thoſe who perform the office of marſhals, and the nuntios ſummoned by the marſhal of the diet, ſhall receive from the ſecretaries the printed liſt of the candidates, ſtamped with the arms of the republic, ſimilar to that which was diſtributed the preceding day. With theſe liſts they ſhall repair in order, one after the other, to a ſmall table ſurrounded with curtains, upon which table they ſhall ſecretly draw a line under the names of the

perſons

perfons whom they favour; and every one fhall put his lift CHAP.
into a vafe ftanding upon a table in the corner of the hall, V.
which vafe fhall be previoufly opened in the fenate-houfe by
the marfhal who is firft in rank, in order to fhew that it is
empty. The vafe fhall be provided with three different locks,
the keys whereof fhall be given, one to his majefty, a fecond
to the great marfhal, or to him who ftands in his place; and
a third to the marfhal of the diet. At the fame time nine deputies fhall be chofen, three from the fenate by the king, and
fix by the marfhal of the diet from the equeftrian order. As
foon as all the lifts have been delivered, thefe deputies, being
fworn, fhall bring the vafe into the middle of the fenate-houfe,
and having, in the face of the whole affembly, opened it with
the three keys, fhall compare the number of lifts with the
members of the diet who are prefent, count the fuffrages, and
the firft in rank among the deputies fhall openly proclaim the
names of thofe who have the majority. 5. Each elector muft
underline in the printed lift fo many, and fuch perfons as are
required; that is, among the perfons elected fhall be the third
of the members in the late permanent council, to the number
of twelve, namely, fix from the fenate and miniftry, and as
many from the equeftrian order, equally chofen from each
province. All the lifts, in which this rule is not obferved,
and in which there are more or lefs perfons nominated than
the neceffary number, fhall be confidered as null, and be rejected by the deputies. 6. Thofe who have the plurality of
fuffrages fhall be admitted into the council; and it is only in
cafe of an equal number of votes for any candidate or candidates, that the king fhall have the cafting voice.

The neceffary qualifications, which entitle a member of the
equeftrian order to become a candidate for a feat in the council,
are to have belonged to any of the four jurifdictions of the republic,

5

BOOK I.

public, (of the marſhal, of war, of the aſſeſſorium *, and of the treaſury), to have been deputy in any tribunal, nuntio of the diet, or miniſter to a foreign court.   Thoſe who ſhall be elected during the diet, before they enter upon their office ſhall take the following oath.

" I do ſwear, in the name of the Almighty, that I will be
" faithful to you Staniſlaus Auguſtus, my gracious maſter, and
" to the republic of Poland ; that, in the exerciſe of my office
" as counſellor of the permanent council, I will execute with
" zeal all which the laws relative to the permanent council
" ordain ; that I will not ſuffer myſelf to be ſurpriſed either
" by preſents or menaces ; that in giving my advice I will not
" be biaſſed by any perſon, but will act in obedience to the
" laws, and in conformity to juſtice will conſult the good of
" my country ; that if I ſee or know any thing which may
" be either ſerviceable or detrimental to my country, I will
" faithfully acquaint his majeſty, my moſt gracious maſter,
" and his permanent council, and will give my ſuffrage in the
" manner I think moſt likely to prevent the evil.   I will not
" reveal the ſecrets which may be entruſted to me by his ma-
" jeſty and his council.   And ſo help me God."

The council ſhall be compoſed of the following perſons :

1. The king as chief and preſident.   2. Three biſhops, among whom the primate of his own right, ſhall preſide during two years, but ſhall have no ſeat the two following years. 3. Nine lay-ſenators, two of whom may be elected either from the miniſters or ſenators.   4. Four from the miniſtry of the republic, namely, one from each department; of theſe eighteen members of the ſenate, ſix muſt be taken from each of the three † provinces.   5. The marſhal of the equeſtrian order, and, in caſe of his death or abſence, the firſt counſellor of the

---

* Court of Juſtice, having cognizance within a certain diſtance of the ſovereign's place of reſidence. See p. 9. note †.

† Great Poland, Little Poland, and Lithuania.

equeſtrian

equeftrian order, according to the turn of the provinces. 6. Eighteen counfellors of the equeftrian order, including the marfhal. 7. The fecretary of the permanent council fhall be elected from the Referendaries *, and national notaries, &c.

OF THE PENSIONS.

The primate, bifhops, and minifters, enjoying very confiderable revenues derived from their charges, fhall have no penfions. Lay-fenators of the crown, and of Lithuania, fhall annually receive each 14,000 florins †, = £388. 18s. The marfhal of the equeftrian order, as member of the permanent council, 30,000 florins, = £833. 6s. 8d.; and, during his refidence at Warfaw, fhall be allowed a guard of fifteen men, with an officer, from the army of the crown. Each counfellor fhall have 14,000 florins per annum, = £388. 18s. The fecretary of the council fhall receive the fame fum.

Explanation of the duties and prerogatives of the perfons who compofe the Permanent Council.

His majefty the king our moft gracious mafter, as chief of the nation, and the firft eftate, reprefenting the majefty of the republic, fhall, according to ufual practice, convoke by circular letters, and at the time prefcribed by the laws, the ordinary diets; he muft always confult the permanent council upon the matters to be laid before thofe affemblies, in the fame manner as he before took the advice of the fenate, which from henceforth fhall no more be convened. His majefty fhall in like manner fummon the extraordinary diets, either of his own accord, or at the inftance of the permanent council, which the king cannot refufe if the majority demand it. All the laws and conftitutions of the diet, decrees, privileges, and public acts, fhall be iffued in the name of the king, as it has been hitherto

---

* " Referendaries are a kind of mafters of " Requefts, whofe office is to receive peti- " tions made to the king, and to give his " majefty's anfwer: they have a place in any " of the king's courts of juftice." Connor's Poland, v. II. p. 77.

† 36 Polifh florins = a pound fterling.

practifed.

practised. He shall sign all the dispatches passed by order of the council, not having it in his power to put a negative upon them, if they are carried by a majority. He shall give public audience to embassadors and foreign ministers, to envoys or residents, shall treat with them, but cannot conclude without communicating the whole to the council, and following the advice of the majority.

The king, on his part, cedes the following royal prerogatives: 1. For the election of bishops, palatines, castellans, and ministers, the council shall nominate by ballot three candidates, one of whom the king shall appoint to the vacant office *. 2. The power of appointing to all other ecclesiastical and civil offices shall continue, without any diminution, vested in the king, excepting the commissioners of war, of the treasury, those in the department of the marshal, and in the assessorium regni : all these commissioners were before accustomed to be named by him in the intervals between the diets ; but his majesty now consents, that from henceforth the council shall elect three candidates, to be presented in the same manner as in the last mentioned article relative to the nomination of the senators and ministers. 3. With respect to military ranks, his majesty shall appoint the captains in the Polish companies, and the officers of the four companies, which are upon the Polish footing, and bear his name. Excepting these, all other military promotions shall be conferred according to seniority. Nevertheless, his majesty may propose candidates for military promotion, chosen among the young officers in the national service, to be secretly balloted for with that person who has the right of seniority ; provided, at the same time, the great general delivers to his majesty his recommendation in writing, with his reasons for the said recommendation. 4. His majesty renounces the right to dispose of the royal demesnes and sta-

* The king had before the sole disposal of these offices. See p. 9.

rosties,

rofties, with this claufe, that the proprietors of both fexes be
continued during their lives in poffeffion of the faid eftates,
which, from this prefent time, fhall never be granted to any
perfon whatfoever, under the appearance of recompence or
any other pretext ; but they fhall be employed for the public
good, to the great advantage of the country, and with the
confent of the king. 5. Four regiments of guards fhall be
reftored to the command of the great general, as in the time
of Auguftus III. that is, while they preferve the name and rank
of guards, they do not bind themfelves by any new oath ;
and with this difference, that whereas formerly the great generals poffeffed alone the military power in their hands, at
prefent they fhare that power with the committee ; which
committee, as well as the great generals, depend, in virtue of
the prefent law, upon the permanent council.   In return, the
king fhall receive an annual fum fufficient to keep in pay two
thoufand troops, who fhall depend folely upon his majefty ;
but this fum fhall not be included in the additional revenues
granted to his majefty, in compenfation for thofe loft by the
difmemberment of the provinces. 6. Reciprocally the republic
ftipulates on its part, once for all, that all the other royal prerogatives (thofe excepted which the king has gracioufly pleafed
to renounce) fhall remain in full force, and be for ever invio-
late.

The Primate.

The primate, during his office *, muft attend the permanent
council at leaft fix months in the year.   The antient laws
which fecure the prerogatives of the primate during the interregnum remaining in force, he fhall † prefide in the council,
even fhould it not be his turn for fitting in the council. During the interregnum, the permanent council, keeping its

* That is, during the two years in which he fits in the council.
† Namely, as viceroy during the interregnum.

power

power and authority, fhall maintain, in the ufual forms, **the**
tribunals, and all the jurifdictions of the republic, according
to the conftitution of 1768, in all things not contradicted by
this new arrangement.   The primate, during the two years
of his function, figns his name after the king to all the acts of
the permanent council; and, in cafe of the king's abfence, or
during an interregnum, he has two * votes, in order to decide
in cafe of equality of fuffrages.   In the primate's abfence, the
firft fenator in rank, who is member of the council, fupplies
his place.

The MARSHAL of the Equeftrian Order.

The equeftrian order fhall have its marfhal in the permanent council, who is the firft in rank among the members of
that order.   He fhall be elected every two years at the ordinary diet by fecret fuffrages, always from each of the three
provinces by rotation, according to the form prefcribed for the
election of the counfellors.   No fenator or minifter is capable
of being elected marfhal unlefs he before-hand refigns his
charge.

He fhall take the following oath before the fame diet in the
fame manner as the other counfellors.

" I fwear before Almighty God, that I will be faithful to
" you Staniflaus Auguftus my gracious mafter, and to the re-
" public of Poland ; that in the exercife of my office of mar-
" fhal of the permanent council, I will execute with zeal all
" which is ordained by the laws eftablifhed by the council ;
" that in giving my advice, and voting, I will take for the rule
" of my conduct the written laws, and the good of my country,
" from which I will never fwerve, neither induced by intreaties,
" promifes, friendfhip or hatred, or any other fpecies of cor-
" ruption or perfonal attachment whatfoever ; that I will never
" divulge the fecret deliberations of the council ; that I will

---

* That is, I fuppofe, one vote as ufual, and the cafting vote in cafe of equality.

4   " caft

" caft up the votes, and faithfully declare the majority of fuf-
" frages. So help me God."

The marfhal of the equeftrian order in the permanent
council cannot be chofen marfhal or nuntio of the next diet,
nor be re-elected marfhal of the permanent council, excepting
after an interval of four years.

His office. He, as well as each of the counfellors, may remonftrate againft the ill-execution of the laws, and lay before
the council thofe matters of which it has the cognizance. It
is the duty of the whole council to watch over the fecurity
and maintenance of the eftablifhed government, and the prefent conftitution ; and the marfhal, as well as each member,
ought to have at heart the prefervation of the prerogatives of
the three eftates ; but more particularly the chancellor, who
is a member of the council, and the marfhal fhall take care
that the papers fhall be kept in order, and the infpector of
the acts and archives of the permanent council fhall depend
upon the permanent council *in pleno*. The marfhal, as well
as each counfellor, may prefent candidates for fubaltern places
in the permanent council, who fhall be accepted, if the council
is unanimous, and, in cafe of any oppofition, fhall be elected
by the majority of fuffrages. The marfhal and chancellor
fhall take care that the faid fubalterns perform their duties,
recommending to the permanent council to reward or punifh
them according to their deferts. The marfhal diftributes the
votes to the members of the equeftrian order, draws the balls
or the billets from the vafe, in prefence of two deputies from
the fenate and two from the equeftrian order, chofen by the
plurality of voices, counts the number of fuffrages, and declares the majority. The feal of the permanent council, together with the arms of the two nations, fhall remain in the
poffeffion of the firft among the chancellors who are members
of the council. The marfhal fhall fign next to the king and
primate,,

primate, or, in the latter's abfence, next to the fenior fenator, all the acts and refolutions of the permanent council, and fhall the fame day difpatch each act to its refpective department. At the ordinary diet he fhall take his feat at the left hand of the marfhal of the diet, and after his juftification he fhall depart from the affembly, together with all the members of the equeftrian order in the late council. If he exceeds his power, the permanent council may cite him, as well as each counfellor, before the tribunal of the diet, according to the form prefcribed by law.

The Secretary of the Council.

He can only give his opinion, but has no vote in the council. He fhall deliver gratis to the petitioners the refolutions and anfwers of the permanent council, and fhall counterfign all the difpatches. He fhall receive from the fecretaries of the departments (who fhall depend upon him as far as relates to reports which are to be delivered) the reports of all that paffes in the fittings of the different departments, and what is inferted in the regifters; he fhall acquaint the permanent council with the contents, and fhall form a regifter of all the operations according to the decifion of the diet. He fhall be obliged to report to the permanent council every thing that comes to his knowledge, which may be either advantageous or detrimental to the republic. During his abfence, the permanent council fhall elect, by a majority of fuffrages, another perfon, who fhall perform the duties of his office until he returns. The archivift fhall be elected in the permanent council by the majority of fuffrages, in the fame manner as the above-mentioned fubalterns, and he fhall be informed of all by the fecretary. The extracts, as well from the archives of the permanent council, as from the departments which appertain to the council, fhall be delivered gratis.

The fecretary fhall take an oath, fimilar to the foregoing
one,

one, with the addition of the following clause : " I fwear that " I will not entruft, or give to any perfon, the papers which " are configned to me, without the permiflion of the council."

The inftigators * of the two nations † (their ancient duties remaining in force) fhall depend upon the permanent council, and fhall not make their appearance in it without being fummoned. They fhall take the ufual oath, with the addition of the following claufe : " We fwear that we will not abandon any " perfon for prayers, threats, promifes, or perfonal confideration, " nor indict but at the inftance of the permanent council."

The nomination of the fecretaries for the departments, the keeper of the archives, and fcribes (all of whom muft be natives and nobles) as well as the appointment of their duties, fhall depend upon the permanent council.

The INTERPRETERS.

There fhall be two for the Eaftern languages, and one for the Ruffian tongue: they fhall depend upon the permanent council, and particularly upon the department for foreign affairs.

The members of the permanent council fhall not be exempted from appearing in the courts of juftice, &c.

If, in criminal affairs, a counfellor incurs any punifhment, he fhall fubmit to it according to the laws and the nature of the crime, without deriving any benefit from his office, &c.

ARTICLE II. Arrangement, divifion, and mode of procedure in the Permanent Council.

The Permanent Council is divided into five departments.

1. For foreign affairs. 2. Police. 3. War. 4. Juftice. 5. Treafury.

In the department for foreign affairs there fhall be only four members, and eight in each of the other departments, amounting in all to thirty-fix perfons. The election of thefe mem-

---

* Officers of the crown who profecute in cafes of high treafon.
† Poland and Lithuania.

bers

bers fhall be made by the permanent council affembled in a
body, either unanimoufly, or by a majority of open fuffrages.
The prefence of three perfons in each department fhall be
deemed fufficient to proceed upon bufinefs.   The minifters *
(who are of the council) fhall prefide in the departments belonging to their refpective charges, and if any accufation fhall
be brought againft them, they fhall retire from the permanent
council, not having a vote in fuch cafes.

The members of each department fhall receive the memorials and reports which concern their refpective departments :
having examined and made extracts, they fhall add their own
opinion upon each matter, and fhall then lay the whole before
the permanent council for its final decifion.

In the department, when there fhall happen to be no minifter, the fenior fenator fhall prefide.   Each prefident has,
befide his common vote, a cafting voice, in cafe of an equality
of fuffrages.   In all the departments, as well as in the council
in pleno, the loweft member in rank fhall give the firft vote.

The council fhall affemble *in pleno*, as often as neceffity requires, in prefence of the king, when he is pleafed to be prefent ; and in his majefty's abfence, the primate during his turn
fhall prefide ; and in his abfence, the firft fenator.

The king fhall firft propofe whatever he thinks proper,
and the queftion fhall be decided, if not unanimoufly, by a
plurality of voices.   In all cafes, when the king is not prefent,
the primate, or, in his abfence, the firft in rank, fhall have
the power of propofing.   Afterwards, the marfhal of the
equeftrian order, and then each counfellor, fhall fucceffively
have the liberty of propofing.   Then the fecretary of the
council fhall read the regifters of the five departments, that
the affairs which they treat may be finally decided by the

* Namely, one of the great treafurers in the department of the treafury ; one of the
great generals in that of war, &c.

permanent

permanent council *in pieno*, or returned to the department from which it was delivered for more exact information. When the king is not prefent in the council, the firft fenator and the marfhal of the equeftrian order fhall, in the name of the council, make reports of the affairs in agitation to the king. The king, having received them, fhall, if he pleafes, give his two votes in writing, which fhall be as valid as if he had been prefent. If the king gives no vote before the next meeting, the queftion fhall be decided by the majority; and, in cafe of an equality, the firft in rank who prefides in the council fhall have the cafting voice.

If the king is abfent from Warfaw with the permiffion of the council, the council muft repair to the place where he refides; but if his majefty quits Warfaw of his own accord, the election of the candidates, and the diftribution of the charges, fhall be fufpended two months; at the expiration of which term, one of the members of the department for foreign affairs fhall attend his majefty, to the end that a correfpondence be preferved between the king and the council.

The memorials, in all public matters cognizable by the council, may be prefented to any member of the council, or even to the fecretary : but in all private affairs equally cognizable by the council, the memorials muft be prefented by thofe perfons whom they concern. The member who prefents a memorial, having firft figned it, fhall fend it to the fecretary of the council, and the latter, having made extracts from it, fhall read them to the council at the next meeting, bringing with him, however, the original to be examined in cafe of neceffity. But if the counfellor, who fends a memorial to the fecretary, perceives it to be of fuch great importance as to deferve the infpection of the council, he fhall add after his name the following words, " This memorial admits no " delay." But fhould a memorial be of fuch a nature as to require fecrecy, and to be laid before the council in the firft refort, then the counfellor, to whom it has been given, fhall himfelf, without fending it to the fecretary, lay it before the council. In all queftions, if the members of the council are not unanimous, the firft in order, whoever he be, marfhal, minifter, or member of the council, fhall diftribute, in the manner above-mentioned, the votes to the fenators, and the marfhal of the equeftrian order to the perfons of that order, and the majority fhall be collected with the greateft exactnefs. The majority may be afcertained by two modes of decifion; either by fecret, or by open votes, when the perfon who affents, faying, " *I permit*," the fuffrages fhall be infcribed in the regifter by each voter. The *Turnus* can never be employed *in pleno*, excepting the members of the council are fifteen in number; and before the turnus is made ufe of, the perfon who lays any propofition before the council ought to afk the members if they confent; the anfwer, that they confent, or filence, announces unanimity; but if any member fhould oppofe and demand the turnus, then they fhall proceed to open voting.

Each propofition may be the fubject of deliberation during three days; but if any one member objects to that delay, he may propofe to determine, by ballot, whether the affair fhall be taken into confideration, or be immediately decided.

The turnus, once begun, fhall be continued without interruption until the fubject in agitation fhall be finally decided, &c. In all queftions, the decifion by ballot may be infifted on by any one member, but it muft be ufed in the following points. 1. In election of vacant offices referved to the council. 2 In extraordinary expences iffued by the treafury of the republic, not warranted by law. 3. In matters of high treafon, ftate crimes, difturbance of the public tranquillity, and conventicles contrary to law. The votes by ballot fhall be collected
with

with the greateſt precaution and fidelity, and with every mark of neceſſary ſolemnity. For this purpoſe, a table ſhall ſtand in the middle of the apartment, ſurrounded with curtains about the height of a man, which may be drawn and undrawn to admit the counſellors; upon this table ſhall be placed a vaſe, having two openings with inſcriptions affirmative and nega-tive, into which the balls ſhall be put; theſe openings ſhall be only big enough to admit the balls, and not to receive the whole hand. The vaſe ſhall be alſo cloſed with a lock, the key whereof ſhall be placed upon the council table until all the members have given their ſuffrages, and the balls are to be counted. The vaſe being opened, the marſhal miniſter, and the marſhal of the equeſtrian order, ſhall firſt hold it up and invert it to ſhew that it is empty; after which, it ſhall be ſealed by the two marſhals, and covered with the curtains. Next, the ſecretary ſhall diſtribute ivory balls to all who have a vote in the council; and every member, according to his rank, ſhall approach the table, and, firſt holding up his hand to ſhew that he has but one ball, ſhall put it into one of the openings, *permitting*, or *not permitting*, as he ſhall think proper, and ac-cording to his conſcience; and in this manner he cannot ſee how the others give their votes, nor be ſeen himſelf. If there are many candidates, the ſecretary ſhall diſtribute to each mem-ber billets, all written in the ſame hand, containing the names and ſurnames of the candidates; each member ſhall then put into the vaſe the billet containing the names and ſurnames of the candidates whom he favours, and ſhall burn the other bil-lets, a candle being ready for that purpoſe. In caſe of equality of ſuffrages, the king has the caſting vote; and, to the end that each member may ſolicit the vacant charges in the gift of the permanent council, they may all propoſe themſelves, as well as recommend others, giving in their petition to that purpoſe in writing. The ſecret balloting being finiſhed, the

marſhal

marſhal of the equeſtrian order, and the marſhal miniſter,
ſhall break each his ſeal and open the vaſe; and then, in
conjunction with the two deputies from the ſenate and two
from the equeſtrian order, ſhall declare the number of balls
or billets.   After which, the marſhal of the equeſtrian order
ſhall read aloud the names of the candidates, and the number
of votes in favour of each candidate, and ſhall declare for
whom is the majority, which the ſecretary ſhall immediately
regiſter.

The king has the privilege of convening an aſſembly of the
permanent council ; and, in his abſence, the firſt in rank ;
neither of whom can refuſe to ſummon a meeting upon the
requeſt of any one member, repreſenting the neceſſity of diſ-
cuſſing an affair of great importance.   Each member of the
council has the liberty of delivering his opinion in a decent
manner ; but whenever any affair, relative to any member, is
in agitation, that member ſhall have no vote.

Two perſons of the ſame family, and even of the ſame
ſurname, cannot be elected into the council, at the ſame time,
as members of the ſame eſtate, namely, two ſenators, or two
perſons of the equeſtrian order ; but only one perſon for
each eſtate.

All the decrees of the permanent council ſhall be iſſued in
the name of the king, without any payment for the affixing
of the ſeal, in the following manner : " We the king, with
" the advice of the permanent council."

In order to prevent too frequent interruptions, no member
of the council ſhall be abſent more than ſix months in the
year, either at one or at different intervals, but with the conſent of the permanent council granted by the majority.   The
members who exceed their leave of abſence ſhall loſe a proportionate part of their ſalary ; the ſame ſhall be underſtood
of thoſe who, being at Warſaw, do not attend the ſittings of

the

the council; excepting, in both cafes, perfons employed in other public offices, or thofe who produce proof of ficknefs. The deduction of the falaries from the abfent members fhall, at the end of the year, be divided among thofe who have affiduoufly performed their duty.

The members of the permanent council cannot be fent beyond the frontiers as minifters to foreign courts : a perfon may decline being elected a member ; but, when once admitted, he cannot refign upon any pretext.

At each ordinary diet, when the council expires, a third of the members of the laft permanent council, namely, fix from the fenators, and the fame number from the equeftrian order, fhall be continued, by ballot, members for the following years ; and this is done to the end that the council may always contain perfons experienced in bufinefs.

At the next ordinary diet, a particular place in the fenatehoufe fhall be affigned to the council, to anfwer any complaints which may be brought againft it, and to receive a public teftimony to be inferted in the conftitutions of the diet ; either that the diet received no complaints againft the permanent council ; or that, having received them, they were proved upon examination to be ill-founded ; or that, having acknowledged their validity, juftice was accordingly inflicted. The fenators and minifters in the council fhall have their ufual places in the fenate. In the ordinary diets, the counfellors of the equeftrian order fhall fit next to the minifters. None of the counfellors, either fenators, minifters, or thofe of the equeftrian order, fhall be prefent at the dictines, or at the opening of the tribunals. No counfellors fhall accept any other public charges than thofe which appertain to their office. No member of the council fhall oppofe the fignature of privileges, refolutions, or acts decided by the majority ; and if either the king, the fenior fenator, or the marfhal, fhould refufe

fufe to fign, in that cafe, each member fhall fubfcribe for himfelf, and the names of the majority fhall render the act valid.
In cafe of death, the vacancy fhall be filled up within the fpace
of ten weeks by ballot, in the manner above-mentioned.   If
the deceafed be a bifhop or lay-fenator, his fucceffor fhall be
taken from the bifhops or lay-fenators; if a minifter, from the
boards of the faid minifter's office; if a perfon of the equeftrian order, either from the candidates prefented at the laft
diet, or from thofe propofed upon this occafion.

ARTICLE III.

Power, authority, and duties of the Permanent Council.

1. Without enjoying the leaft authority, legiflative or judicial, the council orders the execution of the laws; and, being
the center of public affairs, as well foreign as domeftic, is
bound to determine according to the laws of its prefent eftablifhment.   2. It fhall iffue affignments for the payment of
fums referved to the public treafury, and fpecified in the general table of expences unprovided for in extraordinary circumftances; and the members of the council cannot, during
the holding of their office, partake of the faid affignments.
3. It fhall receive all projects beneficial to the ftate, decide
upon the admiffion of thofe which are confonant to law, and
muft lay thofe which appear advantageous, but which have not
the fanction of law, before the firft diet, for the determination
of the ftates.   4. It fhall form plans for the reformation of
the laws, and fhall prefent them before the next diet: it fhall
frame a new code of laws, public, civil, and criminal, to be
approved by the diet.   5. It fhall fend embaffadors and minifters to foreign courts from the perfons nominated by the
king.   The permanent council fhall give them the neceffary
inftructions, excepting in all cafes referved for the diet.   6.
The permanent council fhall appoint, by ballot, in the manner
above-mentioned, three candidates for the vacant charges, excepting

cepting thofe which are in the king's gift, or are chofen by the nobility in the Palatinates.   7. It fhall take the moft effectual methods to preferve the alliances and treaties of the republic.

ARTICLE IV. Limits of the Permanent Council's authority.

The council has no power in all matters referved to the ftates affembled in diet, and can enact nothing contrary to any liberties and prerogatives juftly conferred.   It muft not ufurp to itfelf the legiflative or judicial authority, nor in any degree take into confideration thofe affairs whofe decifion is referved to the diet alone.   If the council fhould exceed its power, the members fhall be liable to be cited and tried at the diet for high treafon, and, if guilty, to be punifhed according to the antient laws eftablifhed upon this article.   The permanent council fhall remain in full authority for two years without interruption, even fhould one or more extraordinary diets interfere ; and at the ordinary diet until a new council fhall be elected in its place, according to the prefcribed form : then the antient council fhall lay before the diet the fituation of affairs, and give an account of its whole adminiftration. The permanent council can only act according to the laws in being, or carry the faid laws into execution. In all cafes, not exprefsly mentioned by the laws, the permanent council cannot decide ; but in all fuch circumftances it may prepare any propofals for new laws, and publifh them in the circular letters for the convocation of the diet.

DEPARTMENT I. Of foreign affairs in the Permanent Council.

The department of foreign affairs fhall be compofed of four members, amongft whom fhall be one from the duchy of Lithuania, one of the chancellors, and two counfellors of the equeftrian order. To thefe fhall be added one of the national fecretaries, who fhall have no vote : he fhall infpect and expedite all foreign affairs, and fhall take the ufual oath, &c.

This department fhall affemble as occafion may require.

When

BOOK I. When the king is not prefent, a chancellor fhall prefide; and, in the latter's abfence, the firft fenator. The national fecretary fhall make a report of all the letters directed to him, and, if required, fhall lay them before the members of the faid department: he fhall not fend any anfwers without their approbation. He fhall read at the meetings the letters and memorials to the department, which fhall deliberate upon the anfwers: he fhall write down the refolutions, and fhall expedite the difpatches accordingly. In all cafes of public moment, fuch as letters from the king to foreign courts, ftate affairs which require any explanation, memorials and declarations, the department fhall draw them up, and lay them before the council *in pleno*, for its determination. Whenever any information is to be given to the Polifh minifters at foreign courts in the ordinary courfe of affairs, the prefident of this department, having firft heard the obfervations of each member, fhall form the refult. All inftructions for foreign minifters fhall be firft drawn up in this department, and then prefented to the permanent council for its decifion. If any member of this department dies, the permanent council fhall, without delay, elect one of its counfellors in his place. The fecretary of this department fhall be nominated by the king from the national fecretaries, or notaries. He fhall maintain the correfpondence with the foreign minifters of the republic, and to him fhall be addreffed all letters and memorials. In the fame manner as the fecretary, the fubalterns in this department fhall be chofen by the king.

DEPARTMENT II. Committee of the marfhals of Poland and Lithuania.

1. The great marfhals fhall act according to the conftitution of 1768, reftraining, however, the affociation of the affeffors *

in

* Before 1768, the great marfhals were fole judges in all criminal caufes cognizable by their tribunals: but in the diet of 1768 the following claufe enacts, that " fix affef-
" fors

in the following cafes. In criminal affairs.—In all taxes *
upon provifions and merchandize only in the place of the
king's refidence, excepting corn, and the productions belonging to the nobility.—In all cafes of debt or borrowings, only
ex vi infcripti fori, when one of the parties appeals from the
firft inftance, and the fum exceeds 500 florins = £13. 17s. 9d.
—All appeals from the firft inftance, relative to the non-
payment of taxes, fhall be brought before the tribunal of the
marfhal with his affeffors, in the prefence of the judge or the
notary, neither of whom fhall have a vote. In this and fimilar
cafes of appeal, the opinion fhall be given openly, and then
finally decided by ballot. 2. The committee of the marfhals
fhall be compofed of the great and little marfhals (or of their
colleagues the marfhals of the crown), of two fenators, and
four perfons of the equeftrian order. Thefe fix affeffors fhall
be chofen at the ordinary diet, according to the form above
prefcribed for the election of the members of the permanent
council. 3. The marfhals fhall be bound to fix months refidence near his majefty, and each of the affeffors to four months,
to the end that there may always be the complete number of
five perfons, including the marfhals, requifite to form a fitting.
4. No member of this committee can be elected a nuntio for
the next diet; but the nuntios may be appointed members of
this committee by ballot, and half of the antient affeffors, both
fenators and nobles of the equeftrian order, may be continued
in their office for the two following years. 5. Solely in the
cafes of *denegati judicii et corruptionis judicis, perjurii et oppref-
fionis civis liberi*, complaints againft the decifions of this committee can be brought before the permanent council; and

---

" fors fhall be added to the jurifdiction of the
" great marfhal: they fhall be elected in each
" ordinary diet; they fhall judge all caufes
" in conjunction with the great marfhal:
" and fhall decide by the majority."

* The great marfhal ufed before, of his
own authority, to impofe prices on merchants
wares, who generally made him great prefents and bribes to augment their profit:
Connor's Hiftory of Poland, v. II. p. 69.

caufes of this nature fhall be tried by the permanent council, in the manner prefcribed by the law concerning the *denegatum judicium, et corruptionem judicis et perjurium.* 6. Each month the great marfhal fhall lay before the permanent council the report of his decifions, made in conjunction with the affeffors. 7. In cafe the marfhal fhould difobey the laws in any of thefe articles, the permanent council may remonftrate; and if he perfifts in infringing them, he fhall be liable to be cited before the diet as guilty of high treafon. 8. In all other points, not contrary to thefe articles, the antient prerogatives of the marfhals fhall continue in force.

Department of the Police in the Permanent Council.

1. When the great marfhal fhall be a member of the permanent council, he fhall prefide in the department of the police; and in his abfence the firft fenior in rank, who is member of the faid department. 2. If any complaints fhall be urged againft the great or little marfhals, for non-performance of the duties fpecified in the articles of the " committee " of marfhals and their dependence on the permanent coun- " cil," the plaintiffs, if members of the council, fhall not be prefent at the refolutions paffed under fuch circumftances. 3. If this department fhall have occafion for the regifter of the committee of marfhals, it fhall be communicated.

DEPARTMENT III. The Great Generals of the Two Nations.

1. Befide the troops, commanded by the marfhals of the two nations, and by the treafurers, ftationed at Warfaw, there may be quartered in that capital 3000 foldiers, namely, 2000 from the army of the crown, and 1000 from that of Lithuania. The difcipline of the Lithuanian corps fhall depend upon the great general of Lithuania; the chief command fhall devolve upon the great general of the crown. If the king fhall refide in Lithuania, a proportionate number of troops from the army of the crown fhall be ftationed in that duchy,

in

in the same manner as the Lithuanian corps is quartered at Warsaw with the crown soldiers. The great generals shall be obliged to change the garrison of Warsaw at the request of the permanent council. 2. When the great generals shall find it expedient to raise new fortifications, they shall present the plan to the permanent council, and the latter to the diet. 3. The permanent council shall make known to the great general, when he should order the absentees to rejoin their regiments. 4. The permanent council, in concert with the great generals, shall regulate the number of soldiers to be furnished by the regiments for the purpose of making high roads, cleansing rivers, and other public works, a representation being previously made, and a plan prescribed, by the commissioners of the treasury: it shall in the same manner fix the pay of the said soldiers, to be assigned from the public fund destined for extraordinary cases, with this exception, that the troops shall be exempted from such services, during the months in which they are exercised or encamped. 5. In case the great generals should act counter to these articles, the permanent council shall first remonstrate, and if that should have no effect, may accuse them of high treason before the diet; if, during the intervals of the ordinary diet, it should be thought necessary to call them to account, the permanent council shall assemble an extraordinary diet for that purpose. 6. The list of extraordinary expences shall be communicated, by the great generals, to the permanent council, before it is laid before the ordinary diet. 7. The discipline, subordination, exercise, and clothing of the troops, the appointment of the spots for the encampment of the divisions, (with this proviso, that never more than one division shall encamp in the same place) in a word, the chief command of the troops shall be vested in the great generals. 8. The nomination and creation of the officers and subalterns, belonging to the committee of war, shall

L 2

reside

reſide in the great generals.   9. In other points, the generals retain all their antient rights and privileges, not contradicted by theſe articles.

Explanation and changes of the Conſtitution of 1768, relative to the Committee of War of both nations.

1. The committee of war ſhall be compoſed of ſix commiſſioners, as enjoined by the diet of 1768, one half to be taken from perſons in the civil line, and the remainder from officers not employed. Among the three military commiſſioners ſhall be included of courſe the generals of the artillery, but without receiving the ſalary of commiſſioners. Three commiſſioners are ſufficient to make a board; and if only two ſhould meet, then the notaries of the committee of war of the crown ſhall aſſume the place of the abſent commiſſioner, and have a vote; but when there is a requiſite number, then the notaries ſhall only have a deliberative voice. 2. This committee of war ſhall keep in order, and have the direction of, the military archives. 3. Twice a year it ſhall receive the reports of the troops relative to the diſcharge of their pay, and ſhall ſend them to the permanent council. 4. Since the troops cannot ſubſiſt without pay, nor ſuffer the leaſt delay in that article, it is enacted, once for all, that the committee of the treaſury ſhall be obliged to employ, for the payment of the ſaid troops, the firſt money which it receives, and which ſhall be regularly delivered to the troops every year on the 1ſt of April and the 1ſt of October. If it happens that this payment ſhall not be made at theſe ſtipulated times, the great general and the council of war ſhall be bound to acquaint the permanent council with this delay; and the permanent council ſhall immediately authorize the great general and the council of war to procure the ſums deſtined for the pay of the troops. 5. The committee of war ſhall have the care of the military cheſt, and ſhall pay all the troops according to the eſtabliſhed calculation. The cheſt ſhall

be

be provided with three keys ; one whereof fhall be kept by the great general, or, in his abfence, by the prefident of the council of war ; the fecond by one of the commiffioners of war ; and the third by the cafhier. 6. The commiffioners of war fhall judge, as well all caufes between foldiers according to the military articles, as all proceffes brought by the citizens againft a foldier in his military capacity : but in cafe a foldier in his military capacity fhould aggrieve a citizen, then the plaintiff fhall apply to the commander for redrefs ; and if he obtains none, he may cite him before the court of juftice of the place where the affault was committed, referving the appeal to the committee of war. 7. No member of the faid committee can be capable of being elected nuntio at the next diet ; but the commiffioners may be taken from the nuntios of the diet, or from other nobles, promifcuoufly. A third part of the commiffioners may be continued for the next two years, if they have the plurality of ballots in their favour. The fame holds good in refpect to the fenators : and thofe, who are thus confirmed in their feats for two more years, cannot be elected the third time for the two next years. 8. In other points, not contradictory to thefe articles, the committee of war of both nations are maintained in their antient rights.

Eftablifhment of the Military Department in the Permanent Council.

1. The military department in the permanent council fhall receive, twice a year, from the great general, the lift of the army, to be examined and inferted in the acts. 2. The great general, having a feat in the council, fhall prefide in the military department, or, in his abfence, the fenior of the faid department. 3. If any complaints fhall be urged againft the great or little generals for not fulfilling the articles prefcribed under the title of " The great generals of both nations," the accufed, if members of the permanent council, fhall not be prefent

fent at the difcuffion of the faid complaints.

DEPARTMENT IV. The Great Chancellors of both Nations.

1. Each great chancellor, or his colleague the vice-chancellor occupying his place, fhall have a committee compofed of two fenators, and four perfons of the equeftrian order, to be chofen during the fitting of the diet by ballot, according to the form prefcribed in the permanent council, &c.   2. Each of thofe minifters fhall be bound to at leaft fix months refidence at Warfaw, upon the affignment of falaries, and each commiffioner or affeffor to at leaft four months ; that the requifite number of three perfons, including the great chancellor, or vice-chancellor, may be prefent at each meeting.   Thefe affeffors fhall receive each 6000 florins *per annum*, = £166. 13s. 4d. and thefe falaries fhall be divided between the affeffors who attend.   3. No member of the equeftrian order in this committee can be elected nuntio of the next diet, &c.   4. Every month the chancellors fhall fend to the permanent council a lift of all the privileges which have paffed the feal. 5. The feals fhall remain in the hands of the great and vice-chancellors.   The chancellor and vice-chancellor of the crown fhall feal, as before, the privileges referved to the king, and thofe of Lithuania fhall, in the fame manner, feal the privileges of that duchy, &c.   6. The great chancellors and vice-chancellors, in cafe of non-compliance with any of thefe articles, fhall be liable to be cited by the permanent council before the diet. 7. In all other points the chancellors are maintained in their antient privileges, not contradictory to thefe articles juft enumerated.

DEPARTMENT V. Great Treafurers of both Nations.

1. The department of the treafury, compofed of members of the permanent council, fhall receive from the committee of the treafury of the crown the lifts of the ordinary expences, &c. and fhall take care that the receipts and expenditures are

authorized

authorized by the laws. 2. Every month the great treasurer of the crown, and the great treasurer of Lithuania, shall send a report of all the transactions of this department to the permanent council, &c. 3. Whenever one or both the great treasurers are elected members of the permanent council, the first in rank shall preside in this department, composed of the members of the permanent council. 4. The commissioners of the treasury shall receive, and, upon proper deliberation, admit or reject all memorials and plans relative to commerce, the augmentation of the revenues, the establishment of manufactures, cleansing rivers, cutting canals, forming harbours, making bridges and high roads, erecting buildings, and all other public works, &c. always under the controul of the permanent council. 5. The commissioners of the two nations shall pay from the public funds, destined for that purpose, the extraordinary expences and gratifications, in compliance with the resolutions of the permanent council *in pleno,* &c. 6. The clerks in the committees of the treasury of both nations shall provide for themselves proper securities. The appointment of these clerks shall belong to the great treasurer; but the examination of their qualifications, the approbation or rejection of their securities, shall wholly rest with the committee. The qualifications are,

1. That they are gentlemen. 2. That they find proper securities. 3. That their characters are not infamous. 4. That they are able to write. 5. That they are able to cast accounts. In case these clerks should discover any notorious incapacity, the committee shall have it in their power to deprive them of their charges. 7. All the writings, decrees, and circular letters, issued by the committee, shall be signed by the treasurers alone; or, in their absence, by the first in rank. In case the treasurers refuse to put the seal to any resolutions passed by the committees, it shall be esteemed valid, if signed

by

by the firſt in rank next to the treaſurer, even in the preſence of the latter; and complaints may be urged againſt the treaſurer, for refuſing to ſign ſuch reſolutions. 8. If the great treaſurers remove from the place where the committees aſſemble, they ſhall be accompanied in their route by fifteen of the treaſury troops, provided that no extraordinary expence on that account be incurred by the treaſury, and that no damage be ſuffered by the inhabitants. 9. The troops of the committee of the treaſury ſhall continue in the ſame obedience to the great treaſurer, and the committee, as enjoined by the diet of 1768 ; and if any of the officers, appointed by the king's patent, ſhall deſerve puniſhment, he ſhall be judged by a court martial, compoſed of the officers of the ſame corps, according to the military articles, and the ſentence ſhall be ſent to the committee of war. The number of this corps ſhall not exceed 500 men, and the ſum appropriated for their ſupport ſhall not ſurpaſs that which is ſettled by the conſtitution of 1768. 10. If the treaſurers diſobey any of theſe articles, the permanent council is bound to remonſtrate, and, in caſe of ſtill further diſobedience, to cite them before the diet as guilty of high treaſon. 11. In other points, the great treaſurers are maintained in their antient privileges.

Changes and Explanation of the Conſtitution of 1768, relative to the eſtabliſhment of the Committee of the Treaſury of both Nations.

1. The commiſſioners of the treaſury of the crown ſhall be compoſed of the great treaſurer of the crown, and of nine commiſſioners, three ſenators, and ſix from the equeſtrian order, &c. 2. The great treaſurers ſhall be bound to at leaſt four months reſidence, under pain of loſing their ſalaries proportionable to the time of their abſence, and theſe deductions ſhall not be divided among the commiſſioners who are preſent, but ſhall be left in the cheſt. The commiſſioners are equally bound

bound to four months refidence, in order that there may be
always prefent five commiffioners (including one or both treafurers), the requifite number for holding a board. The deductions of the falaries for the abfent commiffioners fhall be
divided amongft thofe who are prefent. 3. None of the commiffioners of the equeftrian order can be elected a nuntio for
the next diet, &c. 4. From this time there fhall be a regifter
apart for thofe decrees of the committee, which relate to foreign affairs, commerce, and notes of exchange.

What caufes fhall be brought before the Committees of the
Treafury.

1. Thofe relative to the unpacking of merchandize which
occafion any delays of tranfport. 2. Impofts of all forts pay-
able by the nobility, clergy, and towns. 3. Of contracts of
merchants. 4. Of letters of exchange, which fhall be further
explained in a law apart. 5. Of debts of merchants and work-
men. 6. Of weights and meafures. 7. Of damages caufed
to the treafury, or of thefts and negligences of the fubalterns,
&c. In all other points, the committees of both nations fhall
be maintained in all their antient privileges, not contradictory
to hefe articles above-mentioned.

C H A P. VI.

Supreme authority refides in the diet.—Origin of the die..—
Place and time of affembling.—Ordinary and extraordinary.
—Convoked by the king.—Conftituent parts.—King, fenate,
and nuntios.—Proceedings.—Liberum Veto.—Hiftory and
caufes of its introduction.—Its dreadful effects.—How reme-

VOL. I. M *died.—*

died.—Diet of confederacy.—The plain of Vola *where the kings
are elected.—Account of the diets of convocation and election.*

THE general diet of Poland enjoys, as I have before observed, the supreme authority: it declares war, makes
peace, levies soldiers, enters into alliances, imposes taxes, enacts
laws, in a word, it exercises all the rights of absolute sovereignty.

Some historians place the earliest diet in the reign of Casimir
the Great; but it is very uncertain whether it was first convened in his time; and still more doubtful, of what members
it consisted. Thus much is unquestionable, that it was not
until the reign of Casimir III. that this national assembly was
modelled into its present form [*].

The place of holding the diets depended formerly upon the
will of the kings; and Louis even summoned two in Hungary.
In those early times Petricau was the town in which they were
most frequently assembled; but in 1569, at the union of Poland and Lithuania, Warsaw was appointed the place of meeting; and in 1673, it was enacted, that of three successive diets,
two should be held in this capital, and one at Grodno [†] in Lithuania. This regulation has been generally followed, until
the reign of his present majesty, when the assemblies have been
uniformly summoned to Warsaw [‡].

Diets are ordinary and extraordinary; the former are convened every two years, the latter as occasion requires. In 1717
the usual season for the meeting of the ordinary diets was fixed
for Michaelmas; but during the present reign it has been oc-
casionally changed to the month of October or November.

The king, with the advice of the permanent council, convokes the diet, by means of circular letters issued to all the
Palatines in their respective provinces at least six weeks before
the time appointed for its meeting: these letters are accom-

---

[*] See p. 5.   [†] Lengnich, Hist. Pol. p. 262.   [‡] See Book II. Chap. VI. Art. Grodno.

panied

panied with a fhort fketch of the bufinefs to be agitated in the diet.

The conftituent parts of the diet are the three eftates of the realm, namely, the king, the fenate, and the nobles or gentry, by their nuntios or reprefentatives.

1. The king, confidered in his capacity of prefident, is only, as it were, the chief of the diet: he fubfcribes all acts; figns all decrees agreed to by the affembly; iffues out all ordinances in his own name, and that of the republic, without enjoying the right of a negative in any of thofe particulars. In all queftions he has no vote, excepting upon an equality of fuffrages; but is at liberty to deliver his fentiments upon any queftion. His prefent majefty is efteemed one of the moft eloquent among the Polifh orators; he has an agreeable tone of voice, and much fkill in fuiting and varying his cadence to the fubjects of his difcourfe; he harangues with great energy of ftyle and dignity of manner; and his fpeeches always make a confiderable impreffion upon the members of the diet. When he is difpofed to fpeak, he rifes from his feat, advances a few fteps, and cries out, " I fummon the mi- " nifters of ftate to the throne." Then the great officers of the crown, who are fitting at the lower end of the fenate- houfe, come forward and ftand near the king. The four great marfhals ftrike the ground at the fame time with their ftaffs of office; and the firft in rank fays, " The king is going to " fpeak;" after which his majefty begins.

2. The fecond eftate, or the fenate, is compofed of fpiritual and temporal fenators.

1. The bifhops or fenators fpiritual have the precedence over the temporal fenators. The archbifhop of Gnefna is primate and chief of the fenate, and is viceroy in cafe of an interregnum. 2. The temporal are Palatines, Caftellans, and the great officers of ftate. The palatines are the governors of the pro-

vinces,

vinces, who hold their offices for life.   In time of war, when
the army of the republic is fummoned, the palatines levy and
lead the force of their palatinates into the field, according to
the tenure of feudal fervices; in time of peace, they convoke
the affemblies of the palatinates, prefide in the county courts
of juitice, and judge the Jews within their refpective jurifdictions, &c.   The Caftellans are divided into Grand and Petty
Caftellans: their office, in time of peace, is merely nominal;
but when the military or feudal fervices are required, they are
the lieutenants of the palatines, under whom they command
the troops of the feveral diftricts in the palatinates.

The great officers of the republic, who fit in the fenate, are
ten in number, namely, the two great marfhals of Poland and
Lithuania, the two great chancellors, the two vice-chancellors,
the two great treafurers, and the two fub-marfhals.

All the fenators were formerly appointed by the king; but
by the late change of government, his majefty's choice is re-
ftricted to one of three candidates prefented by the permanent
council [*].   The fenators, once nominated, cannot be deprived
of their charges, excepting by the diet.

3. The third eftate is formed by the nuntios or reprefentatives of the equeftrian order.   Thefe reprefentatives are chofen
in the dietines or affemblies of each palatinate, in which every
noble or gentleman, at the age of eighteen, has a vote, or is
capable of being elected.   There is no qualification in point
of property required, either for the electors, or elected; it is
only neceffary that the nuntio fhould be a noble, that is, a perfon not engaged in trade or commerce, poffeffing land himfelf,
or the fon of a perfon poffeffing land, or of an antient family
which formerly poffeffed land [†].   Each nuntio muft be twenty-
three years of age.

[*] See p. 57.
[†] Eft autem nobilis qui patre nobili natus in fuis poffeffionibus vivens juribus nobilium mutur. Leng. J. P. v. II. p. 8. Les nobles qui ont des terres, leurs enfans males, leurs freres, et autres qui font reconnus pour avoir leurs poffeffions et être de race ancienne et noble. Loix et Conf. de la Diete de 1768, p. 62.

The

The general proceedings of the diet are as follow: The king, senate, and nuntios, first meet altogether in the cathedral of Warsaw, and hear mass and a sermon. After service, the members of the senate, or upper-house, repair to the senate-house; and the nuntios, or lower-house, to their chamber, when the latter choose, by a majority of voices, a marshal, or speaker of the equestrian order: in order to preclude unnecessary delays, the election is required to take place within three days after their meeting *. Two days after the choice of their speaker, the king, senate, and nuntios, assemble in the senate-house, which is called the junction of the two houses. The nuntios then kiss the king's hand, and the members of the diet take their places in the following order.

The king is seated, in regal state, upon a raised throne, under a canopy at the upper end of the apartment. At the lower end, opposite the throne, sit in armed chairs the ten officers of state. The bishops †, palatines, and Castellans, are ranged in three rows of armed chairs, extending from the throne on each side; and behind these are placed the nuntios upon benches covered with red cloth. The senators have the privilege of wearing their caps, but the nuntios remain uncovered.

* Formerly, it being stipulated that the election of the marshal should take place as soon as possible, in most diets much time elapsed before a marshal was chosen; and as the sitting of the national assembly is confined to six weeks, it sometimes happened, that the nuntios could never agree in the choice; and several diets broke up without transacting any business. Connor, who visited Poland in John Sobieski's reign, says upon this head, " He that designs to be elected " marshal, must treat the gentry all the " while, otherwise he would have no vote for " him; and commonly they prolong the " election, that they may live the longer at " the candidates charges." V. II. p. 92.

In order to remedy this inconvenience, it was enacted in 1690, that the marshal must be chosen on the first day of the meeting; but in 1768, the time allowed for the election was extended to three days. See Leng. J. P. II. p. 322. and Loix et Const. de 1768, p. 52.

† Including the archbishops of Gnesna and Vilna, each at the head of his respective suffragans.

The reader will find a print which gives a faithful representation of the diet in Connor's History of Poland, v. II. p. 82. One trifling error must be corrected: the seats mark d 1111 are for the members of state, when not standing near the throne.

All

All the members being feated, the *Pacta Conventa* are read,
when the fpeaker of the equeftrian order, as well as each
nuntio, is empowered to interrupt the perufal by remonftrat-
ing againft the infringement of any particular article, and demanding at the fame time a redrefs of grievances. Then the
great chancellor propofes, in the king's name, the queftions to
be taken into confideration ; after which, his majefty nomi-
nates three fenators, and the fpeaker fix nuntios, to prepare
the bills. The diet, by majority of voices, chufes a committee to examine the accounts of the treafury. The members *
of the permanent council are elected in the manner mentioned
in the preceding chapter.

These preliminary tranfactions muft be difpatched in the
fpace of three weeks ; at which period the two houfes feparate : the nuntios retire into their own chamber, and all the
bills undergo a feparate difcuffion in both houfes. Thofe
which relate to the treafury are approved or rejected by the
fentiments of the majority. But in all ftate-matters † of the
higheft importance no refolution of the diet is valid, unlefs
ratified by the unanimous affent of every nuntio, each of whom
is able to fufpend all proceedings by his exertion of the *Liberum Veto.*

The diet muft not fit longer than fix weeks : on the firft
day, therefore, of the fixth week the fenate and nuntios meet
again in the fenate-houfe. The ftate-bills (provided they are

---

* The equeftrian members of the laft permanent council are permitted to be prefent
in this affembly, without having any vote,
until the refolutions of the council are approved by the diet. The fenators, who have
a feat in the council, are prefent of courfe.

† Matters of ftate are thus defined by the
conftitution of 1768. 1. Increafe or alteration of the taxes. 2. Augmentation of the
army. 3. Treaties of alliance and peace with
the neighbouring powers. 4. Declaration of
war. 5. Naturalization and creation of no-

bility. 6. Reduction of the coin. 7. Augmentation or diminution in the charges of the
tribunals, or in the authority of the minifters
of peace and war. 8. Creation of places. 9.
Order of holding the diets or dietines. 10.
Alterations in the tribunals. 11. Augmentation of the prerogatives of the fenatus-
confulta. 12. Permiffion to the king to purchafe lands for his fucceffors. 13. Arrier-ban,
or fummoning the nobles to arms.

In all thefe cafes unanimity is requifite. See
Loix et Conft. de la Diete de 1768, p. 46.

unanimoufly

unanimoufly agreed to by the nuntios, an event which feldom
happens in a free diet) are paffed into laws; but if that unanimity be wanting to them, they ftand rejected; and the bufinefs relating to the treafury, which has been carried by a
majority, is read and regiftered.

While the bills are debating in the lower-houfe, the king,
fenate, and eighteen nuntios, form a fupreme court of judicature, by which all nobles accufed of capital crimes are tried;
and all appeals from inferior courts determined in the laft refort. The majority decides, and the king gives fentence.

At the conclufion of the fixth week the laws, which have
paffed, are figned by the fpeaker and nuntios, and the diet is
of courfe diffolved.

The extraordinary diets are fubject to the fame regulations
as the ordinary diets, with this difference, that they cannot, by
the conftitutions of 1768, continue longer than a fortnight.
The fame day in which the two houfes affemble in the fenate-
houfe, the queftions are to be laid before them; and the nuntios return immediately to their own chamber. On the thir-
teenth day from their firft meeting, the two houfes are again
united; and on the fifteenth day, after the laws have been
read and figned, the diet breaks up as ufual.

The moft extraordinary characteriftic in the conftitution of
Poland, and which feems peculiarly to diftinguifh this government from all others, both in ancient and modern times, is
the *Liberum Veto*, or the power which each nuntio enjoys in
a free diet *, not only like the tribunes of antient Rome, of
putting a negative upon any law, but even of diffolving the
affembly. That every member of a numerous fociety fhould
be invefted with fuch a dangerous privilege, in the midft of
the moft important national tranfactions, is a circumftance in

---

* A free diet, in which unanimity is requifite, is diftinguifhed from a diet of confederacy, in which all bufinefs is carried by the
majority.

itfelf

itfelf fo incredible, as to deferve a minute enquiry into the
caufes which introduced a cuftom fo pregnant with anarchy,
and fo detrimental to public welfare.

The privilege in queftion is not to be found in any period of
the Polifh hiftory antecedent to the reign of John Cafimir.
It was under his adminiftration, that in the year 1652, when
the diet of Warfaw was debating upon tranfactions of the utmoft importance which required a fpeedy determination, that
Sicinfki, nuntio of Upita in Lithuania, cried out, " I ftop the
" proceedings *." Having uttered thefe words, he quitted the
affembly, and, repairing immediately to the chancellor, pro-
tefted ; that as many acts had been propofed and carried contrary to the conftitution of the republic, if the diet continued
to fit, he fhould confider it as an infringement of the laws.
The members were thunderftruck at a proteft of this nature,
hitherto unknown.   Warm debates took place about the propriety of continuing or diffolving the diet : at length, however, the venal and difcontented faction, who fupported the
proteft, obtained the majority ; and the affembly broke up in
great confufion.

This tranfaction changed entirely the conftitution of Poland,
and gave an unlimited fcope to mifrule and faction.   The
caufes which induced the Poles to acquiefce in eftablifhing the
Liberum Veto, thus cafually introduced, were probably the
following.

1. It was the intereft of the great officers of ftate, particularly the great general, the great treafurer, and great marfhal,
in whofe hands were vefted the adminiftration of the army,
the finances, and the police, to abridge the fitting of the diet.
Thefe great officers of ftate, being once nominated by the king,
enjoyed their appointments for life, totally independent of his
authority, and liable to no controul during the intervals of the

* Leng. Jus Pub. v. II. p. 215.

I   diets,

diets, to which alone they were refponfible. This powerful body accordingly ftrongly efpoufed the *Liberum Veto*, confcious they could eafily, and at all times, fecure a nuntio to proteft; and by that means elude all enquiry into their adminiftration. 2. By a fundamental law of the republic, all nobles accufed of capital crimes can only be brought to trial before the diet; and as, at the period juft mentioned, many perfons ftood under that defcription, all thefe and their adherents naturally favoured an expedient tending to diffolve the only tribunal, by which they could be convicted and punifhed. 3. The exigences of the ftate, occafioned by the continual wars in which Poland had been engaged, demanded, at this particular crifis, an impofition of feveral heavy taxes: as the fole power of levying all pecuniary aids refided in the diet; all the nuntios, therefore, who oppofed the raifing of additional fubfidies, feconded the propofal for fhortening the duration of that affembly. 4. But the principal reafon, which carried through, and afterwards fupported the power of diffolving diets, is to be derived from the influence of fome of the great neighbouring powers, interefted to foment anarchy and confufion in the Polifh counfels. Before this period, if they wifhed to form a cabal, and to carry any point in the national affembly, they were obliged to fecure a majority of votes: under the new arrangement they were able to attain their end on much eafier terms, and to put an end to any diet unfriendly to their views, by the corruption of a fingle member.

The bad effects of the *Liberum Veto* were foon felt by the nation to fuch an alarming degree, that all the members in the diet of 1670 bound themfelves by an oath not to exert it, and even paffed a refolution, declaring its exertion entirely void of effect in the courfe of that meeting. Notwithftanding, however, thefe falutary precautions, one Zabokrzifki, nuntio from the palatinate of Bratlau, interpofing his negative, brought this very diet to a premature diffolution *.

This *Liberum Veto*, indeed, has been always confidered by the moft intelligent Poles as one of the principal caufes, which has contributed to the decline of their country. From the æra of its eftablifhment public bufinefs has continually fuffered the moft fatal interruption; it abruptly broke up feven diets in the reign of John Cafimir; four under Michael; feven under John Sobiefki; and thirty during the reigns of the two Augufti: fo that, within the fpace of 112 years, 48 diets have been precipitately diffolved by its operation; during which period Poland has continued almoft without laws, without juftice, and, excepting the reign of John Sobiefki, with few fymptoms of military vigour. Yet fo ftrongly did the motives above difplayed attach the Poles to this pernicious privilege, that in the act of confederacy, framed in 1696 after the deceafe of John Sobiefki, the *Liberum Veto* is called the deareft and moft invaluable palladium of Polifh liberty †.

The Poles, however, having fatally experienced the diforders arifing from the *Liberum Veto*, would certainly have abolifhed it, if they had not been prevented by the partitioning powers: and it ftill exifts in its full force ‡. I ought not to

* Zawodchi Hift. Arcana.

† Unicum et fpecialiffimum Jus Cardinale.

‡ It would appear, at firft fight, as if, by the following regulation, eftablifhed by the diet of 1768, the exertion of the *Liberum Veto* was in fome inftances reftrained. " The ab-" fence of a nuntio, who has interrupted the " proceedings of the diet, fhall be no hin-" drance to the tranfaction of treafury mat-" ters." Loix et Conft. de la Diete de Var-fovie, 1768, p. 56. But this reftriction of the *Liberum Veto*, in effect, is of no validity.

For among the cardinal laws eftablifhed by the fame diet, it is enacted, " that matters of " ftate cannot be paffed but by a free diet and " unanimous confent;" p. 18. And again, " that after the treafury bufinefs, matters of " ftate fhall be brought forward, when the " oppofition of a fingle nuntio fhall ftop all " proceedings;" p. 56. And in another place,

it is decreed, " that in free diets, the *Libe-*" *rum Veto* fhall hold good in all matters of " ftate:" p. 44. When we recollect the de-finition of ftate matters (p. 86, note †), we cannot but perceive, that the power of inter-pofing a negative fiill effectually exifts. To abate its exertion in fmall points, and to efta-blifh it in the moft important affairs, is no real prevention of the evil.

In fact, as a proof that it continues in its full force, we may obferve, that fince the year 1768, no free diet has been convened; I mean before I vifited Poland. An account of what has paffed fince I quitted the country, does not fall under my plan. I recollect in-deed to have feen, in fome foreign Gazette, that a free diet had been lately affembled, but that nothing material had been tranfacted in it.

omit

omit obferving, that neither the king nor the fenate, but only the nuntios, enjoy the power of interpofing this negative upon the proceedings of the diet *.

It will naturally ftrike the reader, that if every reprefentative poffeffes the *Liberum Veto*, how can any tranfaction be carried on ? or how is it poffible that any one bill fhould pafs into a law ? for no motion can be conceived which is not liable to be oppofed by the intrigues of party, or the jealoufy of the neighbouring powers. In order, therefore, to avoid the anarchy attendant upon free diets through the operation of the *Liberum Veto*, the Poles have lately had recourfe to diets by confederacy ; which, though compofed of the fame members, and held under the fame exterior forms as free diets, differ from them in the effential circumftance of allowing bufinefs to be determined by the plurality of votes. Thefe diets have long been known to the conftitution, and have at times been ufed upon extraordinary emergencies ; but within thefe ten years they have been regularly held at the ftated time for fummoning ordinary diets. Indeed, according to the true principles of the Polifh government, no confederacy ought to be entered into excepting upon the following occafions : in defence of the king's perfon, upon any foreign invafion or domeftic confpiracy ; and during an interregnum at the diets of convocation and election †. But as no other means have been found to prevent perpetual anarchy, the nation is obliged to fubmit to an infrigement of the conftitution, which operates for the general good ‡.

* Lengnich fays, that the fenators have the power of breaking up the diet ; but he adds, that they never make ufe of this privilege ; Jus Pub. II. p. 46. which amounts to the fame as their not having it.

† It is decreed, however, by the code of 1768, that in every diet of convocation all ftate matters muft pafs unanimoufly, p. 58.

‡ But as it is enacted by the diet of 1768, that all matters of ftate muft be carried unanimoufly in free diets, I prefume that the diets by confederacy only tranfact the common bufinefs, without making any new laws, or repealing old ftatutes.

N 2   Diet

DIET OF ELECTION.

During my continuance at Warſaw I viſited the ſpot where the kings of Poland are choſen. I was ſo fortunate as to be accompanied by a nobleman of the ſenate, who obligingly explained all the forms and ceremonies of the election, and anſwered all the queſtions which my curioſity ſuggeſted to me upon the occaſion. Immediately upon my return to Warſaw, while my memory was yet warm, I noted down the following account of the place and mode of election : I was more circumſtantial than uſual, as well becauſe the ſubject is intereſting, as becauſe moſt of the deſcriptions which I have read of this ceremony abound with errors.

The ſpot, which is ſettled by the conſtitution for the place of election, is the plain of Vola, about three miles from the capital. In the midſt of this plain are two encloſures of ground, one for the ſenate, and the other for the nuntios. The former is of an oblong ſhape, ſurrounded by a kind of rampart or ditch ; in the midſt of which is erected, at the time of election, a temporary building of wood, called *ſzopa*, covered at top and open at the ſides. Near it is the other encloſure for the nuntios, of a circular ſhape, from which it derives its name of *kola* or circle, within which there is no building erected, the nuntios aſſembling in the open air. When the two chambers are joined, they meet within the *kola*, the ſenators chairs and the benches for the nuntios being ranged in the ſame regular order as in the ſenate-houſe at Warſaw, while the ſeat of the primate is placed in the middle. The *ſzopa* is always pulled down at the concluſion of the election ; ſo that I could only trace the ſite of the incloſures, the ramparts of earth remaining in the ſame ſtate. I had an opportunity, however, of ſeeing a painting repreſenting the *ſzopa* and whole ſcene of election, which, as I was informed, was perfectly accurate.

But

But before I defcribe the election, it may be neceffary to give a fhort detail of the principal occurrences which precede that ceremony.

Upon the king's demife the interregnum commences : the regal authority is then vefted in the archbifhop of Gnefna primate of Poland, as interrex or regent. He announces the death of the king by circular letters, convokes the dietines and diets of convocation ; and, in a word, performs all the functions of royalty during the vacancy in the throne.

The diet, which is firft convened upon the fovereign's deceafe, is called the diet of convocation, and is always held at Warfaw, previous to the diet of election, which affembles in the plain of Vola. The fovereign authority refides in this affembly, in the fame manner as in thofe which are fummoned while the throne is filled. The primate prefides like the king, with this difference, that he does not place himfelf upon the throne, but fits in an armed chair ftationed in the middle of the fenate-houfe. The diet iffues out acts or ordinances, arranges or changes the form of government, fettles the *Pacta Conventa*, and appoints the meeting of the diet of election. The interval between the death of the king and the nomination of his fucceffor is uncertain ; its longer or fhorter duration depending upon the intrigues and cabals of the candidates, or the pleafure of thofe foreign powers, who give law to Poland. It is always a ftate of turbulence and licentioufnefs ; the kingdom is divided into parties and factions ; juftice is in a manner fufpended ; and the nobles commit every diforder with impunity.

Unanimity * being requifite in all matters of ftate, it is eafy to conceive the delays and cabals, the influence and cor-

* This unanimity, in fact, does not exift ; for the ftrongeft fide forces the weaker to accede or to retire. Yet in the diet of 1768 it was enacted, that in the diets of convocation ftate queftions could only be carried unanimoufly. Several diets of convocation have been frequently affembled before all the affairs could be finally arranged.

ruption,

ruption, employed to gain the members in the diet of convocation. As foon as all the points are adjufted, whether the
acts have paffed unanimoufly or otherwife, the members,
previous to their feparation, enter into a general confederacy
to fupport and maintain the refolutions of the diet.

At the appointed day the diet of election is affembled,
during which Warfaw and its environs is a fcene of confufion,
and frequently of bloodfhed. The chief nobility have large
bodies of troops in their fervice, and repair to the diet attended
by their numerous vaffals and a large retinue of domeftics;
while each petty baron, who can afford to maintain them, pa-
rades about with his retainers and flaves.

On the day in which the diet of election is opened, the
primate, fenate, and nobility, repair to the cathedral of Warfaw, to hear mafs and a fermon; from whence they proceed
in due order to the plain of Vola. The fenators enter the
fzopa, and the nuntios take their places within the *kola*; while
the other nobles are ftationed in the plain. The fenate and
the nuntios, after having paffed their refpective refolutions, as
in the ordinary diets, affemble together in the *kola*, when the
primate, feated in the middle, lays before them the objects to
be taken into confideration; the *Pacta Conventa*, fettled at
the diet of convocation, are read and approved, all neceffary
arrangements made, and the day of election appointed. The
diet then gives audience to the foreign minifters, who are
permitted by recommendation to interfere in the choice of a
king, and to the advocates of the feveral candidates. All thefe
affairs take up feveral days; and would perhaps never be terminated, as unanimity is requifite, if the affembly was not
overawed by the foreign troops, who are always quartered
near the plain of election.

Upon the day appointed for the election, the fenate and
nuntios affemble, as before, in the *kola*, while the nobles are
ranged

ranged in the open field in feparate bodies, according to their feveral palatinates, with ftandards borne before them, and the principal officers of each diftrict on horfeback. The primate, having declared the names of the candidates, kneels down and chants a hymn ; after which the fenators and nuntios join the gentry of their refpective palatinates : then the primate, on horfeback, or in a carriage, goes round the plain to the different bodies of the gentry as they are ftationed according to their palatinates ; and, having collected the votes, proclaims the fuccefsful candidate. Each noble does not give his vote feparately, for that would be endlefs ; but when the primate goes round, the collected body of each palatinate name the perfon they efpoufe. At the conclufion of this ceremony the affembly breaks up.

On the following day the fenate and nuntios return to the plain ; when the fuccefsful candidate is again proclaimed, and a deputy difpatched to acquaint him of his election, as no candidate is allowed to be prefent. After the proclamation, the gentry retire ; and the diet, having appointed the diet of coronation, is diffolved.

All elections are contefted : but for fome time they have always been unanimous upon the fpot, from the terror of a neighbouring army. In cafe of an oppofition, the party who will not accede retire from the plain, and remonftrate againft the election ; and, if they are fufficiently ftrong, a civil war enfues. If it were not for the interference of foreign troops, the confufion, diforder, and bloodfhed attending fuch a popular election (as was formerly the cafe), would be better conceived than defcribed : and thus the country draws fome advantage from an evil, which is confidered by the Poles as the difgrace and fcandal of every election.

3

CHAP.

C H A P. VII.

I. Finances and taxes of Poland.—*Revenue of the king.—II. Commerce.—General exports and imports.—Caufes of the low ſtate of trade.—Failure of the plan of opening the navigation of the Dnieſter.—Navigation of the Notez.—III. Military eſtabliſhment.—Corps of Ulans.—State of the army.—Confederacies.—*Ruſſian *troops.*

I. FINANCES and TAXES of POLAND.

BOOK
I.

THE following extract from the proceedings of the diet of 1768 will ferve to ſhew the annual receipts and diſburſements of government before the diſmemberment: " The " annual revenues of the treaſury of the crown *, amount to " 10,748,245 florins = £298,562. 7s. 2¼d. The expences " to 17,050,000 = £473,611. 2s. 2¼d. It would be neceſ- " ſary, therefore, to increaſe the revenues, ſo as to anſwer the " exceſs of the expences above the receipts, namely, 6,301,755 " florins = £175,048. 15s. but as a part of the antient reve- " nues muſt be aboliſhed, the new taxes muſt yield 10,236,737 " florins = £284,353. 13s. 4d.

" The treaſury of Lithuania produces the annual ſum of " 3,646,628 = £101,295. 4s. 6d. the expences amount to " 6,478,142 = £179,948. 7s. 6d. The revenues ought " therefore to be augmented 2,831,514 = £78,653. 3s. 4d. " But as ſome antient impoſts muſt be aboliſhed, the new " taxes muſt yield 4,250,481 = £118,068. 18s. 4d. †"

Poland, by the late diſmemberment, loſt nearly half of her annual income ; namely, that part ariſing from the ſtaroſties now occupied by the partitioning powers, from the duties ‡

---

* Poland, excluſive of Li·huania.　　　‡ The greateſt part of theſe duties are now
† Loix et Conſt. de la Diete de 1768, p. 70.　paid to the king of Pruſſia.

upon

upon merchandize fent down the Viftula to Dantzic, and particularly from the profits of the falt mines in Auftrian Poland. Thofe of Wieliſka * alone amounted to 3,500,000 Poliſh florins, or £97,222 fterling, which was nearly equal to a fourth part of the government revenues before the partition.

In order to fupply this deficiency, it became neceffary to new-model and increafe the taxes. Accordingly, in the diet of 1775, a few of the old taxes were abolifhed, fome were augmented, and others were added, fo as to make the neat revenues as high as they were before the difmemberment.

The principal taxes are as follow :

Poll tax of the Jews. Each Jew, both male and female, infants and adults, pays three Polifh florins, or about 1s. 8d. *per annum*; this impofition, which is of very old ftanding, was augmented in 1775 a florin per head.

A fourth of the ftarofties. Thefe are the great fiefs of the crown, in the king's gift, holden by the poffeffors during life. The ftaroft enjoys, befide large eftates in land, territorial jurifdiction; the fourth of his revenues arifing from the land is paid into the treafury of the republic. By the late change of government thefe ftarofties, after the demife of the perfons now enjoying them, and of thofe who have the reverfion, are to revert to the public, and their whole amount to be appropriated to the expences of government †.

Excife of beer, mead, and fpirituous liquors diftilled from corn. This article muft not be inconfiderable, confidering the quantity of corn grown in Poland, which, for want of external commerce, cannot be exported, and the propenfity of the people to fpirituous liquours.

Monopoly of Tobacco. Different Duties upon Importation and Exportation. Formerly all the nobles were permitted to

* See Book II Chapter II.
† See the account of the Permanent Council, p. 58.

import

import and export foreign goods and merchandize free of duty, a privilege which effectually diminished, and almost abforbed, the profits of the tax in queftion.   In 177 .   right was abolifhed; and all imported and exported commodities now pay duty without any diftinction.   Confidering the great quantity of foreign manufactures introduced into Poland, and chiefly for the ufe of the nobility, this alteration muft make a confiderable addition to the revenues of government:

Tax upon Chimnies.   Before the partition, this tax exifted only in Lithuania; in 1775 it was rendered general and confiderably augmented; it is the moft profitable of all the taxes, but lies very heavy upon the common people and peafants. Each chimney is affeffed in the following proportion.   In palaces, or houfes of the chief nobility, at 16 Polifh florins *per ann.* = about 8*s.* 2$\frac{1}{4}$*d.*; houfes of the principal merchants in Warfaw at 15 = 7*s.* 7*d.*; other brick houfes from 10 to 14 = from 5*s.* 7$\frac{1}{4}$*d.* to 7*s.* 3$\frac{1}{4}$*d.*; wooden houfes from 6 to 8 = from 3*s.* 4*d.* to 4*s.* 6$\frac{1}{2}$*d.*; beft houfes in other large towns 12 = 6*s.* 8*d.*; in the fmall towns and villages from 6 to 8 = 3*s.* 4*d.* to 4*s.* 6$\frac{1}{2}$*d.*; peafants cottages from 5 to 7 = 2*s.* 9$\frac{1}{2}$*d.* to 4*s.* The peafants pay no other tax to government; and indeed, confidering their poverty, and the oppreffion of their lords and great nobility, this addition is more than they can well fupport.

All thefe feveral impofts amount to 11,628,461 Polifh florins, or £323,012 fterling.

The king received before the partition a neat revenue of 7,000,000 Polifh florins, or £194,500, which arofe from the royal demefnes and the profit of the falt-works.   In order to imdemnify him for the lofs of the falt-works, and the royal eftates fituated in the difmembered provinces, he draws from the public treafury 2,666,666 florins, or £74,074 fterling; which, in addition to the remaining royal demefnes, and fome ftarofties granted for his ufe, make his prefent income the fame

as

as before the difmemberment. Out of this income he only pays his houfhold expences and menial fervants ; the falary of the great officers of ftate, and the other general expences, being fupplied from the public fund. The whole revenue of go- vernment, including the royal demefnes and ftaroflies lately granted to the king, amount to 15,961,795 florins, or £443,938 ; and by extracting the 7,000,000 florins appro- priated to the king's privy purfe, there remains for the fup- port of the army, the falaries of the great officers of ftate, and other general charges, only 8,961,795 florins, or £248,938. 1s. a fum fo fmall, that it hardly feems in any wife equal to the purpofes for which it is defigned. And yet it is nearly adequate to the ordinary current expences : for the regular army is fmall, the great officers of ftate receive little or nothing from the public treafury, being amply re- warded with the royal fiefs which are fo numerous and pro- fitable ; each palatinate pays its own officers from its private treafury ; while the feveral judges, juftices of the peace, and other civil officers who enjoy territorial jurifdiction, may en- rich themfelves fufficiently by extortions and oppreffions with- out any falary.

II. Commerce of Poland.

Poland contains feveral navigable rivers, which flow through its dominions in all directions, and convey its exports to the havens of the Baltic. By means of the Viftula and the rivers falling into it, the productions of the palatinates of Cracow, Lublin, and Mafovia, are fent to Thorn, and from thence to Dantzic and Konigfburg. By the Niemen the commodities of Lithuania are tranfported to Memmel ; and by the Duna thofe of Eaftern Lithuania and White Ruffia to Riga. The chief exports of Poland are all fpecies of grain, hemp, flax, cattle, mafts, planks, timber for fhip-building, pitch and tar, honey, wax, tallow, pot-afh, and leather : its imports are foreign

O 2

wines,

wines, cloths, ſtuffs, manufactured ſilks and cotton, fine linen, hardware, tin, copper, ſilver and gold, glaſs ware, furs, &c.

From the various productions and great fertility of Poland, its trade might be carried to a conſiderable height; but the following cauſes tend to ſuppreſs the ſpirit of commerce.

1. The nobles are degraded if they engage in any kind of traffic. 2. The burghers of the large towns are not rich enough to eſtabliſh any manufactures; and either through want of induſtry, or through dread of exceſſive extortions from the principal nobility, leave almoſt all the retail-trade in the hands of foreigners and Jews. The inhabitants of the ſmall towns, who are expoſed to greater oppreſſions, are ſtill more diſqualified from purſuing any branch of commerce. 3. The peaſants being ſlaves, and the property of their maſter, cannot retire from the place of their nativity without his conſent. John Albert, obſerving that commerce could never flouriſh while this reſtriction ſubſiſted, enacted, that one peaſant in a family ſhould be permitted to quit his village, either for the purpoſe of trade or literature; but the clauſe, which ordered them to requeſt and obtain the conſent of the lord, fruſtrated the purpoſe of this excellent law, and rendered it abſolutely nugatory *.

As the Poles are obliged to draw from foreign countries the greateſt part of the manufactured goods neceſſary for their interior conſumption, the ſpecie which is exported exceeds the imported more than 20,000,000 Poliſh florins, or £555,555.

Poland has been called the granary of the North, an appellation which it ſeems to deſerve rather from its former than from its preſent fertility. For its lands not being ſufficiently cultivated, as well on account of the ſlavery of the peaſants, as the unequal diſtribution of property, the exportation of corn

---

* Stat. Reg. Pol. p. 169.

is by no means anfwerable to the general nature of the foil, or the extent of its provinces, which, if properly improved, would be capable of fupplying half Europe with grain. Several palatinates in Poland, and more particularly Podolia and Kiovia, are extremely adapted to the production of grain: though many parts of thefe provinces remain uncultivated, yet the portion which is in tillage yields a greater fupply than is neceffary for the confumption of the inhabitants. The only method of employing the overplus is to extract from it a fpirituous liquor. But an ingenious Polifh author * has fhown, that the provinces in queftion might undoubtedly fend their grain down the Dniefter through Turkifh Moldavia; and open an intercourfe with the ports of the Black Sea. This project was formerly in agitation.

During the reign of Sigifmond Auguftus, Cardinal Commandon, in travelling through Podolia, being much ftruck with the fertility of that province, firft fuggefted the meafure; and Sigifmond, having obtained the concurrence of the grand feignor, actually difpatched fome Poles down the Dniefter, to explore the ftate of the river. But the perfons employed on this occafion, happening after a few days voyage to meet with fome impediments from rocks and fand banks, declared, without any further examination, that the Dniefter was not navigable; and although Commandon reprefented to the king, that the obftacles pointed out might, without any great difficulty, be furmounted; yet the project was poftponed, and never again revived †.

The judicious author above-mentioned ‡, in touching upon this fubject, laments the ignorance of his countrymen; and ridicules the precipitation with which they abandoned a plan

* Mr de Wiebitfki, a Polifh gentleman of great learning and information. The treatife alluded to in this and other places of this work, is written in the Polifh language, and called Patriotic Letters, addreffed to the Chancellor Zamoifki.

† Vie de Commandon.

‡ Mr. de Wiebitfki.

fo

fo favourable to the improvement of their commerce. He
fhows, that the inattention of the Poles to the natural advantages of their country has been exemplified in another inftance
of a fimilar kind.   By means of the Notez, a river of Great
Poland, which falls into the Oder, the Poles might have conveyed grain into Silefia, and from thence down the Oder into
other parts of Germany.   But they never attempted the navigation of the Notez, from an ill-founded perfuafion of its not
being practicable.   No fooner, however, had the king of
Pruffia acquired the country through which that river takes
its courfe, than it was inftantly, and without undergoing the
leaft alteration, covered with veffels.

III. MILITARY ESTABLISHMENT.

The king has a corps of 2000 troops in his own pay, and
entirely dependent upon himfelf.   Thefe troops confift chiefly
of Ulans or light horfe, who furnifh alternately the efcort
which accompanies his majefty.   We faw a fmall party, about
thirty, who were encamped near his villa, and had afterwards an
opportunity of examining them more minutely.   The Ulans are
chiefly Tartars, many of them Mahometans, and are greatly
to be relied on for their fidelity.   The corps is compofed of
gentlemen and vaffals :   they all form in fquadron together,
but are differently armed ;   they both indifcriminately carry
fabres and piftols, but the gentlemen only bear lances of about
ten feet long ;   inftead of which, the others are armed with
carabines.   Their drefs is a high fur cap, a green and red
jacket, pantaloons of the fame colour, which cover the boots
as low as the ankle ;   and a petticoat of white cloth defcending
to the knee.   Their heads are all fhaved after the Polifh manner [*].   Their lances, at the end of which is faftened a long
fwallow-tailed flag of black and red cloth, are fhorter and
weaker than thofe of the Auftrian Croats ;   but they carry and

* See Book II. Chapter II.

7   ufe

ufe them much in the fame manner, and with no lefs dexte-
rity. The men were of different fizes, and feemed fine and
well grown, but were greatly disfigured with their petticoats
and pantaloons. The horfes on which they were mounted
were about fourteen hands high, of remarkable fpirit, with
great ftrength of fhoulder. Poland is much efteemed for its
breed of horfes; and the king of Pruffia procures his light
cavalry from this country. The breed, however, has been almoft ruined during the late civil wars, and the nobility are
now chiefly fupplied from Tartary.

The armies of Poland and Lithuania are independent of each
other, being feparately commanded, and under the direction
of the refpective great generals. In time of war the king in
perfon may lead the forces of the republic. Formerly the
power of thefe great generals was uncontrouled, excepting by the
diet, to which alone they were amenable for their adminiftration.
Their enormous authority, however, underwent fome limitation
in 1768, by the appointment of a committee of war, of which
they are perpetual prefidents; and was ftill further circum-
fcribed by the eftablifhment of the military department in the
permanent council, whofe office has been already defcribed*.

In 1778 the following was the ftate of the Polifh army.

Troops of Poland.

	Complement.	Effective men.	Wanting.
Staff officers	27	27	
Cavalry	4997	4708	289
Infantry, including artillery	7286	6703	583
Total of Poland -	12310	11438	872

Army of Lithuania.

	Complement.	Effective men.	Wanting.
Staff officers	25	25	
Cavalry	2670	2497	173
Infantry, including artillery	4770	4465	305
Total of Lithuania	7465	6987	478

* See p. 54.

Total

Total of the Polish and Lithuanian troops,

19775   18425   1350

The standing army of Poland being so inconsiderable, the defence of the country, in case of invasion, is left to the gentry at large, who are assembled by regular summons from the king with the consent of the diet. Every palatinate is divided into districts, over each of which proper officers are appointed; and every person possessing free and noble tenures is bound to military service, either singly or at the head of a certain number of his retainers, according to the extent and nature of his possessions. The troops thus assembled are obliged only to serve for a limited time, and are not under the necessity of marching beyond the limits of their country. The mode of levying and maintaining this army is exactly similar to that practised under the feudal system. At present, though it is almost totally unfit for the purposes of repelling a foreign enemy, it is yet a powerful instrument in the hands of domestic faction : for the expedition with which it is raised under the feudal regulations, facilitates the formation of those dangerous confederacies, which suddenly start up on the contested election of a sovereign, or whenever the nobles are at variance with each other.

There are two sorts of confederacies. The first are those formed with the consent of the king, senate, or equestrian order, assembled in the diet; by which the whole nation confederates for the good of the country. The second are the confederacies of the several palatinates, which unite for the purpose of redressing any grievances, or remonstrating against encroachments of the sovereign power. These may be particular, or general, and are usually the forerunners of a civil war. The general confederacy, which is always in opposition to the king, is called Rokoz, and is formed by the union of the particular confederacies.

5

As

As every Polifh gentleman has a right to maintain as many troops as he chufes, it may eafily be conceived, that each palatinate is the fcene of occafional difputes and petty contentions between the principal nobles, and fometimes even between their refpective retainers. In fuch a dreadful ftate of anarchy, it is a wonder that the whole kingdom is not a perpetual fcene of endlefs commotions, and that the nation is compofed of any thing elfe but lawlefs banditti. It redounds, therefore, greatly to.the honour of the natural difpofition of the Poles, that amid all thefe incentives to confufion, a much greater degree of tranquillity, than could be well expected, is maintained.

As I am now delineating the military eftablifhment, I muft not omit the Ruffian troops, which have been fo long quartered in this country, that they may almoft be confidered as forming part of the national army. The whole kingdom is entirely under the protection, or, in other words, under the power of Ruffia, who rules over it with the fame unbounded authority as over one of its own provinces. The king is in effect little more than a viceroy; while the Ruffian embaffador has the real fovereignty, and regulates all the affairs of the kingdom according to the direction of his court. The emprefs maintains within the country about 10,000 foldiers. Every garrifon is compofed of Ruffian and native troops; a thoufand of the former are ftationed at Warfaw; and each gate of the town is guarded by a Ruffian and Polifh centinel. In a word, the Ruffian troops hold the nobles in fubjection, and for the prefent keep under internal feuds and commotions. But when Poland (if ever that event fhould happen) is again left to herfelf, the fame fury of contending parties, now fmothered, but not annihilated, will probably break out with redoubled fury; and again generate thofe difturbances which have long convulfed this unhappy kingdom: and to what a wretched ftate is that country reduced, which owes its tranquillity to the interpofition of a foreign army?

C H A P. VIII.

Wretched state of Poland.—*Division of the inhabitants into*
I. Nobles or gentry; II. Clergy; III. Burghers; IV. Peasants.
—State of Vassalage.—Its fatal effects.—Instances of a few
nobles who have given liberty to their peasants.—Advantages
resulting from that practice.—V. Jews.—Population of Poland.

BOOK
I.

I Consider Polish liberty as the source of Polish wretchedness; and Poland appears to me, as far as I can judge by the specimens which fell under my observation, of all countries the most distressed. Nor indeed do the natives themselves attempt to palliate or deny this melancholy fact. Upon expressing my surprize at one instance of the abuse of liberty, to which I had been myself a witness, to a person well versed in the laws of the country, he returned for answer, " If you " knew the confusion and anarchy of our constitution, you " would be surprised at nothing: many grievances necessarily " exist even in the best regulated states; what then must be " the case in ours, which of all governments is the most de- " testable?" Another lamenting the dreadful situation of his country, said to me, " The name of Poland still remains, but " the nation no longer exists: an universal corruption and " venality pervades all ranks of people. Many of the first no- " bility do not blush to receive pensions from foreign courts. " One professes himself publicly an Austrian, a second a Prus- " sian, a third a Frenchman, and a fourth a Russian."

The present situation of the Polish nation impressed my mind with the most pathetic ideas of fallen greatness; and I could not consider, without a mixture of regret and sympathy, a people, who formerly gave law to the North, reduced to so

low

low a ſtate of inſignificance and domeſtic miſery. The nation
has few manufactures, ſcarcely any commerce ; a king almoſt
without authority ; the nobles in a ſtate of uncontrouled anarchy ; the peaſants groaning under a yoke of feudal deſpotiſm
far worſe than the tyranny of an abſolute monarch. I never
before obſerved ſuch an inequality of fortune, ſuch ſudden
tranſition from extreme riches to extreme poverty ; wherever
I turned my eyes, luxury and wretchedneſs were conſtant
neighbours. In a word, the boaſted Poliſh liberty is not enjoyed
in the ſmalleſt degree by the bulk of the people, but is confined
among the nobles or gentry. The truth of theſe remarks will
beſt appear from the following account of the inhabitants.

The inhabitants of Poland are nobles, clergy, citizens, and
peaſants.

I. The nobles are divided into two claſſes : the members
of the ſenate, and of the equeſtrian order. Having, upon a
former occaſion *, deſcribed the powers which ſenators enjoy
in their collective capacity, it will be unneceſſary to repeat
them in this place.

We ſhould be greatly deceived if we were to underſtand
the word *noble* in our ſenſe of that term. In the laws of
Poland a noble is a perſon who poſſeſſes a freehold † eſtate, or
who can prove his deſcent from anceſtors formerly poſſeſſing
a freehold, following no trade or commerce, and at liberty to
chooſe the place of his habitation. This deſcription includes
all perſons above burghers and peaſants. The members of

---

* See p. 83.

† Some citizens have the right of poſſeſſing lands within a league of the town which
they inhabit ; but theſe lands are not free
and noble, and are always diſtinguiſhed from
the freeholds of the nobles ; the latter are
called in the ſtatute law terrigenæ, or earth-
born, free to live where they pleaſe, to diſtin-
guiſh them from perſons neceſſarily inhabiting
towns, " Quos leges nominant terrigenas,

" non alii ſunt, quam nobiles ; exprimitque
" prius vocabulum, polonicum *Ziemiánin*, quo
" in agris ſibi et ſuo jure vivens intelligitur,
" quæ nobilium in Polonia eſt conditio, qui
" non civitates & oppida, ſed ſua prædia ha-
" bitantes, vitam ſuo arbitrio diſponunt."
Leng. Jus Pub. I. p. 297. a true feudal diſtinction. They are alſo ſtyled indigenæ or
natives, and concives or fellow-citizens of the
republic.

this

this body below the rank of fenators are. called, in a collective
ftate, the equeftrian order;. and in their individual capacities.
nobles, gentlemen, freemen, or land-holders, which appellations.
are fynonymous.

All the nobles or gentry are, in the ftrict letter of the law,
equal by birth; fo that all honours and titles are fuppofed to.
add nothing to their real dignity *. By means of their reprefentatives in the diet, they have a fhare in the legiflative authority, and in fome cafes, as in the election of a king, they
affemble in perfon, when each noble is capable of being elected:
a nuntio, of bearing the office of a fenator, and of prefenting
himfelf as a candidate upon a vacancy in the throne. No
noble can be arrefted without being previoufly convicted, except in cafes of high treafon, murder, and robbery on the
highway, and then he muft be furprifed in the fact; nor can.
he be capitally punifhed but by order of the diet. The de-
finition of a noble being thus applied not only to perfons.
actually poffeffing land, but even to the defcendants of former
landholders,. comprehends fuch a large body of men, that.
many of them are in a ftate of extreme indigence; and as,.
according to the Polifh law, they lofe their nobility if they
follow trade or commerce, the moft needy generally devote
themfelves to the fervice of the richer nobles, who, like the;

---

* It is particularly ftipulated, that titles
give no precedence; which is called in the
Pacta Conventa of Auguftus III. " Jus æqua-
" litatis inter cives regni," &c. upon which
Lengnich makes the following remark, " Om-
" nis hæc nobilitas natura eft æqualis, quod
" omnes ex illâ, ad eadem jura, in eandem
" fpem nafcuntur. Tituli Principum, Mar-
" chionum, Comitum, quibus alii præ aliis
" infigniuntur, vocabula funt, quæ ftatum
" non immutant, & qui illis gaudent, non
" alio, quam nobilium jure, fua tenent. Ne-
" que Polonia alias Principum, alias Marchi-
" onum, alias Comitum, alias Equitum leges
" novit; fed omnibus una nobilium lex

" fcripta eft. Inde in conclavi Nunciorum.
" Principum & Comitum nominibus fulgen-
" tes, cæteris permixtos videmus. Nullum
" ibi inter modici agelli & paucorum juge-
" rum, ac aliquot oppidorum multorumque
" vicorum dominum, obfervatur difcrimen.
" Præcedunt alii, alii fequuntur non ex titulis
" familiarum, fed ad palatinatuum terrarum-
" que, ex quibus nuntii miffi, ordinem. Ea-
" dem in fenatu ratio. Affignat loca, mune.
" iis non ftemmatis dignitas. Et qui fenator;
" non princeps, non comes, præcedit princi.
" pem, ac comitem, non fenatorem." Pac.
Con p. 31.

old;

old feudal barons, are conftantly attended by a large number of retainers. As all nobles, without any diftinction, enjoy the right of voting, as well for the choice of nuntios, as at the election of a king, their poverty and their number is frequently productive of great inconvenience. Hence the king, who has juftly conceived a great veneration for the Englifh conftitution, wifhed to introduce into the new code a law fimilar to ours relating to county elections, that no perfon fhould be intitled to a vote in the choice of a nuntio but thofe who poffeffed a certain qualification in land *. This propofition, however, has been received with fuch marks of diffatisfaction, that we may conclude it will never be allowed to pafs into a law.

II. The Clergy. Miciflaus, the firft fovereign of Poland who embraced Chriftianity, granted feveral immunities and eftates to the clergy. His fucceffors and the rich nobles followed his example; and the riches of this body continued increafing as well from royal as private donations, until the diet, apprehenfive left in procefs of time the greateft part of the eftates fhould pafs into the hands of the clergy, forbad by different laws, and particularly in 1669, the alienation of lands to the church, under penalty of forfeiture: and under the prefent reign feveral eftates have been confifcated which had been beftowed upon the clergy fince that period.

From the time of the firft eftablifhment of the catholic religion by Cardinal Ægidius, nuntio from Pope John XII. the bifhops have been admitted into the fenate as king's counfellors. They were ufually appointed by the king, and confirmed by the pope; but, fince the creation of the perma-

---

* Connor mentions a fimilar attempt of John Cafimir, which failed of fuccefs. "King Cafimir obferving the great abufes "that fpring from every little gentleman's "pretended privilege to fit in the little diets, "ordered that none fhould have a vote there, "in electing a deputy or nuntio, but fuch "only as had at leaft two hundred crowns a "year; whereupon the palatine of Pofnania, "offering to put this law in execution in his "province, was not only affronted, but alfo "narrowly efcaped with his life." Hift. of Poland, v. II. p. 104.

5

nent

nent council, they are nominated by his majesty out of three candidates chosen by the council : a bishop, the moment he is appointed, is of course entitled to all the privileges of a senator. The archbishop of Gnesna is primate, as we have before observed, the first senator in rank, and viceroy during an interregnum.

The ecclesiastics are all freemen, and, in some particular instances, have their own courts of justice, in which the canon law is practised. Of these courts of justice peculiar to the clergy, there are three sorts ; I. The confistorial, under the jurisdiction of each bishop in his diocese ; II. The metropolitan, under the primate, to which an appeal lies from the bishop's court ; III. That of the pope's nuntio, which is the supreme ecclesiastical judicature within the kingdom, to which an appeal may be made both from the decision of the bishop and of the primate. In cases of divorce, dispensations for marriages, and in other instances, the parties, as in all catholic countries, must apply to the pope ; by which means no inconsiderable portion of money is absorbed by the see of Rome.

In most civil affairs the clergy are judged in the ordinary courts of justice. In criminal causes, an ecclesiastic is first arrested by the civil powers, then judged in the consistory, and, if convicted, he is remitted to the civil power, in order to undergo the penalty annexed to the crime of which he has been found guilty. One great ecclesiastical abuse, which has been abolished in most other catholic countries, still exists in this kingdom : when the Pope sends a bull into Poland, the clergy publish and carry it into execution, without the confirmation or approbation of the civil power. Before 1538 ecclesiastics were allowed to hold civil employments ; but in that year priests were declared incapable of being promoted to secular offices. They were also exempted from paying any taxes ; but this exemption has been wisely taken off, and they

are

are now rated in the fame manner as the laity, with this difference, that their contributions are not called taxes, but charitable fubfidies.

III. The next clafs of people are the burghers, inhabiting towns, whofe privileges were formerly far more confiderable than they are at prefent.

The hiftory of all countries, in which the feudal fyftem has been eftablifhed, bears teftimony to the pernicious policy of holding the lower claffes of men in a ftate of flavifh fubjection. In procefs of time a concurrence of caufes * contributed gradually to foften the rigour of this fervitude with regard to the burghers, in feveral of the feudal kingdoms. Among other circumftances tending to their protection, the moft favourable was the formation of feveral cities into bodies politic, with the privilege of exercifing municipal jurifdiction. This inftitution took its rife in Italy, the firft country in Europe which emerged from barbarifm; and was from thence transferred to France and Germany. It was firft introduced into Poland about 1250, during the reign of Boleflaus the chafte, who being inftructed in the Teutonic or German laws by Henry the bearded duke of Wratiflaw, granted firft to Cracow, and afterwards to feveral other towns, the privileges poffeffed by the German cities: this body of rights is called in the ftatutes of Poland. *Jus Magdeburgicum et Teutonicum*; and the caufe affigned for its introduction is, that no city could flourifh and increafe under the feudal laws †. In the 13th and following centuries the kings and great barons built feveral towns, to all which they granted a charter of incorporation, conceived in the following terms ‡: " *Transfero hanc villam ex jure Polonico in* " *jus Teutonicum.*" The beneficial tendency of this political

---

* It does not enter into the plan of this work to defcribe thefe caufes: the reader will find them amply and ably illuftrated in a View of the State of Europe, prefixed to Dr.

Robertfon's Hiftory of Charles V.
† Leng. Jus Pub. p. 524.
‡ Chromer.

regu-

regulation foon appeared : by a fudden increafe of population
and wealth, the burghers of fome of the principal free towns
acquired fuch a degree of importance and confideration, as to
give their affent to treaties, and fend deputies to the national
affembly ; a noble was not degraded by being a burgher, and
a burgher was capable of being an officer of the crown.   A
treaty * which Cafimir the Great entered into with the knights
of the Teutonic order, was not only figned by the king and
the principal nobles, but alfo by the burghers of Cracow,
Pofin, Sandomir, and other towns ; and under the fame monarch Wiernefk †, burgomafter of Cracow, was fubmarfhal
and treafurer of the crown.

The burghers enjoyed the privileges juft mentioned during
the Jaghellon line, as appears from the different acts of Sigifmond I. and his fon Sigifmond Auguftus.   During the reign
of the former the nobles endeavoured to exclude the deputies
of Cracow from the diet ; but that monarch not only confirmed the right of that city to fend reprefentatives, but even
decreed, that the citizens were included within the clafs of
nobles ‡.

When the crown became wholly elective, the burghers
fuffered continual encroachments on their privileges at every
nomination of a new fovereign ; they loft the right of poffeffing lands, excepting within a fmall diftance of their towns,
of fending deputies to the diets, and were of courfe excluded
from all fhare of the legiflative authority.   The principal
caufe of this exclufion was, that as the burghers were not

* Dlugoffius L. IX. p. 1067.
† This Wiernefk was fo rich, that in 1363,
when the emperor Charles IV. married at
Cracow Elizabeth grand daughter of Cafimir,
he gave a moft fumptuous entertainment to
his fovereign, to the emperor, kings of Hungary, Denmark, Cyprus, and other princes,
who were prefent at the marriage : befide
other magnificent gifts which he beftowed
upon the company, he prefented Cafimir with
a fum equal to the portion of the bride.
Chromer, p. 324.
‡ Confules Cracovienfes, &c. debere et
poffe omnibus confiliis, quibus alii nuntii ter-
reftres aderunt, &c. more folito confultari,
Statuta Pol. p. 8   Cracovia eft incorporata
et unita nobilitati ; ib. terrarumque civita-
tumque nuntii, p. 353.

obliged,

obliged, by the nature of their tenures, to march againſt the enemy, but were only under the neceſſity of furniſhing arms and waggons for the uſe of the army; they incurred, therefore, the contempt of the warlike gentry, who, in the true ſpirit of feudal arrogance, conſidered all occupations, but that of war, as beneath a freeman, and all perſons, not bound to military ſervices, as unqualified for the adminiſtration of public affairs.

The burghers, however, ſtill enjoy a conſiderable portion of freedom, and poſſeſs the following immunities: they elect their own burgomaſter and council; they regulate their interior police, and have their own criminal courts of juſtice, which decide without appeal. A burgher, when plaintiff againſt a noble, is obliged to carry the cauſe into the courts of juſtice belonging to the nobles, where the judgement is final: when defendant, he muſt be cited before the magiſtrates of his own town, from whence an appeal lies only to the king in the aſſeſſorial tribunal. To this exemption from the juriſdiction of the nobles, though only in one ſpecies of cauſes, the burghers owe whatever degree of independence they ſtill retain; as without this immunity they would long ago have been reduced to a ſtate of vaſſalage.

IV. The peaſants in Poland, as in all feudal governments, are ſerfs or ſlaves; and the value of an eſtate is not eſtimated ſo much from its extent, as from the number of its peaſants, who are transferred from one maſter to another like ſo many head of cattle.

The peaſants, however, are not all in an equal ſtate of ſubjection: they are diſtinguiſhed into two ſorts; 1. German; 2. Natives.

1. During the reign of Boleſlaus the Chaſte, and more particularly in that of Caſimir the Great, many Germans ſettled in Poland, who were indulged in the uſe of the German

laws *; and their defcendants ftill continue to enjoy fevera? privileges not poffeffed by the generality of Polifh peafants. The good effects of thefe privileges are very vifible in the general ftate of their domeftic œconomy: their villages are better built, and their fields better cultivated, than thofe which belong to the native Poles; they poffefs more cattle, pay their quit-rents to their lords with greater exactnefs; and, when compared with the others, are cleaner and neater in their perfons.

2. The flavery of the Polifh peafants is very antient, and was always extremely rigorous. Until the time of Cafimir the Great, the lord could put his peafant to death with impunity, and, when the latter had no children, confidered himfelf as the heir, and feized all his effects. In 1347 Cafimir prefcribed a fine for the murder of a peafant; and enacted, that, in cafe of his deceafe without iffue, his next heir fhould inherit †. The fame fovereign alfo decreed, that a peafant was capable of bearing arms as a foldier, and that therefore he ought to be confidered as a freeman. But thefe and other regulations, by which that amiable monarch endeavoured to alleviate the miferies of the vaffals, have proved ineffectual againft the power and tyranny of the nobles, and have been either abrogated or eluded. That law, which gives the property of a peafant dying without iffue to the next of kin, was inftantly rendered nugatory by an old Polifh maxim, " That " no flave can carry on any procefs againft his mafter;" and even the fine for his murder was feldom levied, on account of the numerous difficulties which attend the conviction of a noble for this or any other enormity. So far indeed from being inclined to foften the fervitude of their vaffals, the nobles have afcertained and eftablifhed it by repeated and pofi-

* Lubienfki, p. 108.　Florus Pol. p. 118.　Chromer, 319.
† Stat. Pol. I. p. 24.

tive ordinances. An able Polish writer, in a benevolent treatife * addreffed to the chancellor Zamoifki, obferves, that in the Statutes of Poland there are above an hundred laws unfavourable to the peafants, which, among other grievances, erect fummary tribunals fubject to no appeals, and impofe the fevereft penalties upon thofe who quit their villages without leave. From thefe numerous and rigorous edicts to prevent the elopement of the peafants, the fame humane author juftly infers the extreme wretchednefs of this oppreffed clafs of men, who cannot be detained in the place of their nativity but by the terror of the fevereft punifhment.

The native peafants may be divided into two forts : 1. Peafants of the crown ; 2. Peafants belonging to individuals.

1. Peafants of the crown are thofe who are fettled in the great fiefs of the kingdom, or in the royal demefnes, and are under the jurifdictions of the ftarofts. If the crown-peafants are oppreffed by thefe judges, they may lodge a complaint in the royal courts of juftice ; and, fhould the ftaroft endeavour to obftruct the procefs, the king can order the chancellor to iffue a fafe conduct, by which he takes the injured perfon under his protection : and although in moft cafes the corrupt adminiftration of juftice, and the fuperior influence of the ftarofts, prevent a complainant from obtaining any effectual redrefs even in the king's courts ; yet, the very poffibility of procuring relief is fome check to injuftice, and fome alleviation of diftrefs.

2. Peafants belonging to individuals are at the abfolute difpofal of their mafter, and have fcarcely any pofitive fecurity, either for their properties or their lives. Until 1768 the Statutes of Poland only exacted a fine from a lord who killed his flave ; but in that year a decree paffed, that the murder of a peafant was a capital crime ; yet, as the law in

* Patriotic Letters.

Q 2

queſtion requires ſuch an accumulation of evidence * as is
ſeldom to be obtained, it has more the appearance of protection than the reality.

How deplorable muſt be the ſtate of that country, when a
law of that nature was thought requiſite to be enacted, yet is
found incapable of being enforced.   The generality, indeed,
of the Poliſh nobles are not inclined either to eſtabliſh or give
efficacy to any regulations in favour of the peaſants, whom
they ſcarcely conſider as entitled to the common rights of humanity †.   A few nobles, however, of benevolent hearts and
enlightened underſtandings, have acted upon different principles, and have ventured upon the expedient of giving liberty
to their vaſſals.   The event has ſhowed this project to be no
leſs judicious than humane, no leſs friendly to their own intereſts than to the happineſs of their peaſants : for it appears
that in the diſtricts, in which the new arrangement has been
introduced, the population of their villages is conſiderably increaſed, and the revenues of their eſtates augmented in a triple
proportion.

The firſt noble who granted freedom to his peaſants was
Zamoiſki, formerly great chancellor, who in 1760 enfran-
chiſed ſix villages in the palatinate of Maſovia.   Theſe villages were, in 1777, viſited by the author of the Patriotic Letters, from whom I received the following information : On
inſpecting the pariſh-regiſters of births from 1750 to 1760,
that is, during the ten years of ſlavery immediately preceding
their enfranchiſement, he found the number of births 434;
in the firſt ten years of their freedom, from 1760 to 1770,
620; and from 1770 to the beginning of 1777, 585 births.

* The murderer muſt be taken in the fact;
which muſt be proved by two gentlemen or
four peaſants ; and if he is not taken in the
fact, and there are not the above-mentioned
number of witneſſes, he only pays a fine.

† Zamoiſki, in his new code of laws, has
warmly ſpoken in favour of the peaſants;
but ſuch are the national prejudices, that it
is uncertain whether the diet will receive
this code, and confirm its decrees, though
formed upon the common and natural rights
of mankind.

By

By thefe extracts it appeared that

During the firft period there were only 43 births⎫
    fecond period   62   ⎬ each year.
    third period   77 ⎭

If we fuppofe an improvement of this fort to take place throughout the kingdom, how great would be the increafe of national population!

The revenues of the fix villages, fince their enfranchife-ment, have been augmented in a much greater proportion than their population. In their ftate of vaffalage Zamoifki was obliged, according to the cuftom of Poland, to build cottages and barns for his peafants, and to furnifh them with feed, horfes, ploughs, and every implement of agriculture; fince their attainment of liberty they are become fo eafy in their circumftances, as to provide themfelves with all thefe neceffa-ries at their own expence; and they likewife cheerfully pay an annual rent, in lieu of the manual labour, which their mafter formerly exacted from them. By thefe means the receipts of this particular eftate have been nearly tripled.

Upon figning the deed of enfranchifement of the fix vil-lages, their benevolent mafter intimated fome apprehenfions to the inhabitants, left, encouraged by their freedom, they fhould fall into every fpecies of licentioufnefs, and commit more dif-orders than when they were flaves. The fimplicity and good fenfe of their anfwer is remarkable, " When we had no other " property," returned they, " than the ftick which we hold " in our hands, we were deftitute of all encouragement to a " right conduct; and, having nothing to lofe, acted on all " occafions in an inconfiderate manner; but as foon as our " houfes, our lands, and our cattle, are our own, the fear of " forfeiting them will be a conftant reftraint upon our actions." The fincerity of this affertion was manifefted by the event. While they were in a ftate of fervitude, Zamoifki was occa-

5   fionally

fionally obliged to pay fines for diforders * committed by his
peafants, who, in a ftate of drunkennefs, would attack and
fometimes kill paffengers : fince their freedom he has feldom
received any complaints of this fort againft them. Thefe circumftances decifively confute the ill-grounded furmifes entertained by many Poles, that their vaffals are too licentious and
ungovernable not to make an ill ufe of freedom. Zamoifki,
pleafed with the thriving ftate of the fix villages, has enfran-
chifed the peafants on all his eftates.

The example of Zamoifki has been followed by Chrep-
towitz, vice-chancellor of Lithuania, and the abbé Bryzotowfki,
with fimilar fuccefs. I was informed by a perfon who had
vifited the abbé's eftate at Pawlowo near Vilna, that the happy
countenance and comfortable air of thefe peafants made them
appear a different race of men from the wretched tenants of
the neighbouring villages. The peafants, penetrated with a
fenfe of their mafter's kindnefs, have erected, at their own expence, a pillar with an infcription expreffive of their gratitude
and affection.

Prince Staniflaus, nephew to the king of Poland, has warmly
patronized the plan of giving liberty to the peafants. His
own good fenfe and natural humanity, improved during his
refidence in England by a view of that equal liberty which
pervades every rank of men, have raifed him above the prejudices too prevalent among his countrymen : he has enfran-
chifed four villages not far from Warfaw, in which he has
not only emancipated the peafants from their flavery, but even
condefcends to direct their affairs. I had the honour of holding feveral converfations with him upon this fubject ; he explained to me, in the moft fatisfactory manner, that the grant
of freedom was no lefs advantageous to the lord than to the
peafant, provided the former is willing to fuperintend their

* Called, in the Polifh law, Pro incontinentiá fubditorum.

conduct

conduct for a few years, and to put them in a way of acting for themfelves; for fuch is the ignorance of the generality among the boors, arifing from the abject flavery in which they are held, and fo little have they been ufually left to their own difcretion, that few at firft are equal to the proper management of a farm. From a conviction of thefe facts, the prince, whofe knowledge and benevolence I fhall ever revere, continues his attention to their concerns; he vifits their cottages, fuggefts improvements in agriculture, inftructs them in the mode of rearing cattle and bees, and points out the errors into which ignorance and incapacity occafionally betray them.

The example of this prince, great by his rank, but ftill greater by his humanity, can fcarce fail of producing its due effect, efpecially as he intends giving to the public his arrangements and regulations, and will fhow how much he has increafed his eftate and the happinefs of his peafants. Still, however, the condition of thefe peafants is not permanent; for though a lord grants their freedom, yet he cannot entail it upon them, as his fucceffor may again reduce them to their original ftate of vaffalage. It is, however, in agitation to fecure the perpetuity of their liberty, when they are once rendered free; but this attempt is of fo delicate a nature, that it muft be introduced with great caution, and can only be the work of time.

V. In giving an account of the different claffes of men who inhabit this country, I ought not to omit the Jews, as they form no inconfiderable part of its prefent inhabitants. This people date their introduction into Poland about the time of Cafimir the Great, and as they enjoy privileges which they fcarcely poffefs in any other country excepting England and Holland, their numbers have furprizingly increafed. Lengnich, whom I have often quoted, fays of them, that they "monopolize * the

* Pac. Con. Aug. III. p. 128.

"commerce

" commerce and trade of the country, keep the inns and ta-
" verns, are ftewards to the nobility, in ſhort, they ſeem to
" have ſo much influence, that nothing can be bought or ſold
" without the intervention of a Jew." Under John Sobieſki
they were ſo highly favoured, that his adminiſtration was
invidiouſly called a Jewiſh junto : he farmed to the Jews the
royal demeſnes, and put ſuch confidence in them as raiſed
great diſcontents among the nobility. After his death, an
antient law of Sigiſmond I. was revived and inſerted in the
Pacta Conventa of Auguſtus II. that no Jew or perſon of low
birth ſhould be capable of farming the royal revenues.

In ſome towns, as at Caſimir, Poſen, &c. the Jews are permitted to ſettle, but in other places they are only allowed to
reſide during the time of fairs, or when the dietines are aſſembled; but the laws are ſeldom put in force againſt them.
I endeavoured to obtain a probable account of their number,
but I found this to be no eaſy matter, although all Jews, as
well male as female, pay an annual poll-tax, and therefore
muſt be regiſtered. According to the laſt capitation there
were 166,871 Jews in Poland, excluſive of Lithuania, who
paid that tax; but this cannot be their full complement, as
it is their intereſt to diminiſh their number ; and it is a well-
known fact, that they conceal their children as much as poſſible. Perhaps the following calculations will aſſiſt us in this
reſearch. Of 2,580,796 inhabitants in Auſtrian Poland,
144,200, or about an eighteenth, were Jews [*]. The eighteenth of the preſent population of Poland will give near
500,000 : allowing therefore, for omiſſions in the capitation,
as well as for thoſe who migrated into Poland from the Ruſſian diſmembered province [†], we may fairly eſtimate the
number of Jews at 600,000.

[*] See Compend Geog. Sclavoniæ, Gallicæ, &c. p. 66.
[†] Jews are not tolerated in Ruſſia.

Before

Before the late partition Poland contained about 14,000,000 of inhabitants *. As far as I could collect from various conversations with several intelligent Poles, its present population amounts to 9,000,000.

While I am giving my principal attention to the history and constitution of Poland, I cannot but remark, that the feudal laws, formerly so universal, and of which some traces are still to be discovered in most countries, have been gradually abolished in other nations, and given place to a more regular and just administration; yet in Poland a variety of circumstances has concurred to prevent the abolition of those laws, and to preserve that mixture of liberty and oppression, order and anarchy, which so strongly characterized the feudal government. We may easily trace in this constitution all the striking features of that system. The principal are, an elective monarchy with a circumscribed power; the great officers of state possessing their charges for life, and independent of the king's authority; royal fiefs; the great nobility above controul; the nobles or gentry alone free and possessing lands; feudal tenures, military services, territorial jurisdiction; commerce degrading; oppressed condition of the burghers; vassalage of the peasants. In the course of this book I have had occasion to make mention of most of these evils as still existing in Poland, and they may be considered as the radical causes of its decline; for they have prevented the Poles from adopting those more stable regulations, which tend to introduce order and good government, to augment commerce, and to increase population.

---

* Busching gives the following estimate of the population of Poland since the partition :

Males	— —	4,396,969
Females	— —	4,298,083
Ecclesiastics { Secular	18,369	
Regular	10,189	31,137
Nuns	2,579	

Jews { Males	300,612	601,479	
Females	300,867		

Total number of inhabitants   9,327,668

See Busching, His. Magazin. v. XVI. p. 28.

T R A V E L S

I N T O

P O L A N D.

B O O K   II.

C H A P.   I.

Entrance into Auftrian Poland.—*Limits of the difmembered province.*—*Its population and productions.*—*Arrival at* Cracow. —*Defcription of that city.*—*Univerfity.*—*Palace.*—*Citadel occupied by the confederates in the late troubles.*—*Hiftory of that tranfaction.*—*Cathedral.*—*Tombs and characters of feveral* Polifh *fovereigns,* &c.

JULY 24, 1778. We entered Poland juft beyond Bilitz, having croffed the rivulet Biala, which falls into the Viftula, and purfued our journey to Cracow through the territories which the houfe of Auftria fecured to itfelf in the late partition.

The diftrict claimed by the emprefs of Germany in her manifefto is thus defcribed: " All that tract of land lying on
" the

4

" the right fide of the Viftula from Silefia above Sandomir
" to the mouth of the San, and from thence by Franepole,
" Zamoifc, and Rubieffow, to the Bog. From the Bog the li-
" mits are carried along the frontiers of Red Ruffia to Zabras
" upon the borders of Volhynia and Podolia; and from Zabras
" in a ftraight line to the Dnieper, where it receives the rivulet
" Podhorts, taking in a fmall flip of Podolia, and laftly, along
" the boundaries feparating Podolia from Moldavia."

A remarkable circumftance attended the taking poffeffion
of this diftrict, which will fhew with what uncertainty the
limits were at firft traced. The partition being made according to the map of Zannoni, the river Podhorts was taken as
the eaftern boundary of this difmembered province : but when
the Auftrian commiffioners vifited the fpot, where, according
to Zannoni, the Podhorts flowed into the Dnieper, they found
no river known to the inhabitants which anfwered to that
name. They advanced, therefore, the frontiers ftill more
eaftwards, and adopting the Sebrawce or the Sbrytz for the
boundary, called it the Podhorts. This ceded country has,
fince the partition, changed its name; and is now incorporated
into the Auftrian dominions under the appellation of the kingdoms of Galicia and Lodomeria, which kingdoms fome antient diplomes reprefent as fituated in Poland, and fubject to
the kings of Hungary : the moft convincing proof that there
ever exifted fuch kingdoms, that they depended upon Hungary, and ought, by virtue of an hereditary, though dormant
title, to revert to the emprefs as fovereign of Hungary, was
derived from the Auftrian army; for what people can refift
an argument backed by 200,000 troops, unlefs they can defend their fide of the queftion by an equal number?

The importance of this acquifition to the houfe of Auftria
will beft appear from the number of inhabitants, which, ac-

cording to the numeration made in 1776[*], amounted to
2,580,796. The mountainous parts of Galicia and Lodomeria produce fine pasture; the plains are mostly sandy, but
abound in forests, and are fertile in corn. The principal articles of traffic are cattle, hides, wax, and honey. These
countries contain mines of copper, lead, iron, and salt, of
which the latter are the most valuable.

We crossed only a narrow slip of Austrian Poland of about
86 miles in length from Bilitz to Cracow, leaving on our right
hand a chain of mount Crapak, or the antient Carpathian
mountains. The country we passed through was at first some-
what hilly, but afterwards chiefly plain, covered with forests.
The roads were bad, the villages few and wretched beyond
description; the hovels all built of wood seemed full of filth
and misery, and every thing wore the appearance of extreme
poverty.

July 25. About noon we arrived at the Vistula, the limits
of the Austrian dominions, which reach to its southern banks.
According to the partition treaty, this river was marked as
forming the limits between the Austrian and Polish territories:
the house of Austria at first construed the Vistula to mean the
old channel of that river now dry, called the Old Vistula;
and by force of this strained interpretation included Casimir in
the dismembered province; but not long afterwards the empress of Germany restored Casimir to the Poles; and accepted
the Vistula as it now flows, for the boundary of her dominions.

Having crossed the Vistula by a bridge, at one end of which
was an Austrian soldier, and at the other a Polish centinel, into
Casimir, we passed the above-mentioned dry channel, termed
the Old Vistula, by a second bridge, and entered Cracow.

Cracow is a curious old town: it was formerly the capital
of Poland, where the kings were elected and crowned, and was

[*] Comp. Regn. Sclavoniæ, Galiciæ, Lodomeriæ, &c. p. 66, note *m.*

once

once almoft the center of the Polifh dominions, but is now a frontier town ; a proof how much the power of this republic has been contracted !

Cracow ftands in an extenfive plain, watered by the Viftula, which is broad but fhallow : the city and its fuburbs occupy a vaft track of ground, but are fo badly peopled, that they fcarcely contain 16,000 * inhabitants. The great fquare in the middle of the town is very fpacious, and has feveral well-built houfes, once richly furnifhed and well inhabited, but moft of them now either untenanted, or in a ftate of melancholy decay. Many of the ftreets are broad and handfome ; but almoft every building bears the moft ftriking marks of ruined grandeur : the churches alone feem to have preferved their original fplendour. The devaftation of this unfortunate town was begun by the Swedes at the commencement of the prefent century, when it was befieged and taken by Charles XII. ; but the mifchiefs it fuffered from that ravager of the North were far lefs deftructive than thofe it experienced during the late dreadful commotions, when it underwent repeated fieges, and was alternately in poffeffion of the Ruffians and Confederates. The effects of cannon, grape, and mufket-fhot are ftill difcernible on the walls and houfes. In a word, Cracow exhibits the remains of antient magnificence, and looks like a great capital in ruins : from the number of fallen and falling houfes one would imagine it had lately been facked, and that the enemy had left it only yefterday. The town is furrounded with high walls of brick, ftrengthened by round and fquare towers of whimfical fhapes in the antient ftyle of fortification : thefe walls were built by Venceflaus † king of Bohemia during the fhort period in which he reigned over Poland.

In Cracow there was a Ruffian garrifon of 600 men, who

---

* The city, exclufive of the fuburbs, contained in 1778 only 8394 fouls.
† Cracoviam muro circumdedit. Lengnich, Hift. Pol. p. 20.

were

were ftationed at the guard-houfe in the center of the town : at all the gates a Ruffian centinel ftood on one fide, and a Polifh centinel on the other.   The citadel was entirely occupied by Ruffian troops.

I did not omit vifiting the univerfity founded and endowed by Cafimir the Great, and improved and completed by Ladiflaus Jaghellon.   The librarian told me that the number of ftudents amounted to 600.   I examined the library, which was neither remarkable for the number nor rarity of its books.   Among the principal objects of attention, the librarian pointed out a Turkifh book, of no intrinfic value, but efteemed a curiofity becaufe found among the fpoils at the battle of Chotzim, and prefented by John Sobiefki to the univerfity, as the memorial of a victory which faved his country from defolation, and raifed him to the throne of Poland.   The univerfity of Cracow was formerly, and not unjuftly, called the mother of Polifh literature, as it principally fupplied the other feminaries with profeffors and men of learning ; but its luftre has been greatly obfcured by the removal of the royal refidence to Warfaw, and ftill more by the late inteftine convulfions.

In this city the art of printing was firft introduced into Poland by Haller ; and one of the earlieft books was the conftitutions and ftatutes compiled by Cafimir the Great, and afterwards augmented by his fucceffors.   The characters are Gothic, the fame which were univerfally ufed at the invention of printing : the great initial letters are wanting, which fhews that they were probably painted and afterwards worn away. The year in which this compilation was printed is not pofitively known ; but its publication was certainly anterior to 1496, as it does not contain the ftatutes paffed by John Albert in that year.

The moft flourifhing period of the univerfity was under Sigifmond Auguftus in the fixteenth century, when feveral
of

of the German reformers fled from the perfecutions of the emperor Charles V. and found an afylum in this city. They gave to the world feveral verfions of the facred writings, and other theological publications, which diffufed the reformed religion over great part of Poland. The protection which Sigifmond Auguftus afforded to men of learning of all denominations, and the univerfal toleration which he extended to every fect of Chriftians, created a fufpicion that he was fecretly inclined to the new church, and it was even reported that he intended to renounce the catholic faith, and publicly profefs the reformed religion *.

Towards the fouthern part of the town near the Viftula rifes a fmall eminence or rock, upon whofe top is built the palace, furrounded with brick walls and old towers, which form a kind of citadel to the town. This palace owes its origin to Ladiflaus Jaghellon ; but little of the antient ftructure now appears, as the greateft part was demolifhed by Charles XII. in 1702, when he entered this town in triumph after the battle of Cliffow. It has been fince repaired : the remains of the old palace confift of a few apartments, which are left in their antient ftate as they exifted in the laft century. The walls of the firft of thefe apartments are decorated with paintings of tilts and tournaments; thofe of the fecond with a reprefentation of the coronation of a king of Poland, affirmed, by the perfon who fhewed the palace, to be that of Ladiflaus the Firft, and to have been drawn in his time ; but the ftyle of the painting befpeaks it of a more modern date. The cieling of the third apartment is divided into different compartments, ornamented with carved heads of extraordinary fhapes and grotefque appearances. All the rooms in the palace are of fine dimenfions, containing feveral remains of antient magnificence, but totally without furniture.

* See p. 17.

This

This palace was formerly the refidence of the kings of Poland, who, from the time of Ladiflaus Loketec, have been
crowned at Cracow. The Polifh and German hiftorians differ
concerning the time when the title of king was firft claimed
by the fovereigns of this country ; but the moft probable account is, that in 1295 Premiflaus affumed the regal title, and
was inaugurated at Gnefna by the archbifhop of that diocefe.
He was fucceeded by Ladiflaus Loketec, who, offending the
Poles by his capricious and tyrannical conduct, was depofed
before he was crowned ; and Venceflaus king of Bohemia,
who had married Richfa daughter of Premiflaus, being elected
in his ftead, was in 1300 confecrated at Gnefna. Ladiflaus,
after flying from his country, and undergoing a feries of ca-
lamitous adventures, was at length brought to a fenfe of his
mifconduct. Having regained the affection of his fubjects,
he was reftored, in the life-time of Venceflaus, to part of his
dominions ; and he recovered them all upon the demife of
that monarch in the year 1305 : he governed, however, for
fome years without the title of king ; but at length in 1320
was crowned at Cracow, to which place he transferred the ceremony of the coronation ; and afterwards enacted, that for
the future his fucceffors fhould be inaugurated in the cathedral of this city *.

Since that period, the laws of Poland have exprefsly enjoined that Cracow fhould be the place of coronation ; and
fuch has been the fuperftitious attachment of the Poles to this
ufage, that when John Sobiefki was defirous of being crowned
at Leopold, on account of its vicinity to the army, which he
was to command againft the Turks at the time of his election,
the Polifh patriots ftrongly oppofed any innovation † ; and
that monarch was under the neceffity of repairing to Cracow

---

* Dlugoffus, lib. IX. p. 971.   Lengnich, Hift. Pol. p. 19—22.
† Lengnich, Jus Publicum.

for the performance of the ceremony.

Since Ladiflaus, all the fucceeding fovereigns have been confecrated at Cracow *, excepting the prefent king. Previous to his election a decree was iffued by the diet of convocation, that the coronation fhould be folemnized for this turn at Warfaw, without prejudice in future to the antient right of Cracow; a provifo calculated to fatisfy the populace, but which will not probably prevent any future fovereign from being crowned at Warfaw, now become the capital of Poland, and the refidence of its kings. The diadem and other regalia ufed at the coronation are ftill kept in the palace of Cracow, under fo many keys, and with fuch care, that it was impoffible to obtain a fight of them.

From the apartments of the palace we commanded an extenfive view of the neighbouring country, which is principally a large fandy plain. We obferved particularly two very large mounds of earth, or barrows, one of which is by tradition called the burial-place of Cracus duke of Poland, who is fuppofed to have built the town of Cracow in the year 700; the other is called the fepulchre of his daughter Venda, who is reported to have drowned herfelf in the Viftula, that fhe might not be compelled to marry a perfon for whom fhe had entertained an averfion. The whole hiftory of Cracus and Venda is involved in impenetrable darknefs, and thefe barrows, which are common in different parts of Europe, were probably anterior to the Chriftian æra. The practice of raifing barrows over the bodies of the deceafed was almoft univerfal in the earlier ages of the world. Homer mentions it as a common practice among the Greeks and Trojans; Virgil alludes to it as ufual in Italy in the times treated of in the Æneid; Xenophon relates that it obtained among the Perfians; the Roman

---

* I do not mention Staniflaus Letzinfki, only a temporary fovereign, and was foon who was crowned at Warfaw, becaufe he was obliged to retire from Poland.

hiftorians record that the fame mode of interring took place among their countrymen; and it appears to have prevailed no lefs among the antient Germans, and many other uncivilized nations. In general, popular tradition allows fome favourite characters in national hiftory, like Cracus and Venda, to ufurp the honour of being buried under the moft confpicuous of thefe monuments.

At fome diftance from Cracow we noticed the fortrefs of Landfkron fituated upon a rock, which the confederates poffeffed during the late troubles; and from whence they made excurfions as occafion offered againft the Ruffian and Polifh troops in the fervice of the king. By a detachment of troops from this fortrefs, the citadel of Cracow was taken by furprize; a gallant exploit, and which merits a particular defcription. The perfon who fhewed us the palace was himfelf prefent, when the Polifh troops iffued from a fubterraneous paffage, and furprized the Ruffian garrifon, confifting of 87 troops. About four in the morning a party of 76 confederates, all of whom were Poles, led by a lieutenant *, whofe name was Bytranowfki, entered the palace through a common fewer, without being difcovered, and repairing to the main guard inftantly fell upon the Ruffians: the latter were fo confounded with the fuddennefs of the affault, that they all yielded themfelves prifoners without the leaft refiftance, and the Poles became mafters of the citadel. Two or three Ruffians were killed at the firft onfet, and the remainder were

---

* In moft of the accounts publifhed of this tranfaction, it is faid that the confederates were led by a French officer, and that there were feveral Frenchmen amongft them. I have related fimply the account which I received from the fteward of the palace, who repeatedly affured me, that there was not one Frenchman amongft them; that they were led by a Polifh lieutenant, whofe name was Bytranowfki. The fteward was himfelf prefent at the tranfaction, and as he was no foldier, was not confined with the garrifon in the dungeon; he had, therefore, every opportunity of being informed of the truth: at the fame time it is poffible, that his partiality to his countrymen might have induced him to give the whole honour to the Poles. Monfieur Viofmenil is the French officer, generally mentioned as leading this enterprifing band of confederates through the fubterraneous paffage.

confined

confined in a dungeon. One foldier, however, found means to efcape by climbing the wall of the citadel, and alarmed the Ruffian foldiers within the town; thefe without delay attacked the caftle, but, receiving a warm fire from the confederates, they imagined the enemy to be more numerous than they really were, and defifted from the affault. This event happened on the 2d of February, 1772. The fame evening Monfieur de Choify, in the fervice of the confederates of Land-fkron, being made acquainted with the fuccefs of the enterprize, advanced towards Cracow at the head of 800 confederates (amongft whom were 30 or 40 Frenchmen, moft of them officers), and, having defeated a detachment of 200 Ruffians, was received into the citadel. But the Ruffian garrifon in the town, which before confifted of only 400 men, being likewife reinforced, the confederates in the citadel underwent a regular fiege: they defended themfelves with the moft undaunted fpirit for the fpace of three months; and at length capitulated upon the moft honourable terms.

I examined the fubterraneous paffage through which the 76 confederates introduced themfelves into the palace: it is a drain which conveys all the filth from the interior part of the palace to a fmall opening without the walls near the Viftula. They entered this fmall opening, and crawled upon their hands and knees a confiderable way, one behind another, until they came out through a hole in the walls of the palace: fo that if the Ruffians had either been apprized of their attempt, or had over-heard them in their paffage, not one perfon could have efcaped: the danger was great, but it fhews what fpirit and perfeverance will effect.

Having viewed the palace, we vifited the adjoining cathedral, which ftands within the walls of the citadel. In this cathedral *, all the fovereigns, from the time of Ladiflaus

* Lengnich, Jus Publ.

S 2

Loketec,

Loketec, have been interred, a few only excepted, viz. Louis
and Ladiflaus III. who were kings of Hungary as well as of
Poland, and whofe bodies were depofited in Hungary; Alexander, who died and was buried at Vilna; Henry of Valois,
interred in France; and the late monarch Auguftus III. The
laws of Poland are as exprefs and minute in regulating the
burial as the election and coronation of the kings; and, as
many curious circumftances attend their interment, I fhall
take this opportunity of laying the ceremony before the reader.

Since Warfaw has become the royal refidence, and the
place for the election of the kings of Poland, the body of the
deceafed prince muft be carried firft to that city, where it remains until the nomination of the new fovereign has taken
place; it is then tranfported in great ftate to Cracow, and,
two days before the day appointed for the ceremony of the
coronation, the king elect, preceded by the great officers of
ftate, with their rods of office pointing to the ground, joins
the funeral proceffion as it paffes through the ftreets, and follows the body to the church of St. Staniflaus, where the burial
fervice is performed: the remains are then depofited in the
cathedral adjoining to the palace. It is peculiar to the laws
of Poland, that the funeral of the deceafed monarch fhould
immediately precede the coronation of the new fovereign;
and that the king elect fhould be under a neceffity of attending the obfequies of his predeceffor. Hiftorians have
fagely remarked, that this fingular cuftom was inftituted, in
order to imprefs the new king with the uncertainty of human
grandeur; and to remind him of his duty, by mixing the
horrors of death with the pomp and dignity of his new ftation; yet we cannot but obferve, that this precaution has not
hitherto been productive of any vifible effects, as it does not
appear that the kings of Poland have governed with greater
wifdom and juftice than other potentates. But it is moft
probable,

probable, that this cuſtom took its riſe from the habits of exterior homage, which the Poles affect to pay to their ſovereign in compenſation for the ſubſtantial dignity which they withhold from him : this ſpirit of mock-reverence they extend beyond the grave; and while they ſcarcely allow the reigning king the ſhadow of real authority, they heap upon a deceaſed monarch every poſſible trapping of imperial honour.

The ſepulchres of the kings of Poland are not diſtinguiſhed by any peculiar magnificence : their figures are carved in marble of no extraordinary workmanſhip, and ſome are without inſcriptions.

I felt a ſtrong ſentiment of veneration at approaching the aſhes of Caſimir the Great, whom I conſider as one of the greateſt princes that ever adorned a throne.   It was not, however, the brilliancy and magnificence of his reign, his warlike atchievements, nor even his patronage of the arts and ſciences; but his legiſlative abilities, and his wonderful beneficence to the inferior claſs of his ſubjects, that inſpired me with a reverence for his character.

Caſimir was born in 1310; and in 1333 aſcended the throne of Poland, upon the demiſe of his father Ladiſlaus Loketec. The Poliſh hiſtorians dwell with ſingular complacency upon his reign, as the moſt glorious and happy period of their hiſtory; and record with peculiar pleaſure the virtues and abilities of this great and amiable monarch : nor are their praiſes the echoes of flattery, for they were moſtly written ſubſequent to his death, when another family was ſeated upon the throne. In peruſing the reign of Caſimir, we can hardly believe that we are reading the hiſtory of the ſovereign of a barbarous people in the beginning of the fourteenth century; it ſeems as if, by the aſcendancy of his ſuperior genius, he had got the ſtart of the age in which he flouriſhed, and had anticipated the knowledge and improvements of the ſucceeding

3

ceeding

ceeding and more enlightened periods.

From the moment of his acceſſion his firſt care was to ſecure his kingdom againſt foreign enemies ; with this view he attacked the knights of the Teutonic order, with whom Poland had long been in an almoſt continual ſtate of warfare, and .obliged them to purchaſe a peace by the ceſſion of Culm and Cujavia, which they had wreſted from his father ; he then .reduced Red Ruſſia, and annexed the duchy of Maſovia to the dominions of Poland. By theſe acquiſitions he not only extended the frontiers of his empire, but rendered his dominions leſs liable to ſudden invaſions. But theſe great ſucceſſes were not able to excite in his breaſt the fatal ſpirit of military enterprize ; he always conſidered war as a matter of neceſſity, not of choice, and as the means of ſafety rather than of glory *. Having ſecured his frontiers, as well by his victories as by treaties with the neighbouring powers, he turned his whole .attention to the interior adminiſtration of his kingdom ; he built ſeveral towns, enlarged and beautified others : ſo that Dlugoſſius †, who wrote in the following century, ſays of him, " Poland is indebted to Caſimir for the greateſt part of her " churches, palaces, fortreſſes, and towns ;" adding metaphorically, " that he found Poland of wood, and left her of mar- " ble." He patronized letters, and founded the academy of Cracow ; he promoted induſtry, and encouraged trade ; elegant in his manners and magnificent in his court, he was œconomical without meanneſs, and liberal without prodigality.

He was the great legiſlator of Poland : finding his country without any written laws, he reviewed all the uſages and cuſ-

---

* Mitis ingenio, et quietis quam armorum appetentior. Florus Pol. p. 116.

† Tantus enim illi ad magnificandum, loeupletandumque Regnum Poloniæ inerat amor, ut graviſſimos & notabiles ſumptus in erigendis ex muro eccleſiis, caſtris, civitatibus, & curiis, faciendo ad id omnem ſolicitudinem curamque intenderit, ut Poloniam, quam luteam, ligneam, & ſqualidam repererat, lateritiam, glorioſam, & inclytam, ſicut evenit, reliquerit. Nam quicquid Polonia in caſtris, eccleſiis, civitatibus, curiis, & domibus murorum continet, id pro majori parte ab ipſo Caſimiro rege, & ſuis regiis ſumptibus eſt perfectum. Lib. IX. p. 1164.

toms,

toms, and digested them, with some additions, into a regular code, which he ordered to be published. He simplified and improved the courts of justice ; he was easy * of access to the meanest as well as the highest of his subjects, and solicitous to relieve the peasants from the oppressions of the nobility ; such indeed was the tenderness he showed to that injured class of men, and so many were the privileges which he conferred upon them, that the nobles used to call him out of derision *Rex Rusticorum*, the king of the peasants ; perhaps the most noble appellation that ever was bestowed upon a sovereign, and far to be preferred to the titles of magnificent and great, which have been so often lavished rather upon the persecutors than the benefactors of mankind. Human nature is never perfect ; Casimir was not without his failings : voluptuous and sensual, he pushed the pleasures of the table to an excess of intemperance ; and his inordinate passion for women led him into some actions, inconsistent with the general tenor of honour and integrity which distinguishes his character. But these defects influenced chiefly his private, and not his public deportment ; or, to use the expression of a Polish historian, his private failings were redeemed by his public virtues † : and it is allowed by all, that no sovereign more consulted the happiness of his subjects, or was more beloved at home and respected abroad. After a long reign of 40 years he was thrown from his horse as he was hunting, and died after a short illness in the 60th year of his age, carrying with him to the grave the regret of his subjects, and a claim to the veneration of posterity. He is described (for the figure of so amiable a character cannot fail to be interesting) as tall in his person, and inclined to corpulency, with a majestic aspect, thick and curling hair,.

---

* Adeuntibus facilis, querimonias etiam patebat accessus. Dlugossius.
infimorum audivit, &c. Sarnicki. Cuilibet † Redimens vitia virtutibus. Dlugossius.
conditioni, generi, atque ætati facilis ad eum .

long

long beard, with a ftrong voice fomewhat lifping [*].

Next to the remains of Cafimir repofe the afhes of Ladiflaus [†] II. known by the appellation of Jaghellon, the father
of a race of kings called from him the Jaghellon line. This
fovereign was originally duke of Lithuania, and, together
with his fubjects, a worfhiper of idols; but having embraced
Chriftianity, and efpoufed Hedwige fecond daughter of Louis,
he obtained the throne of Poland. This event happened in
1386, in which year he was publicly baptized, married, and
crowned at Cracow, and affumed a new baptifmal name of
Ladiflaus II.; he died in 1434 in a very advanced age, in the
50th year of a long and glorious reign.

Among his pofterity, whofe bodies are depofited in this cathedral, the moft memorable is Sigifmond I. a great and able
monarch, the protector of the arts and fciences, which made
no inconfiderable figure under his aufpices. He is reprefented,
however, as not fufficiently watchful over the royal prerogative [‡]; and as yielding too eafily to the encroachments of the
nobility, to the injury of fucceeding monarchs, and the detri-
ment of the republic. But thefe compliances admit of great
palliation, when we reflect, that the nobles, to whom they
were made, had raifed him to the throne, and were become
nearly uncontroulable by the conceffions of his immediate
predeceffors.

As I viewed the tomb of Sigifmond Auguftus, fon of the
laft mentioned monarch, I recollected, not without a mixture

---

[*] Vir ftaturâ elevatâ, corpore craffo, fronte
venerabili, crine circino et abundante, barbâ
promiffâ, voce aliquantulum balbâ fed fonorâ.

Deceffit Cafimirus 2. 1370, fays Lengnich,
cui Polonia leges, judicia, cultum, plurimas
civitates, arces, et alia edificia, debet. Hift.
Pol. p. 25.

[†] He is fometimes called Ladiflaus IV.
and fometimes Ladiflaus V.; but reckoning
from the time the fovereigns of Poland af-

fumed the regal authority, he ought to be
called Ladiflaus II. Ladiflaus inter Poloniæ
reges illius nominis fecundus. Lengnich,
Hift. Pol. p 31.

[‡] Ab hoc potiffimum rege nimis indul-
gente, licentia nobilitatis incrementa contra
jura majeftatis, cum injuria fuccedentium
regum, et reipub. decremento, fumere et
prævalere cœpit, ut fapientes, &c. De Script.
Pol. &c. p. 4.

of

of regret and fympathy for this unhappy country, that in him terminated that hereditary influence, which had given tranquillity during a long fucceffion of fovereigns to the diets of election; and that upon his death all thofe troubles and confufions, which are infeparable from a crown wholly elective, broke in upon the kingdom. From this period the cabals and convulfions, continually recurring at every appointment of a new fovereign, rapidly impaired the ftrength of the ftate and the dignity of the throne. The Poles gradually loft their confequence among foreign powers; and the authority of fucceeding kings depended more on their own perfonal abilities, and accidental circumftances, than on any permanent principle of vigour inherent in the crown, which has been nearly ftripped of all its prerogatives.

The firft of the new fucceffion, whofe remains are interred in this church, is Stephen Bathori prince of Tranfylvania, elected in 1576, upon the abdication of Henry of Valois: he owed his elevation to his marriage with Anne daughter of Sigifmond I.; a princefs who, being in the 52d year of her age, was not endowed with any winning attractions, if fhe had not brought a kingdom for her portion. The epitaph upon his tomb juftly afcribes to Stephen a long catalogue of civil and military virtues.

I came next to the fepulchre of his fucceffor Sigifmond III. fon of John III. king of Sweden, and of Catharine daughter of Sigifmond I.: elected king of Poland in 1587, he revived in his perfon, on the female fide, the race of the Jaghellon family. He was raifed to the throne of this country while he was prince royal of Sweden; and, upon the death of his father in 1592, poffeffed both crowns; but he gradually loft all authority in Sweden, and was at length formally depofed by the ftates of that kingdom. He owed his expulfion from Sweden to his partiality for Poland, to his bigoted zeal for the catholic religion, and above all to the superior genius of his uncle and rival Charles IX.   He expired in the 46th year of his reign, and in the 67th of his age.

Near the body of Sigifmond lie thofe of his two fons ; the eldeft named Ladiflaus IV. elected king of Poland upon the demife of his father, fupported the dignity of his crown with reputation and honour ; the fecond, John Cafimir, was a prince, whofe character and adventures are too fingular to be paffed over without particular notice.

John Cafimir, fon of Sigifmond III. by a fecond wife Anne, fifter of the emperor Ferdinand II. was educated in his father's court, upon whofe death his mother endeavoured, but without effect, to procure his election to the throne, in oppofition to his elder brother Ladiflaus IV.   Repulfed from the throne, he contracted a difguft to Poland, and undertook a journey to Spain with a view of offering his fervices to his coufin Philip IV. then at war with France.   Paffing through Auftria and Trent into Italy, at Genoa he embarked in a veffel bound for Spain ; but, prompted by curiofity, he ventured to land incognito at Marfeilles : being difcovered, he was arrefted by order of the court of France, and, on account of his connection with the houfe of Auftria, clofely imprifoned for the fpace of two years *.   Being at length releafed at the interceffion of his brother the king of Poland, he repaired to Rome, and there, either out of devotion or caprice, entered into the order of the Jefuits.   Afterwards, grown weary of his function, he quitted that order, and was promoted to the rank of cardinal. Upon the death of his brother Ladiflaus IV. being abfolved from his vows by the pope, he was elected king of Poland ; and, having obtained a difpenfation, married his brother's widow Louifa Maria daughter of the duke of Nevers, a woman of great beauty and ftill greater fpirit, who blended de-

* Florus Polon. p. 437, & feq.

votion

votion with a ſtrong propenſity to political intrigues : the ſoul of her huſband's councils, ſhe may be ſaid to have reigned over Poland, while he was only nominal king. Such was her aſcendancy, that ſhe prevailed upon him to ſolicit the nomination of the duke of Enguien ſon of the great Condé for his ſucceſſor ; a meaſure ſo contradictory to the firſt principles of the Poliſh conſtitution, as well as to his coronation oath, excited a general diſcontent, and threw the kingdom into the moſt violent commotions.

The reign of John Caſimir was active and turbulent, memorable for the revolt of the Coſſacs of the Ukraine, for the unſucceſsful wars with Sweden, and for the inſurrections of the nobility. Though, ſo far from being deficient in military courage, that in every deſperate emergency he always commanded his troops in perſon ; though, to uſe his own expreſſion, " he was the firſt to attack, and the laſt to retreat * ;" yet as he preferred peace to war, and wanted the enterprizing ſpirit of his brother Ladiſlaus IV. he was accuſed by the Poles of indolence and puſillanimity. His political ſagacity appears from his predictions, that Poland, enfeebled by the anarchy of its government, and the licentiouſneſs of the nobles, would neceſſarily be diſmembered by the neighbouring powers. Worn out at length with the cares of royalty, ſhocked at the diſtreſſed ſtate of the kingdom, diſcontented with the factions of the nobility, afflicted at the death of his wife, and impelled by the verſatility of his diſpoſition, he abdicated the throne in the 20th year of his reign, and in the 68th of his age. This extraordinary event happened on the 27th of Auguſt, in the year 1668, before a general diet aſſembled at Warſaw : the ſcene was affecting ; the conduct of the king manly and reſolute ; and his ſpeech upon that event is the fineſt piece of pathetic eloquence that hiſtory has ever recorded †.

* " Eum me eſſe, qui primus in praeliis, " poſtremus in diſcrimine et receſſu." Za   luſki Ep. vol. I. p. 57.
† See Zaluſki Epiſt. v. I. p. 57.

Soon after his abdication he retired into France, and again
embraced the ecclefiaftical profeffion. Louis XIV. who prided
himfelf in affording an afylum to abdicated fovereigns, gave
him the abbeys of St. Germain and St. Martin, without which
he would have had no means of fubfiftence, as Poland foon
with-held his penfion; a proof that the tears which were
fhed at his abdication were not fincere. Notwithftanding his
ecclefiaftical engagements, John Cafimir could not withftand
the attractions of Marie Mignot, a woman, who, from being a
laundrefs, had been married firft to a counfellor of Grenoble,
and afterwards to the marfhal de L'Hofpital. She was a widow when fhe attracted the notice of the abdicated king, and
fo powerful was the impreffion he received, that it was fufpected he was fecretly married to her. Cafimir is reprefented,
by thofe who knew him in his retirement, as eafy and familiar
in his converfation, and difpleafed with receiving any honours
or titles due to his former rank *. He furvived his abdication
only four years, and died at Nevers on the 16th of December,
1672. His body was brought to this city, and buried in the
cathedral at the fame time with that of his fucceffor Michael,
the day before the coronation of John Sobiefki.

Upon approaching the remains of John Sobiefki, I recollected that when Charles XII. of Sweden entered Cracow he
vifited thefe tombs, in order to pay a mark of refpect to the
memory of that great monarch : he is reported, as he hung
with reverence over his fepulchre, to have cried out, " What
" a pity that fo great a man fhould ever die !" May we not
alfo exclaim, what a pity that a perfon, fo impreffed with a
fenfe of Sobiefki's virtues, fhould adopt only the military part
of his character for the object of his imitation! How infinitely inferior is the Swedifh to the Polifh fovereign ! The
former, dead to all the finer feelings of humanity, was awake

* Vie de Sobiefki I. p. 135.

only

only to the calls of ambition; every other fentiment being loft in the ardour for military honours. If perfonal courage be fufficient to conftitute an hero, he poffeffed that quality in a fuperior degree; but it was rather the bravery of a common foldier than of a general. Sobiefki, even upon that ground, has an equal title to fame; for his valour was no lefs diftinguifhed, and was fuperior in this refpect, that it was not clouded with rafhnefs, but tempered with prudence. Though the firft general of his age, he placed not his fole ambition in military glory; he was great in peace as well as in war; by the union of talents belonging to each department, he defended his country from impending danger, raifed her from her falling ftate, and delayed during his reign the æra of her decline; while Charles, who was deficient in civil virtues, plunged Sweden, which he found highly profperous, into ruin and defolation: in a word, Charles had the enthufiafm of a knight errant, and Sobiefki the virtues of an hero *.

About an Englifh mile from Cracow are the remains of an old ftructure, called the palace of Cafimir the Great, which my veneration for that fovereign induced me to vifit, as there is a fingular pleafure arifing from feeing the fpot that was once dignified by the refidence of a favourite character. Little, I imagine, of the original palace, as it was built by Cafimir, exifts at prefent. In the inner court are the remains of a corridore with pillars of the Doric order; and upon one of the fide walls I obferved the white-eagle of Poland carved in ftone, and around it an infcription feemingly in old Gothic characters, of which I could only make out Ann. Dom. M.CCCLXVII, which anfwers to the æra of Cafimir, who died in 1370. Several marble columns were fcattered around, which fhowed the antient magnificence of the building. The greateft part of the fabrick was evidently of later date than the reign of

* See an account of Sobiefki's death and family, Chap. IV. of this book.

Cafimir,

Cafimir, and was probably conftructed by fucceeding fove
reigns upon the foundation of the antient palace; perhaps by
Stephen Bathori, as I could trace in one place an infcription,
Stephanus Dei gratia; and alfo by Sigifmond III. as I plainly
difcovered his cypher with the wheat-fheaf, the arms of Guf-
tavus Vafa, from whom he was lineally defcended.

This palace was the principal refidence of Cafimir: in the
garden is a mound of earth, or one of thofe barrows before
mentioned, which is called the tomb of Efther the fair Jewefs,
who was the favourite miftrefs of that monarch. To the influence of Efther it is faid the Jews owe the numerous privileges enjoyed by them in Poland, which is called the paradife
of the Jews. But when I confider the character of Cafimir,
I conceive that they were indebted for their favourable reception in Poland more to his policy than to his affection for
his miftrefs; for in thofe times the Jews were the richeft and
moft commercial individuals in Europe; by allowing them,
therefore, to fettle in Poland, and by granting them fome extraordinary immunities, he introduced trade and much wealth
into his dominions. The number of Jews is now prodigious *,
and they have in a manner engroffed all the commerce of the
country; yet this flourifhing ftate of their affairs muft not be
attributed folely to the edicts of Cafimir in their favour, but
to the induftry of thofe extraordinary people, to the indolence
of the gentry, and the oppreffed condition of the peafants.

* See p. 121.

CHAP.

A POLISH GENTLEMAN.

Published according to Act of Parliament, Jan'y 1784 by T. Iidell in the Strand

C H A P.   II.

Mode of saluting and dress of the Poles.——*Account of the salt-mines of* Wielitska.——*Their extent and profit.——Journey to* Warsaw.

THE Poles seem a lively people, and use much action in their ordinary conversation.   Their common mode of salute is to incline their heads, and to strike their breast with one of their hands, while they stretch the other towards the ground; but when a common person meets a superior, he bows his head almost to the earth, waving at the same time his hand, with which he touches the bottom of the leg near the heel of the person to whom he pays his obeisance.   The men of all ranks generally wear whiskers, and shave their heads, leaving only a circle of hair upon the crown.   The summer dress of the peasants consists of nothing but a shirt and drawers of coarse linen, without shoes or stockings, with round caps or hats.   The women of the lower class wear upon their heads a wrapper of white linen, under which their hair is braided, and hangs down in two plaits.   I observed several of them with a long piece of white linen hanging round the side of their faces, and covering their bodies below their knees: this singular kind of veil makes them look as if they were doing penance.

The dress of the higher orders, both men and women, is uncommonly elegant.   That of the gentlemen is a waistcoat with sleeves, over which they wear an upper robe of a different colour,   which reaches down below the knee, and is fastened round the waist with a sash or girdle ; the sleeves of this upper garment are in warm weather tied behind the shoulders ;

3

a sabre

a fabre is a neceſſary part of their dreſs as a mark of nobility. In ſummer, the robe, &c. is of ſilk ; in winter, of cloth, velvet, or ſtuff, edged with fur. They wear fur-caps or bonnets, and buſkins of yellow leather, the heels of which are plaited with iron or ſteel. The dreſs of the ladies is a ſimple polonaiſe, or long robe, edged with fur.

The Poles, in their features, look, cuſtoms, dreſs, and general appearance, reſemble Aſiatics rather than Europeans ; and they are unqueſtionably deſcended from Tartar anceſtors. A German hiſtorian *, well verſed in the antiquity of nations, remarks, that the manner in which the Poles wear their hair is, perhaps, one of the moſt antient tokens of their origin. So early as the fifth century ſome nations, who were comprehended under the name of Scythians, had the ſame cuſtom. For Priſcus Rhætor, who accompanied Maximus in his embaſſy from Theodoſius II. to the court of Attila, deſcribes a Scythian lord, whoſe head was ſhaved in a circular form †, a mode perfectly analogous to the preſent faſhion in Poland.

Before we quitted this part of Poland, we viſited the celebrated ſalt-mines of Wielitſka, which are ſituated within eight miles of Cracow. Theſe mines are excavated in a ridge of hills at the Northern extremity of the chain which joins to the Carpathian mountains : they take their appellation from the ſmall village of Wielitſka ; but are ſometimes called in foreign countries the mines of Cracow, from their vicinity to that city.

Upon our arrival at Wielitſka we repaired to the mouth of the mine ‡. Having faſtened three ſeparate hammocks in a circle round the great rope that is employed in drawing up the ſalt, we ſeated ourſelves in a commodious manner, and were let down gently without the leaſt apprehenſion of danger, about 160 yards below the firſt layer of ſalt. Quitting our ham-

* Maſcow.
† Capite in rotundum raſo.
‡ There are two other openings, down one of which the miners deſcend by ſtairs, down the other by ladders.

mocks,

mocks, we paſſed a long and gradual deſcent, ſometimes through broad paſſages or galleries capable of admitting ſeveral carriages abreaſt; ſometimes down ſteps cut in the ſolid ſalt, which had the grandeur and commodiouſneſs of the ſtair-caſe in a palace. We each of us carried a light, and ſeveral guides preceded us with lamps in their hands: the reflection of theſe lights upon the glittering ſides of the mine was extremely beautiful, but did not caſt that luminous ſplendour, which ſome writers have compared to the luſtre of precious ſtones.

The ſalt dug from this mine is called *Ziebna* or Green Salt, for what reaſon I cannot determine; for its colour is an iron grey; when pounded it has a dirty aſh colour like what we call brown ſalt. The quality improves in proportion to the depth of the mine: towards the ſides and ſurface it is mixed with earthy or ſtony particles; lower down it is ſaid to be perfectly pure, and requires no other proceſs before it is uſed than to be pounded. The fineſt of this grey ſalt, however, is of a weak quality when compared with our common ſea-ſalt: it is therefore undoubtedly by no means perfectly pure, but is blended with extraneous mixtures, though it ſerves very well for common purpoſes. Being almoſt as hard as ſtone, the miners hew it with pick-axes and hatchets, by a tedious operation, into large blocks, many of which weigh ſix or ſeven hundred pounds. Theſe large maſſes are raiſed by a windlas, but the ſmaller pieces are carried up by horſes along a winding gallery, which reaches to the ſurface of the earth.

Beſide grey ſalt, the miners ſometimes diſcover ſmall cubes of white ſalt, as tranſparent as chryſtal, but not in any conſiderable quantity; they find likewiſe occaſionally pieces of coal and petrified wood buried in the ſalt.

The mine appears to be inexhauſtible, as will eaſily be conceived from the following account of its dimenſions. Its

known breadth is 1115 feet; its length 6691 feet; and·
depth 743 ; and the beſt judges on the ſpot ſuppoſe, with the
greateſt appearance of probability, this ſolid body of ſalt to
branch into various directions, the extent of which cannot be
known : of that part which has been perforated, the depth
is only calculated as far as they have hitherto dug; and who
can aſcertain how much farther it may deſcend?

Our guide did not omit pointing out to us, what he conſidered as one of the moſt remarkable curioſities of the place,·
ſeveral ſmall chapels excavated in the ſalt, in which maſs is
ſaid on certain days of the year ; one of theſe chapels is above
30 feet long and 25 broad; the altar, the crucifix, the orna-
ments of the church, the ſtatues of ſeveral ſaints, are all
carved out of the ſalt.

Many of the excavations or chambers, from whence the
ſalt has been dug, are of an immenſe ſize; ſome are ſupported with timber, others by vaſt pillars of ſalt, which are
left ſtanding for that purpoſe : ſeveral of vaſt dimenſions are
without any ſupport in the middle. I remarked one of this
latter ſort in particular, which was certainly 80 feet in height,
and ſo extremely long and broad, as almoſt to appear amid
the ſubterraneous gloom without limits. The roofs of theſe
vaults are not arched, but flat. The immenſe ſize of theſe
chambers, with the ſpacious paſſages or galleries, together
with the chapels above mentioned, and a few ſheds built for
the horſes which are foddered below, probably gave riſe to
the exaggerated accounts of ſome travellers, that theſe mines
contain ſeveral villages inhabited by colonies of miners, who
never ſee the light. It is certain that there is room ſufficient
for ſuch purpoſes ; but the fact is, that the miners have no
dwellings under ground, none of them remaining below more
than eight hours at a time, when they are relieved by others
from above. In truth, theſe mines are of a moſt ſtupendous

extent

extent and depth, and are sufficiently wonderful without the least exaggeration. We found them as dry as a room, without the least damp or moisture; obferving only in our whole progrefs one fmall fpring of water, which is impregnated with falt, as it runs through the mine.

Such an enormous mafs of falt exhibits a wonderful phænomenon in the natural hiftory of this globe. Monfieur Guetard, who vifited thefe mines with great attention, and who has publifhed a treatife upon the fubject, informs us, that the uppermoft bed of earth at the furface immediately over the mines is fand, the fecond clay occafionally mixed with fand and gravel and containing petrefactions of marine bodies, the third calcarious ftone. From all thefe circumftances he conjectures that this fpot was formerly covered by the fea, and that the falt is a gradual depofit formed by the evaporation of its waters *.

Thefe mines have now been worked above 600 years, for they are mentioned in the Polifh annals fo early as 1237, under Boleflaus † the Chafte, and not as a new difcovery : how much earlier they were known cannot now be afcertained. Their profits had long been appropriated to the king's privy purfe : before the partition they furnifhed a confiderable part of his prefent majefty's revenue, who drew from them an annual average profit of about 3,500,000 Polifh florins, or £97,222. 4s. 6d. fterling. They now belong to the emperor, being fituated within the province which he difmembered from Poland; but at the time we vifited them they were far from yielding a revenue equal to that which they had afforded to the king of Poland ; for the Auftrian commiffioners imprudently raifed the price of falt, from an idea that Poland could not exift without drawing that commodity as ufual from Wie-

* See Memoire fur les Mines de Sel de for 1762.
Wielittka in Hift. de l'Acad. des Sciences † Lengnich, Jus Pub. vol. I. p. 249.

litfka,

litfka, and would therefore be obliged to receive it at any price. This mode of proceeding offending the Poles, the king of Pruffia, with his ufual fagacity, did not neglect this opportunity of extending his commerce; he immediately imported large quantities of falt, which he procured chiefly from Spain, to Dantzic, Memmel, and Koningfburg, from whence it was conveyed up the Viftula into the interior provinces: by thefe means he furnifhed great part of Poland with falt, at a cheaper rate than the inhabitants could procure it from the houfe of Auftria; and in 1778 the mines of Wielitfka only fupplied the diftricts which immediately border upon Auftrian Poland.

I never faw a road fo barren of interefting fcenes as that from Cracow to Warfaw; there is not a fingle object throughout the whole tract, which can for a moment draw the attention of the moft inquifitive traveller. The country, for the moft part of the way, was level, with little variation of furface: it was chiefly overfpread with vaft tracts of thick gloomy foreft; and even where the country was more open, the diftant horizon was always fkirted with wood. The trees were moftly pines and firs, intermixed with beech, birch, and fmall oaks. The occafional breaks in the foreft prefented fome pafture ground, with here and there a few meagre crops of corn.

Without having actually traverfed it, I could hardly have conceived fo comfortlefs a region: a forlorn ftillnefs and folitude prevailed almoft through the whole extent, with few fymptoms of an inhabited, and ftill lefs of a civilized country. Though in the high road, which unites Cracow and Warfaw in the courfe of about 258 Englifh miles, we met in our progrefs only two carriages and about a dozen carts. The countrry was equally thin of human habitations: a few ftraggling villages, all built of wood, fucceeded one another at long intervals, whofe miferable appearance correfponded to the wretchednefs of the country around them. In thefe affemblages of

huts,

huts, the only places of reception for travellers were hovels, belonging to Jews, totally deſtitute of furniture and every ſpecies of accommodation. We could ſeldom procure any other room but that in which the family lived ; in the article of proviſion eggs and milk were our greateſt luxuries, and could not always be obtained : our only bed was ſtraw thrown upon the ground, and we thought ourſelves happy when we could procure it clean. Even we, who were by no means delicate, and who had long been accuſtomed to put up with all inconveniences, found ourſelves diſtreſſed in this land of deſolation. Though in moſt countries we made a point of ſuſpending our journey during night, in order that no ſcene might eſcape our obſervation ; yet we here even preferred continuing our route without intermiſſion to the penance we endured in theſe receptacles of filth and penury : and we have reaſon to believe that the darkneſs of the night deprived us of nothing but the ſight of gloomy foreſts, indifferent crops of corn, and objects of human miſery. The natives were poorer, humbler, and more miſerable than any people we had yet obſerved in the courſe of our travels : wherever we ſtopped, they flocked around us in crouds ; and, aſking for charity, uſed the moſt abject geſtures. The road bore as few marks of induſtry as the country which it interſects. It was beſt where it was ſandy ; in other parts it was ſcarcely paſſable ; and in the marſhy grounds, where ſome labour was abſolutely neceſſary to make it ſupport the carriages, it was raiſed with ſticks and boughs of trees thrown promiſcuouſly upon the ſurface, or formed by trunks of trees laid croſsways. After a tedious journey we at length approached Warſaw ; but the roads being neither more paſſable, nor the country better cultivated, and the ſuburbs chiefly conſiſting of the ſame wooden hovels which compoſe the villages, we had no ſuſpicion of being near the capital of Poland until we arrived at its gates.

GHAP.

C H A P.   III.

Arrival at Warfaw.—*Defcription of the city* —*Journal of occur-*
rences.—*Prefentation to the king of* Poland.—*Palace.—*
Portraits of the kings of Poland. — *Literary fociety.*—*Enter-*
tainment at the king's villa.—*Supper in prince* Poniatoufki's
garden.—*Defcription of a fête champêtre given at* Povonfki
by the princefs Zartorifka, &c. &c.

BOOK
II.

THE fituation of Warfaw is not unpleafant : it is built
partly in a plain, and partly upon a gentle afcent rifing
from the banks of the Viftula, which is about as broad as the
Thames at Weftminfter-Bridge, but very fhallow in fummer.
The city and its fuburbs occupy a vaft extent of ground ; and
are fuppofed to contain between fixty and feventy thoufand
inhabitants, among whom are a prodigious number of foreigners. The whole town has a melancholy appearance, ex-
hibiting that ftrong contraft of wealth and poverty, luxury
and diftrefs, which pervades every part of this unhappy country. The ftreets are fpacious, but ill-paved ; the churches
and public buildings are large and magnificent ; the palaces
of the nobility are numerous and fplendid ; but the greateft
part of the houfes, particularly in the fuburbs, are mean and
ill-conftructed wooden hovels.

August 2. The Englifh minifter being abfent in the
country, we carried our letters of recommendation to Count
Rzewufki great marfhal of the crown, who received us with
much civility, and appointed Sunday morning to prefent us
to the king at his levee. At the hour appointed we repaired
to court, and were admitted into the audience-chamber, where
the principal officers of the crown were waiting for his majefty's

STANISLAUS of AUGUSTUS
KING POLAND

Teighe sculpsit London 1783

Published according to Act of Parliament, Jan.¹ 1ˢᵗ 1784. by T. Cadell, in the Strand.

jefty's appearance. In this chamber I obferved four bufts, placed by order of his prefent majefty; namely, thofe of Elizabeth queen of England; Henry IV. of France; John Sobiefki; and the prefent emprefs of Ruffia.

At length the king made his appearance; and we were prefented. His majefty talked to each of us a confiderable time in the moft obliging manner; he faid many handfome things of the Englifh nation, mentioned his refidence in London with great appearance of fatisfaction, and concluded by inviting us to fupper in the evening, of which honour we had before had previous intimation from the great marfhal. The king of Poland is handfome in his perfon, with an expreffive countenance, a dark complexion, Roman nofe, and penetrating eye: he is uncommonly pleafing in his addrefs and manner, and poffeffes great fweetnefs of condefcenfion, tempered with dignity. He had on a full dreffed fuit; which circumftance I mention becaufe he is the firft king of this country who has not worn the national habit, or who has not fhaved his head after the Polifh cuftom. His example has of courfe had many imitators: and I was much furprized to fee fo few of the chief nobility in the national garb. The natives in general are fo attached to this drefs, that in the diet of convocation which affembled previous to the election of his prefent majefty, it was propofed to infert in the *Pacta Conventa* an article, whereby the king fhould be obliged to wear the Polifh garment: but this motion was over-ruled; and he was left at liberty to confult his own tafte. At his coronation he laid afide the antient regal habit of ceremony, and appeared in robes of a more modern fafhion, with his hair flowing upon his fhoulders.

The levee being ended, we went over the palace, which was built by Sigifmond III. and which fince his time has been the principal refidence of the Polifh monarchs. Warfaw is far

6

more

more commodious for the capital than Cracow, becaufe it is fituated nearer to the center of the kingdom, and becaufe the diet is affembled in this city. The palace ftands upon a rifing ground at a fmall diftance from the Viftula, and commands a fine view of that river and of the adjacent country. Next to the audience-chamber is an apartment fitted up with marble, which his majefty has dedicated, by the following infcription, to the memory of his predeceffors the kings of Poland: *Regum Memoriæ dicavit Staniſlaus Auguſtus hocce monumentum,* 1771. The portraits of the fovereigns are ranged in chronological order: the feries begins from Boleflaus, and is carried down to his prefent majefty, whofe picture is not yet finifhed. Thefe heads are all painted by Bacciarelli, and well executed: the portraits of the earlier kings are fketched from the painter's imagination; but that of Ladiflaus II. and moft of his fuccef-fors are copied from real originals. They altogether produce a pleafing effect, and may be confidered as an agreeable fpecies of genealogical table. In this apartment the king gives a dinner every Thurfday to the men of letters who are moft confpicuous for their learning and abilities: his majefty him-felf prefides at table, and takes the lead in the graces of con-verfation as much as in rank; and, though a fovereign, does not think it beneath him to be a moft entertaining companion. The perfons who are admitted to this fociety read occafionally treatifes upon different topics of hiftory, natural philofophy, and other mifcellaneous fubjects: and as a code of laws was at that time compiling in order to be prefented to the next diet, parts of that code, or obfervations relating to legiflation in general, and the conftitution of Poland in particular, were in-troduced and perufed. The king ftudioufly encourages all attempts to refine and polifh his native tongue, which had been much neglected during the reigns of his two predecef-fors, who were totally ignorant of the Polifh language. He is

fond

fond of poetry; accordingly that species of composition is much cultivated at thefe meetings. The next apartment was hung with the portraits of the principal members of the society.

In obedience to the king's condefcending invitation, we fat off about eight in the evening, and drove to one of the royal villas, fituated in the midſt of a delightful wood about three miles from Warfaw. The villa is fmall, confifting of a faloon, and four other apartments upon the firſt floor, together with a bath, from which it takes its name of *la Maifon de Bain:* above ſtairs are the fame number of rooms; each of them fitted up in the moſt elegant manner. The king received us in the faloon with wonderful affability: his brother and two of his nephews were prefent, and a few of the nobility of both fexes, who generally compofe his private parties. There were two tables for whift, and thofe who were not engaged at cards walked about, or ſtood at different fides of the room, while the king, who feldom plays, converfed occafionally with every one. At about half an hour after nine, fupper being announced, we followed the king into an adjoining apartment, where was a fmall round table with eight covers: the fupper confifted of one courfe and a defert. His majefty fat down, but eat nothing; he talked a great deal, without wholly engroffing the converfation. After fupper we repaired to the faloon, part of the company returned to their cards, while we, out of refpect to the king, continued ſtanding, until his majefty was pleafed to propofe fitting down, adding, " we fhall " be more at our eafe chatting round a table." We accordingly feated ourfelves, and the converfation lafted without interruption, and with perfect eafe, till midnight, when the king retired. Before he withdrew, he gave a general order to a nobleman of the party, that we fhould be conducted to fee every object in Warfaw worthy of a ſtranger's curiofity. This extraordinary degree of attention penetrated us with gratitude,

and

and proved a prelude to ſtill greater honours.

August 5. We had the honour of dining with his majeſty at the ſame villa, and experienced the ſame eaſe and affability of reception as before. His majeſty had hitherto talked French, but he now did me the honour to converſe with me in Engliſh, which he ſpeaks remarkably well. He expreſſed a great predilection for our nation: he ſurprized me by his extraordinary knowledge of our conſtitution, laws, and hiſtory, which was ſo circumſtantial and exact, that he could not have acquired it without infinite application: all his remarks were pertinent, juſt, and rational. He is familiarly acquainted with our beſt authors, and his enthuſiaſtic admiration of Shakeſpeare gave me the moſt convincing proofs of his intimate acquaintance with our language, and his taſte for the beauties of genuine poetry. He inquired much about the ſtate of arts and ſciences in England, and ſpoke with raptures upon the protection and encouragement which our ſovereign gives to the liberal arts, and to every ſpecies of literature. After we had taken our leave, we drove round the wood to ſeveral other villas, in which the king occaſionally reſides. They are all conſtructed in different ſtyles with great taſte and elegance. His majeſty is very fond of architecture, and draws himſelf all the plans for the buildings, and even the deſigns for the interior decorations of the ſeveral apartments.

In the evening we had the pleaſure of meeting his majeſty at his brother's, prince Poniatoſki, who gave us a moſt elegant entertainment at a garden which is ſituated near his villa, and is richly ornamented with buildings. The taſte of the Poliſh nobility is not to be controuled by want of any materials; for if they cannot procure them from nature, they make a repreſentation of them by art. In the preſent inſtance, as there are no quarries of ſtone near Warſaw, the prince has ſubſtituted a compoſition ſo nearly reſembling ſtone, that the moſt minute
                                                            obſerver

observer can scarce discover the difference. We arrived at the garden about nine; it was a beautiful evening of one of the most sultry days we had experienced this summer. After walking about the grounds, we came to a grotto of artificial rock, where a spring of water dripped through the sides, and fell into a bason with a pleasing murmur. We were scarcely assembled in this delightful spot, when the king made his appearance: we rose up to meet him; the usual compliments being passed, we attended his majesty about the grounds, and then returned to the grotto, round which we ranged ourselves upon a bank covered with moss. The moon was now risen, and added greatly to the beauty of the scene. I happened to be seated next to the king (for all form and ceremony was banished), who talked with me as usual, in English, on the arts and sciences, literature, and history. In the course of this conversation I ventured to ask whether there was any good poetry in the Polish language. His majesty told me, " We " have some lighter pieces of poetry, by no means contemp- " tible, and an indifferent epic poem; but the work of chief " poetical excellence in our tongue is a fine translation of the " *Gerusalemme Liberata* of Tasso, far superior to any transla- " tions of that admirable poem in other languages; some Ita- " lians of taste and judgement have esteemed it not much in- " ferior to the original performance." I then took the liberty of inquiring about the historical productions of Poland; when the king informed me, that they had no good history of their country in Polish, which he looked upon as a national reflec- tion, though he flattered himself it would soon be removed, as a person of genius and erudition, admirably calculated for the undertaking, was now employed in that work. Upon ex- pressing my surprize at a circumstance almost peculiar to Po- land, that they had no history in their native tongue, his ma- jesty condescended to acquaint me, that they had several excel-

lent

lent hiftorians, all of whom however had written in Latin;
" the knowledge of this language," his majefty remarked,
" is very general among the Poles * ; the earlieft laws are all
" drawn up in Latin until the reign of Sigifmond Auguftus,
" when they began to be compofed in the vernacular lan-
" guage; the old *Pacta Conventa* are all in Latin; thofe of
" Ladiflaus IV. being the firft that appeared in Polifh." This
converfation, in which I was at a lofs whether to admire moft
the knowledge or condefcenfion of the king, was interrupted
by the prince, who propofed a turn in the garden before fupper: his highnefs led the way, and the company followed;
we paffed through a fubterraneous paffage, long and winding,
with here and there a fingle lamp, which fhed a glimmering
light; we came at length to a wooden door, which feemed the
entrance into fome hovel; it opened, and we found ourfelves,
to our great aftonifhment, in a fuperb faloon, illuminated with
innumerable lamps. It was a rotunda, with an elegant dome
of the moft beautiful fymmetry; in the circumference were
four open receffes between pillars of artificial marble † : in the
receffes were fophas, with paintings *in frefco*, reprefenting the
triumphs of Bacchus, Silenus, Love, and the victory of the Emprefs of Ruffia over the Turks. As we were all admiring the
beauty and elegance of the rotunda, our ears were on a fudden
regaled with a concert of exquifite mufic from an invifible
band. While we were liftening to this agreeable performance,
and conjecturing from what quarter it came, a magnificent
table was fuddenly fpread in the midft of the faloon with fuch
expedition, as to refemble the effects of enchantment. We
immediately fat down to fupper with the king, the prince, and
a chofen company : our fpirits were elevated by the beauty of

---

* I had feveral opportunities of remarking
the prevalency of the Latin tongue in Poland;
when I vifited the pinions, I converfed in that
language with a common foldier, who ftood
guard at the entrance : he fpoke it with

great fluency.

† Thefe pillars are of the fame compofi-
tion and colour with thofe of the Pantheon
in Oxford-Street.

the faloon, by the hofpitality of the prince, and by the affability of the king; who, fo far from being a conftraint to the fociety, greatly enlivened it by his vivacity, and feemed the foul of the party. I never paffed a more agreeable evening; the converfation was animated and rational; while the focial eafe and freedom, which diffufed itfelf through every part of the company, realized this beautiful convivial picture;

> La Liberté convive aimable
> Met les deux coudes fur la table *.

Even without the luftre of a crown, which is apt to dazzle our judgements, the king of Poland could not fail of being efteemed one of the moft agreeable and polite gentlemen in Europe: he has a furprizing fund of interefting converfation; and I never had the honour of accefs to his company without being both informed and delighted. His majefty did not retire until one o'clock, when the company feparated, and we returned to Warfaw, highly pleafed with our evening's entertainment.

I have had frequent occafion to mention the elegance and luxury of the Polifh nobility in their houfes and villas; in their decorations and furniture they feem to have happily blended the Englifh and French modes; in their entertainments they are exquifitely refined; and as they fpare no expence, and have a natural good tafte, they generally fucceed in creating pleafure and furprize. We every day experienced the agreeable effects of their hofpitality and politenefs; but by none were we fo elegantly regaled as by the princefs Zartorifka in a *fête champétre*, of which I fhall attempt a defcription.

Povonfki, the villa of prince Adam Zartorifki, is about three miles from Warfaw in the midft of a foreft: the fituation is almoft level, with here and there a gentle flope, which produces an agreeable variety. A river runs through the grounds, which are laid out in the Englifh tafte, with a beautiful inter-

* Voltaire.

mixture

mixture of lawn and wood; walks are cut through the wood, and carried along the fide of the water.

The houfe, which ftands upon a gentle rife, has the appearance of a cottage, conftructed like thofe of the peafants, with trunks of trees piled upon each other, and thatched with ftraw: befide the principal building, inhabited by the prince and princefs, there are feparate cottages for the children and attendants, each of which has its inclofures and fmall garden; this group of ftructures bears the refemblance of a village, compofed of huts fcattered at a fmall diftance from each other. Other buildings, fuch as fummer houfes, pavilions, ruftic fheds, and ruins, are difperfed throughout the grounds; the ftables are conftructed in the form of an half demolifhed amphitheatre. Several romantic bridges, rudely compofed of the trunks and bent branches of trees, contribute to heighten the rufticity of the fcenery.

Upon our arrival we repaired to the principal cottage, where the princefs was ready to receive us: we expected the infide to be furnifhed in the fimple ftyle of a peafant's hovel, but were furprized to find every fpecies of elegant magnificence which riches and tafte could collect. All the apartments are decorated in the moft coftly manner; but the fplendour of the bath-room was peculiarly ftriking: the fides are covered from top to bottom, with fmall fquare pieces of the fineft Drefden china, each ornamented with an elegant fprig; and the border and cieling are painted with beautiful feftoons. The expence of fitting up this apartment muft have been prodigious; as I was informed that there were at leaft three thoufand fquare pieces of china employed, each of which coft at Drefden three ducats *. After we had furveyed all the apartments, we proceeded to an enclofure near the houfe, furrounded with large blocks of granite heaped one upon another,

* About 1l. 7s. 6d.

ther,

ther, and fallen trees placed in the moſt natural and picturesque ſhapes; here we drank tea upon the lawn. From thence we repaired to the ſeveral cottages inhabited by the children; which are fitted up in different ſtyles, but with equal elegance. Every thing without doors gives one the idea of an happy peaſant's family; within all is coſtlineſs and taſte: I never ſaw ſuch a contraſt of ſimplicity and magnificence.

We next walked round the grounds, which are prettily laid out in our taſte of gardening; the company then all adjourned to a Turkiſh tent of rich and curious workmanſhip, pitched in a beautiful retired field near the ſtables, which repreſent a ruined amphitheatre. This tent belonged to the grand-vizier, and was taken during the late war between the Ruſſians and the Turks: under it was a ſettee, and a carpet ſpread upon the ground. Here we ſtaid converſing until it was quite duſk; when the princeſs propoſed returning; ſhe led us through the houſe to a ſmall ſpot of riſing ground, where we were ſuddenly ſtruck with a moſt beautiful illumination. A ruſtic bridge, conſiſting of a ſingle arch over a broad piece of water, was ſtudded with ſeveral thouſand lamps of different colours; while the reflection of this illuminated bridge in the water was ſo ſtrong as to deceive the eye, and gave the whole the appearance of a brilliant circle ſuſpended in the air: the effect was ſplendid beyond deſcription, and conſiderably heightened by the gloom of the foreſt in the back-ground. While we continued admiring this delightful ſcene, a band of muſic ſtruck up at a little diſtance, and amuſed us with an excellent concert. We were then led from this enchanting ſpot, acroſs the illuminated bridge, to a thatched pavilion, open at the ſides, and ſupported by pillars ornamented with garlands and twiſted feſtoons of flowers: we found within a cold collation, and ſat down to a table covered with all kind of delicacies, with the moſt coſtly wines, and every ſpecies of fruit which art or na-

5

ture,

ture could furnifh.   The evening was delightful, the fcenery picturefque, the fare delicious; the company in good fpirits; for who could be otherwife when every circumftance, which the tafte and ingenuity of our fair hoftefs could invent, confpired to heighten the entertainment?   The collation being ended, we rofe from table: which I concluded to be the clofe of the entertainment, but was agreeably difappointed: the gardens were fuddenly illuminated; we all ranged about as fancy dictated; and were gratified with the found of wind inftruments played by perfons difperfed in different parts of the grounds.   We repaffed the bridge, and returned into the cottage, when the two eldeft daughters of the princefs, who were dreffed in Grecian dreffes of the moft elegant fimplicity, performed a Polifh and a Coffac dance; the former ferious and graceful, the latter comic and lively.   The eldeft fon, a boy about eight years old, next performed an hornpipe with wonderful agility, and afterwards a dance in the ftyle of the Polifh peafants with much humour.   It was now paft two in the morning; we feemed as if we could ftay for ever; but as there muft be an end of all fublunary joys, we took our leave, expreffing our thanks and gratitude in language far unequal to our feelings.   I can fcarce form to myfelf a *fête champêtre* fo elegant: and I am fatisfied, that it will feldom fall to the lot of the fame perfon to partake of fuch a pleafing entertainment twice in his life.

The day before our departure from this town we dined with the bifhop of Plotfko, the king's brother, at his palace of Jablonifka about eight miles from Warfaw.   The palace is an handfome building, conftructed after a defign, and at the expence, of his majefty.   One of the apartments, called the Turkifh faloon, is remarkable for its elegance and fingularity: it is in the Oriental tafte, of an oblong fhape, very high, with a fountain in the middle, furrounded with a *parterre* of flowers.

Between

Between the *parterre* and sides of the room are ranges of
Turkish sophas. The variegated tints and rich fragrance of
the flowers, joined to the transparency and murmurs of the
fountain, produce a most pleasing effect, and, together with
the coolness of the apartment, render it a delicious retreat from
the heats of summer. The Vistula winds along at a small
distance from the palace, through a sandy and almost level
country.

In the evening we accompanied prince Staniflaus to his majesty's villa, secure of passing an interesting evening, but it
was now embittered with the idea that it would never again
be repeated, and that this was the last time of our being admitted to the company of so amiable a monarch. In the following conversation I had an additional proof of his humanity
and condescension : " You have been to the prisons *, and I
" am afraid you found them in a wretched condition." To
have mentioned all their abuses, when I knew that his majesty
could not alter them, would only have been an insult ; I endeavoured therefore to palliate my answer, by remarking, what
is but too true, that in several instances they were not so badly
regulated as in England. " I am surprized," returned the king,
" that a nation, who so justly piques itself for its humanity,
" should be deficient in so effential an article of police." I
then ventured, with as much delicacy as possible, to point out
one material abuse in the prisons of Warsaw, which I thought
might probably be in his majesty's power to alleviate at least,
if not to remedy. The circumstance which I alluded to was,
that there is no separate room for the accommodation of sick
prisoners ; at the same time I begged pardon for this instance
of presumption, which nothing but my compassion for the unfortunate could have extorted from me. " He who pleads the
" cause of the unhappy," replied his majesty, " is always list-

* See the latter part of Chap. V.

Y " ened

" ened to with pleafure ;" an expreſſion I ſhall never forget,
and which convinced me, by the pathetic manner in which
it was uttered, that it was the real ſentiment of his heart.
The turn of the converſation led the king to enlarge upon
the code of laws preparing for the infpection of the approaching diet; when his majeſty expatiated, with peculiar ſatisfaction, upon ſeveral beneficial regulations calculated to promote the impartial adminiſtration of juſtice.   " Happy Eng-
" liſhman !" exclaimed the king, " your houſe is raiſed, and
" mine is yet to build."   Every part of this conference im-
preſſed me with the higheſt opinion of the king's benevolence,
patriotiſm, and legiſlative abilities.

After ſupper, which paſſed off no leſs agreeably than the
preceding entertainments, we were preſented to take leave,
when the king condeſcended to inquire of us the route we
intended to take ;   and to point out what was moſt likely to
occur worthy of obſervation.   " Your majeſty," I ventured to
obferve, " has omitted the manufactures which you have
" eſtabliſhed at Grodno *."   " An Engliſhman," replied the
king, " after having feen the manufactures of his own
" country, will find little deferving his curioſity in any other,
" and particularly in this kingdom, where there is fuch a fet-
" tled averſion to commerce.   The eſtabliſhment at Grodno is
" but a beginning : I confider it only as a pledge of my future
" intentions."   I then mentioned the new regulations in the
univerfity of Vilna, and the foundation of a phyſic-garden at
Grodno.   " You are deceived by the ſimilarity of names.   An
" Engliſh univerfity is as much fuperior to foreign feminaries,
" as your nation excels all others in the cultivation of litera-
" ture, and the encouragement given to genius and abilities.
" The academy at Vilna is more the image of what it was, and
" of what it ought to be, than an object of a traveller's curi-

* See Chap. VI. article GRODNO.

" ofity."

" ofity." He then gracioufly exprefled his regret at our departing fo foon from Warfaw, and, wifhing us a good journey, retired.

I flatter myfelf, that I fhall not appear too minute in relating all thefe circumftances ; the familiar incidents of domeftic life place the character of a fovereign in a truer point of view than the more fplendid occurrences of public grandeur, where the real difpofition is often difguifed by form, or facrificed to policy.

C H A P. IV.

Villanow *the favourite palace of* John Sobiefki.—*Account of that monarch.—Circumftances of his death.—Intrigues of his queen.—Divifion and cabals of his family.—Fortunes of his children.—Extinction of his name.—Genealogical table of his defcendants.*

AUGUST 6. We paffed the day at Villanow, where we dined with prince Zartorifki. He is a fine old man, near fourfcore, and lives in the true ftyle of ancient hofpitality : he is conftantly attended by his own guards, which I mention, not as being peculiar to him, who enjoys the firft offices of the republic, but becaufe it leads me to remark that every Polifh nobleman may have as many guards as he can afford to maintain.

The prince keeps an open table, at which there are feldom lefs than twenty or thirty covers. His revenues are large, amounting to near £100,000 fterling *per annum*; and his ftyle of living correfponds to this great income.

Villanow

BOOK
II.

Villanow was built by John Sobiefki the conqueror of the Turks and deliverer of Vienna: it was the favourite refidence of that great monarch, where he moftly lived when not in arms, and where he clofed his days. The palace, being fold after his death, came by marriage into the family of Zartorifki; it was lent to Auguftus II. who confiderably enlarged it. The outfide is ornamented with feveral baffo relievos, reprefenting the principal victories of John Sobiefki, which were probably added by Auguftus; for the former was too modeft and unaffuming to erect monuments of his own glory.

The æra of John Sobiefki, fplendid in itfelf, appears more luminous, when contrafted with the darknefs which preceded and followed. The reigns of his immediate predeceffor and fucceffor were convulfed with internal commotions; but the fpirit of difcord and anarchy was laid for a time by his tranfcendent genius. Under his aufpices Poland feemed to revive from the calamities which had long oppreffed her, and again to recover her antient fplendour; fuch is the powerful afcendency of a great and fuperior mind. His military talents require no other teftimony than the victory of Chotzim, the recovery of the Ukraine, repeated defeats of the Turks and Tartars, and the delivery of Vienna; while an exact infight into the laws and conftitution of his country, a manly and perfuafive eloquence, a love and protection of literature, an accurate knowledge of foreign languages, and an unceafing habit of affability, moderation, and temperance, render him no lefs an object of our admiration in his civil capacity *. But

* Dr. South, in his Account of Poland, thus defcribes John Sobiefki: " The king is " a very well-fpoken prince, very eafy of ac- " cefs, and extreme civil, having moft of the " qualities requifite to form a complete gen- " tleman. He is not only well verfed in all " military affairs, but likewife, through the " means of a French education, very opu- " lently ftored with all polite and fcholaftical " learning. Befides his own tongue, the " Sclavonian, he underftands the Latin, " French, Italian, German, and Turkifh lan- " guages: He delights much in natural hif- " tory, and in all the parts of phyfic. He " is wont to reprimand the clergy for not ad- " mitting the modern philofophy, fuch as Le " Grand's and Cartefius's, into the univer- " fities and fchools," &c. South's Pofthumous Works, p. 24.

the

the monarch, who could allay the fentiments of public faction, could not fupprefs the domeftic diffentions of his own family; and the fame great prince, who kept a turbulent people in awe, and chaftifed the moft formidable enemies, was himfelf under the controul of his confort, a French lady *, of exquifite beauty and elegant manners, but of reftlefs intrigue, infatiable avarice, and inordinate ambition. This unprincipled woman fomented a fpirit of difunion and jealoufy among her children; and loaded her eldeft fon with every fpecies of indignity. She formed and fupported an adminiftration called, by way of derifion, the Jewifh junto; and introduced into the royal houf-hold a narrow parfimony unbecoming the dignity of a powerful fovereign: in a word, by a feries of offenfive and wicked meafures, fhe loft her hufband the affection of his fubjects; and rendered the clofe of his reign as odious, as the preceding part had been popular and glorious.

The decline of Sobiefki's life was clouded with affliction. He felt himfelf a prey to a lingering difeafe †; yet, inftead of deriving any comfort from his neareft connections, he experienced an aggravation of his diftrefs from the unnatural contefts of his children, and the intriguing fpirit of his queen. The decay of his authority, and the indecent cabals almoft openly carrying on about the choice of his fucceffor, affected in the ftrongeft manner a perfon of his extreme fenfibility: his fubjects, inftead of lamenting, feemed eagerly to anticipate his diffolution. Yet, in this deplorable ftate, the king's equanimity, founded on religion and philofophy, did not forfake him; and he retained, even upon his death-bed, that mixture of ferioufnefs and gaiety, ftrength of reafoning and quicknefs of repartee, which fo ftrongly marked his character. He died on the 17th of June, 1696. Some ftriking incidents, imme-

---

* Marie de la Grange. See p. 168.
† His illnefs was a complication of diforders, gout, ftone, afthma, dropfy.

I

diately

diately preceding his death, are tranſmitted to us by the chancellor Zaluſki biſhop of Plotſko, who was preſent when he
expired.

Some alarming ſymptoms in Sobieſki's diſorder having
awakened the queen's ſolicitude about the ſucceſſion to his
fortune, ſhe earneſtly importuned Zaluſki to preſent himſelf
before the king, and inſinuate ſome advice with reſpect to the
diſpoſition of his affairs. The biſhop, when he entered the
apartment, finding the king in an agony of excruciating pain *,
endeavoured to give him comfort and hopes of recovery. But
Sobieſki replied, " I foreſee my approaching death ; my ſitu-
" ation will be the ſame to-morrow as it is to-day ; all conſo-
" lation is now too late ;" then, fetching a deep ſigh, his majeſty aſked him " why he came ſo ſeldom to court, and in
" what manner he employed himſelf at his dioceſe alone !"
Zaluſki, after expatiating upon the duties of his epiſcopal office and the reſources of literature, artfully turned the diſcourſe
to the buſineſs in queſtion. " Lately," ſaid he, " I have been
" employed in no very agreeable, yet neceſſary duty : weigh-
" ing the frail condition of human nature, remembering, that
" as Socrates and Plato, ſo all men muſt die ; and conſidering
" the diſſenſions which may ariſe among my relations after
" my deceaſe, I have taken an inventory of my effects, and
" have diſpoſed of them by will." The king, who ſaw the
purport of his diſcourſe, interrupted him with a loud laugh,
and exclaimed, in a quotation from Juvenal †, " O medici, me-
" diam contundite venam." " What, my Lord Biſhop ! you
" whoſe judgement and good ſenſe I have ſo long eſteemed,
" do you make your will ? What an uſeleſs loſs of time !" &c.
Not diſcouraged by this ſally, the biſhop perſevered in ſug-
geſting " that in juſtice to his family and country he ought

* Zaluſki Epiſt. vol. III. p. 5—14.   In applying this paſſage, the king meant to
† Juvenal, Sat. VI. l. 40. " Open a vein." inſinuate that the biſhop was mad.

3

" without

" without delay to regulate the difpofition of his effects, and
" to declare his final inclinations." " For God's fake," returned
Sobiefki with a more ferious tone, " do not fuppofe that any
" good will arife in this age! when vice has increafed to fuch
" an enormous degree, as almoft to exclude all hopes of forgive-
" nefs from the mercy of the Deity! Do you not fee how
" great is the public iniquity, tumult, and violence? all ftrive
" who fhall blend good and evil without diftinction : the mo-
" rals of my fubjects are overturned; will you again reftore
" them? My orders are not attended to while I am alive;
" can I expect to be obeyed when I am dead? That man is
" happy, who with his own hand difpofes of his effects, which
" cannot be entrufted with fecurity to his executors; while
" they who leave a will act abfurdly, for configning to the
" care of others what is more fecure in the hands of their
" neareft relations. Have not the regulations of the kings my
" predeceffors been defpifed after their deaths? Where cor-
" ruption univerfally prevails, judgement is obtained by mo-
" ney : the voice of confcience is not heard, and reafon and
" equity are no more." Then fuddenly giving a ludicrous
turn to the converfation, he exclaimed, " What can you fay
" to this, Mr. Will-maker * !"

On the 17th of June, the king growing worfe, the bifhop
was again fummoned to Villanow, when his majefty heard
prayers, and was particularly fervent in his devotion. After
dinner, while he was converfing with his ufual gaiety in the
prefence of Zalufki and the abbé Polignac, he was fuddenly
feized with a ftroke of apoplexy ; but recovering a little, he
confeffed, and, having received abfolution and extreme unction,
expired almoft without a groan, in the 66th year of his age,
and the 23d of his reign, on the fame day in which he was
raifed to the throne. The name of Sobiefki is now extinct.

* Quid ad hæc, Domine teftimentarie !

BOOK
II.

My veneration for this great man prompted me to inquire into the fortunes of his family.

Sobiefki * left behind him his wife Marie de la Grange, three fons, James, Alexander, and Conftantine, and one daughter Therefa Cunigunda. Marie his wife, daughter of Henry de la Grange captain of the guards to Philip duke of Orleans, and of Frances de la Chartre, was maid of honour to Louifa queen of Ladiflaus IV. She was firft married to Radzivil prince of Zamofki; within a month after his deceafe fhe efpoufed John Sobiefki in fecret, and brought him in dower a large portion and the favour of his fovereign. Her influence over her hufband, and the ill ufe fhe made of her power when he afcended the throne, have been already obferved.

James Louis, the eldeft fon of Sobiefki, was born at Paris in 1667. He accompanied his father to the relief of Vienna, in the 16th year of his age, and narrowly efcaped being flain in an action near Banan in Hungary. He afterwards gave fuch fignal proofs of his military talents, that, upon hi+ father's indifpofition in the campaign of 1687 againft the Turks, he was entrufted with the command of the army, although only in the 21ft year of his age; and received from the foldiers all the honours ufually paid only to the kings of Poland : a fingular mark of deference in an elective monarchy, and which gave encouragement to an expectation of the throne at his father's deceafe. His father promoted this view with the utmoft exertion of his intereft; but this project was entirely difconcerted by the indifcretion of the prince, and the reftlefs intrigues of the queen, who, having conceived the ftrongeft antipathy to her eldeft fon, and a no lefs violent predilection in favour of her fecond fon Alexander, a prince of a more tractable difpofition, facrificed the dignity of her family to a blind impulfe of parental partiality.   Sobi-

---

* The abbé Coyer has written the Life of   what is remarkable in a French hiftorian,
Sobiefki with great fpirit and fidelity ; and,   has cited his authorities.

Sobieſki had ſcarcely expired, before the cabals, which even his authority could hardly ſuppreſs, broke out with undiſſembled violence. The diviſion of the king's treaſure cauſed the moſt indecent diſputes and altercations between his widow and children. James, without a moment's delay, endeavoured, though in vain, to ſeize it by force, being anticipated by the queen *, who, by the aſſiſtance of the abbé Polignac, ſent it into France. She had three great objects in view : either to obtain the crown for Alexander, whom ſhe was ſecure of governing ; to promote the election of Count Jablonouſki, great general of the crown, with an intention of marrying him ; or to favour the pretenſions of the prince of Conti, warmly ſupported by Louis XIV. At all events ſhe was firmly reſolved to procure the excluſion of her eldeſt ſon, and this was the only point ſhe carried. Had the family of Sobieſki been unanimous, James muſt have been elected king ; but no ſubmiſſion † could ſoften the implacable reſentment of the queen, who, even when ſhe found it impracticable to ſecure the election of her favourite ſon Alexander, or to compaſs any of her other deſigns, both in ſecret and openly ſet herſelf in oppoſition to the pretenſions of James. When the diet of convocation aſſembled at Warſaw, the queen ſummoned a meeting of ſenators and nuntios in her apartment, whom ſhe addreſſed in regard to her ſon with all the virulence which inve-

---

* The queen ſent 3,000,000 French livres = £125,000 into France. Larrey, Hiſt. Louis XIV. v. II. p. 297.

† Zaluſki has given the following curious inſtance of the queen's implacability. "I "and other ſenators accompanied prince "James to the Queen's at Bieltz, but her "majeſty being informed of our approach, "retired precipitately from the palace in "order to avoid the interview ; we overtook "her about a mile from Bieltz, and ordered "the driver to ſtop, while ſhe repeatedly "urged him to continue his route : at length "the coachman, alarmed by our number and

"threats, ſtopped the carriage. On our ad-"vancing to the queen, ſhe received us with "great marks of diſpleaſure ; and although "the prince proſtrated himſelf before her, "and embraced her feet with the moſt pro-"found reſpect, he was not able to extort "from her more than a ſhort and evaſive "anſwer. Upon his retiring, with his eyes "full of tears, I myſelf uſed ſome endeavours "to ſoften her reſentment ; which, however, "had no other effect than to draw from her "additional expreſſions of diſguſt and indig-"nation." Zaluſki, vol. III. p. 135.

terate

terate fury could infpire, and all the affected candour towards
the Poles which the moſt confummate hypocrify could fug-
geſt *.   " Although I am not by birth a Pole, I am one by
" inclination, and am more attached to this nation than to
" my own family.   Reflect maturely whom you will nomi-
" nate your king in the place of my much-regretted hufband,
" and I fincerely recommend to you not to elect one of my
" children.   I too well know all their difpofitions; and par-
" ticularly caution you not to raife to the throne the eldeſt
" prince James.   His inconfiderate raſhneſs will involve the
" kingdom in fpeedy and inevitable ruin."   The biſhop of
Plotſko, though her creature, difguiſted at thefe appearances
of unnatural rancour, importuned her to defiſt; but ſhe exclaimed with greater violence: " Do not interrupt me; I
" will never retract what I have faid, as I prefer the fafety of
" the republic to my own intereſts and the fplendour of my
" family.   I again exhort the Poles to elect any candidate in
" preference to one of my children."   This virulent oppofition to the views of her eldeſt fon was but too fuccefsful: he
was rejected by a great majority, and the choice of the nation
fell upon Auguſtus elector of Saxony.

The fequel of the hiſtory of Sobiefki's family, now reduced
to a private ſtation, will be comprifed in a ſhort compafs.
After the defeat of Auguſtus II. at the battle of Cliſſow,
Charles XII. determined to give a new king to Poland; and
his veneration for the memory of John Sobiefki induced him
to offer that dignity to his eldeſt fon.   In confequence of this
refolution, Auguſtus was declared by the primate unworthy
to reign; and a diet of election was convened at Warſaw.
James was then at Breſlaw, impatiently expecting his nomination to the throne fo worthily filled by his father, and from
which he had been deprived by the unprecedented malice of

* Zaluſki, vol. III. p. 102.

5   a mother

a mother.   But the ufual fingularity of his ill-fortune ftill
purfued him : as he was hunting with his brother Conftantine, a fmall detachment of Saxon horfemen furprized and
carried him off; and, inftead of receiving a crown, he was
confined in the caftle of Pleiffenburgh near Leipfic.   Conftantine * might have have efcaped ; but, from an impulfe of
fraternal affection, voluntarily accompanied his brother into
confinement, and adminiftered confolation under this grievous
reverfe of fortune.   This event happened on the 28th of
February, 1704.

In the month of September, 1706, the two brothers were
removed to the fortrefs of Koningftein, as to a place of ftill
greater fecurity ; but in December of the fame year fortunately obtained their enlargement, upon the requeft of
Charles XII. at the conclufion of the celebrated treaty with
Auguftus II. in which the latter was compelled to abdicate
the throne of Poland.   This abdication, however, did not revive the pretenfions of James to the crown, the election having fallen, during his confinement, upon Staniflaus Letzinfki.
From this period James paffed a private and retired life, and
feems to have entirely renounced all his views upon the crown
of Poland.   He died in 1737 at Zolkiew in Red Ruffia, in the
70th year of his age ; and in him, as the laft male of his
family, the name of Sobiefki became extinct.   His wife was
Hedwige Eleonora †, daughter of Philip William elector palatine ;

* Lengnich, Hift. Pol. p. 342.
† Sifter of Eleonora Magdalena wife of
the emperor Leopold.   James had been firft
contracted in marriage to the widow of the
elector of Brandenburgh's brother, a rich
heirefs of the houfe of Radzivil in Lithuania,
but upon this occafion he firft experienced
that ill fortune which afterwards attended
him through life.   " An envoy was fent to
" Berlin to negotiate the marriage, which
" was agreed upon by the elector's and her

" confent, and the prince himfelf came thi-
" ther in perfon, with a numerous attend-
" ance, to confummate it.   At the fame time
" came to Berlin the elector palatine's bro-
" ther, prince Charles of Newburg, brother
" to the emprefs, to fee the ceremony of the
" marriage ; but this princefs, taking more
" fancy to him than to the prince of Poland,
" gave him encouragement to make his ad-
" dreffes to her ; which he did with that fuc-
" cefs, that he engaged her fo far and fo un-
                              " expectedly,

Z 2

latine; by her he left two daughters, Mary Charlotte and Clementina Mary.

The eldeſt, Mary Charlotte, married in 1723 Frederic Maurice de la Tour duke of Bouillon, who dying within a few days after the marriage, ſhe eſpouſed, with a diſpenſation from the pope, his brother Charles Godfrey the ſame year. By him ſhe left iſſue a ſon, the preſent duke of Bouillon, married to a lady of the houſe of Lorraine, and a daughter, who eſpouſed the duke of Rohan-Rohan. In theſe noble perſons and their progeny the female line of Sobieſki ſtill exiſts.

Clementina Mary, the youngeſt daughter of prince James, married at Monteſiaſcone, in 1719, James Edward Stuart, commonly known by the name of the Chevalier de St. George, the pretender to the Britiſh throne. This princeſs, though a woman of great perſonal and mental endowments, could not engage the affection of her huſband; and ſhe was ſo offended at his attachment to a favourite miſtreſs, that ſhe withdrew from his houſe, and remained for ſome time in a convent near Rome. Afterwards, being reconciled to him, ſhe died at Rome on the 18th of June, 1735, aged 33; her death, according to the account of a writer * attached to the Stuart family, was occaſioned by religious abſtinence and too ſevere mortifications: her remains were interred with regal pomp in the church of St. Peter, and a ſumptuous monument was erected to her memory. She left two ſons by the Chevalier:

" expectedly, that he was privately married " to her the night before ſhe was to be married to the prince of Poland, ſo that prince " James was forced to return back ſhamefully: which the king his father reſented " ſo highly, that he was reſolved to have ſatisfaction from the elector of Brandenburg, " for ſuffering his ſon to receive ſo notorious " an affront at his court; but the elector, " knowing nothing of that private intrigue,

" juſtified himſelf, and all animoſities were " at laſt adjuſted by prince James's marrying " his rival's ſiſter the princeſs of Newburg, " who was ſent into Poland, and has two " daughters by him." Connor's Hiſtory of Poland, v. II. p. 188, 189.

* Letters from a Painter in Italy, where her funeral and monument is deſcribed v. II. p. 56.

2

Charles,

Charles, ufually termed count of Albany, who died lately; and Henry, cardinal of Yorke, who is ftill alive. Charles married the princefs of Stolberg, by whom he has no children: a mifunderftanding not long after their marriage taking place between them, fhe quitted her hufband, and took fhelter in a convent in the Tufcan dominions; and, as her quarrel was efpoufed by the cardinal of Yorke, fhe obtained a feparation for life. We may therefore forefee the extinction of the Sobiefki line in the Stuart branch. The ample patrimony of James Sobiefki was divided equally between his two daughters. Having lent a confiderable fum to the houfe of Auftria, he obtained in return a mortgage upon certain eftates in Silefia, which, upon the divifion of the property after his deceafe, fell to the Stuart family, and were in their poffeffion when the king of Pruffia fecured Silefia in the year 1740. His Pruffian majefty confifcated thefe lands to himfelf by right of conqueft; and the houfe of Auftria never made any further compenfation for the above-mentioned loan.

Alexander, fecond fon of John Sobiefki, was born at Dantzic in 1677; and as he was brought into the world after his father had been raifed to the throne, he was ufually ftyled by his mother, who adored him, the fon of the king; while fhe affected to call his brother James, who was born before his father's election, the fon of the great marfhal. Excited by his mother's partiality, and inflamed by an ambition natural to youth, he even afpired to the throne in oppofition to his brother James; afterwards however, when a more mature age had corrected his paffions, and his mother's influence had ceafed to miflead him, he declined, from a principal of fraternal affection, the acceptance of that very crown, which had once been the object of his warmeft hopes. When Charles XII. upon the imprifonment of James, offered the crown of Poland to Alexander, the latter, with a difintereftednefs which reflects

the

the higheft honour upon his memory, refufed it with this generous declaration, " that no intereft fhould tempt him to " avail himfelf of his brother's misfortunes *."

Alexander paffed his days principally at Rome with the queen his mother. During his refidence in that city, he never made his appearance at the court of Clement XI. becaufe that pontiff had refufed to receive him with the marks of diftinction which he claimed as a king's fon. But the honours which were withheld from him while alive, were granted unto him when dead ; his body being permitted to lie in royal ftate, and to be interred with the fame ceremonies, which attended the funeral of Chriftina queen of Sweden. He expired in June 1714, having affumed upon his death-bed the habit of a capuchin, from a fuperftitious notion of enfuring his falvation †.

Conftantine, having regained his liberty at the fame time with his brother James, married a German baronefs, maid of honour to the princefs of Neuburg ; a marriage of paffion, foon followed by repentance, and from which he in vain endeavoured to procure a releafe by a divorce. He deceafed in 1726 without children.

Therefa Cunigunda, the daughter of John Sobiefki, married in 1696 Maximilian Emanuel elector of Bavaria, and died a widow 1730. Her fon Charles Albert, who fucceeded to the electorate of Bavaria, was the unfortunate emperor Charles VII. and her grandfon Maximilian Jofeph expired in 1778 without iffue. Her grand-daughter Maria Antonietta married Frederic Chriftian elector of Saxony ; and the blood of John Sobiefki ftill flows in the veins of their progeny, the prefent electoral family.

Marie de la Grange, the confort of John Sobiefki, paffed the firft part of her widowhood at Rome with her father the

* Voltaire's Charles XII. p. 90.   † Vie de Sobiefki, v. III. p. 176.

marquis

marquis of Arquien, who, from being captain of the Swifs
guards to the duke of Orleans, had been promoted by her
intereſt to the dignity of cardinal. She continued to reſide
in that city until the year 1714, when ſhe retired into France,
her native country. Louis XIV. aſſigned the caſtle of Blois
for her reſidence, where ſhe died in 1716 *, above 70 years
of age. Her remains were tranſported to Warſaw, and from
thence conveyed, together with thoſe of her huſband in 1734,
to Cracow, and interred in the cathedral of that city †.

* Vie de Sobieſki, v. III. p. 177.   † Lengnich, Hiſt. p. 390.

Genealogical

Genealogical Table of John Sobieski's Family.

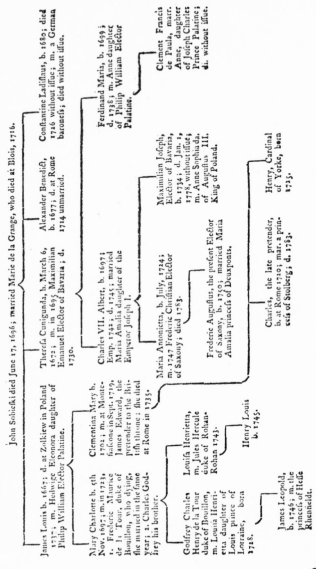

John Sobieski died June 17, 1696; married Marie de la Grange, who died at Blois, 1716.

James Louis b. 1667; d. at Zolkiew in Poland 1737; m. Hedwige Eleonora daughter of Philip William Elector Palatine.

Theresa Cunigunda, b. March 6, 1672; m. in 1695 Maximilian Emanuel Elector of Bavaria; d. 1730.

Alexander Benedict, b. 1677; d. at Rome 1714 unmarried.

Constantine Ladislaus, b. 1680; died 1716 without issue; m. a German baroness; died without issue.

Mary Charlotte b. 5th Nov. 1697; m. in 1723, 1. Frederic Maurice de la Tour, duke of Bouillon, who dying, she married in the same year; 2. Charles Godfrey his brother.

Clementina Mary b. 1701; m. at Montefiascone in Sept. 1719, James Edward, the pretender to the British throne; she died at Rome in 1735.

Charles VII. Albert, b. 1697; Emp. 1742; d. 1745; married Maria Amalia daughter of the Emperor Joseph I.

Ferdinand Maria, b. 1699; d. 1738; m. Anne daughter of Philip William Elector Palatine.

Godfrey Charles Henry de la Tour duke of Bouillon, m. Louisa Henrietta daughter of Louis prince of Lorraine, born 1728.

Louisa Henrietta, m. Jules Hercule duke of Rohan-Rohan 1743.

Maria Antonietta, b. July, 1724; m. 1747 Frederic Christian Elector of Saxony; died 1783.

Maximilian Joseph, Elector of Bavaria, b. 1734; d. Jan. 1, 1778, without issue; m. Anne Sophia da. of Augustus III. King of Poland.

Clement Francis de Paula, marr. Anne, daughter of Joseph Charles Prince Palatine; d. without issue.

James Leopold, b. 1746; m. the princess of Hesse Rheinfeldt.

Henry Louis b. 1745.

Frederic Augustus, the present Elector of Saxony, b. 1750; married Maria Amalia princess of Deuxponts.

Charles, the late pretender, b. at Rome 1720; mar. a princess of Stolberg; d. 1783.

Henry, Cardinal of Yorke, born 1725.

CHAP.

C H A P.   V.

Coins of Poland.—*Public library.*—*State of learning.*—*Literature encouraged by the king.*—*Wretched adminiſtration of
juſtice.*—*Priſons of* Warſaw.—*Puniſhments for criminal offences.*—*Torture aboliſhed.*—*Laws relating to debtors.*

BEFORE our departure from Warſaw we viſited ſome objects
of literary curioſity uſually ſeen by foreigners.   We firſt
adjourned to the palace to examine ſome coins and medals relative to the hiſtory of Poland.   The count of Mazinſki, natural ſon of Auguſtus III. purchaſed the greateſt part of this
collection, and preſented it to his preſent majeſty.   I ſhall not
enter upon any account of the foreign coins and medals, but
content myſelf with mentioning a few which relate to Poland.

The earlieſt coin is that of Boleſlaus I. ſon of Miciſlaus, the
firſt Poliſh prince converted to Chriſtianity : this piece of money was ſtruck in 999, probably ſoon after the introduction of
coining into Poland.   There was no head of the ſovereign upon it, only the Poliſh eagle on one ſide, and a crown on the
reverſe.   The ſeries of coins is broken until Sigiſmond I. from
whoſe acceſſion it is continued in an uninterrupted line, Henry
of Valois excepted ; during whoſe ſhort reign no money was
ſtruck in Poland.   I noticed a curious piece of Albert of Brandenburgh as duke of Pruſſia, after he had wreſted that country
from the Teutonic knights.   The Pruſſian eagle is marked
with an S, to ſhew that Albert held his lands as feudal and
tributary to Sigiſmond I.   There was a fine medal in honour
of John Sobieſki's raiſing the ſiege of Vienna, with the following punning inſcription : *Urbem ſervaſtis et orbem.* I likewiſe obſerved a medal of his preſent majeſty, caſt in the late

VOL. I.   A a   turbulent

turbulent times; it had a well-executed likenefs of the king on one fide, and on the reverfe an emblem of civil commotions, a fhip in a ftorm with the claffical allufion, *Ne cede malis.*

The public library next engaged our attention.   The collection owes its beginning to the private bounty of two bifhops of the family of Zalufki; the following infcription is over the door; " *Civium ufui perpetuo Zaluficorum par illuftre dicavit* " 1714." It has fince received feveral large additions from various benefactors; and, as the librarian informed me, contains above 100,000 volumes.   It is very rich in books and manufcripts relating to the Polifh hiftory.

I have only a few obfervations to make upon the general ftate of literature in Poland, my ftay in this country not being long enough to collect a more circumftantial account.

There are two univerfities, one at Cracow, and the other at Vilna; the former was under the direction of priefts, called Academicians; and the latter was fuperintended by the Jefuits; but in both, the courfe of ftudies was chiefly confined to theology.   Since the fuppreffion of the Jefuits, the king has eftablifhed a committee of education, compofed of members diftinguifhed either by high ftation, or enlightened underftandings.   The committee has an abfolute power in matters of education; appoints profeffors; regulates their falary; and directs their ftudies.   The advantages of this regulation have already been experienced.

Although from the nature of the government learning has never been widely diffufed in Poland, yet there never have been wanting men of genius and literature, who have been an ornament to their country : and perhaps no nation can boaft a more regular fucceffion of excellent hiftorians *; or a greater variety of writers deeply converfant in the laws, ftatutes, and conftitution.   Under Sigifmond I. and his fon Sigifmond Au-

* See p. 155.

6   guftus,

guftus, the arts and fciences began to be greatly diftinguifhed
by royal patronage; they were cherifhed by fome of the fucceeding monarchs, particularly John Sobiefki; but no prince
has paid them more attention than the prefent king Staniflaus
Auguftus. His munificence in this particular has been attended with the happieft effects. The Polifh literati have,
within a few years, given to the public a much greater variety
of elegant performances than ever appeared in any former
period of the fame length. What is more material, a tafte for
fcience has fpread itfelf among the nobles, and begins to be
regarded as an accomplifhment. The enlargement of mind,
derived by thefe licentious fpirits from this new purfuit, has
already weaned feveral of them from their habits of barbarous
turbulence, and greatly humanized their civil deportment.
It may in time teach them thoroughly to comprehend the true
intereft of their country, and the expedience of due fubordi-
nation, hitherto deemed incompatible with liberty : thefe petty
defpots will, perhaps, be induced to lay afide that contempt
for their vaffals; they will perceive that the burghers and peafants are the true fupports of their country; and that Poland
wants nothing but juftice and order to become as flourifhing
as the neighbouring ftates.

During my ftay at Warfaw I vifited the feveral prifons;
and made inquiries into the nature of the various tribunals,
and into the different modes of punifhment for criminal offences: my engaging in this employment was principally
owing to a cafual meeting I had at Vienna with the benevolent
Mr. Howard, whofe humane attention to the outcafts of fociety has reflected fo much honour on himfelf and his country.
Informing him that I was proceeding to the Northern kingdoms, I intimated an intention to examine the ftate of the prifons and penal laws in thofe countries; and profeffed a readi-
nefs to lay before him the refult of my obfervations. Mr.

A a 2　　　　　　　　　Howard

Howard approved my defign, fuggefted feveral ufeful hints,
and even dictated fome fpecific queftions tending greatly to
facilitate my inquiries.

I fhall not enter upon a defcription of the prifons in Warfaw, as they afforded fcarcely any thing worthy of particular
obfervation ; I fhall therefore confine myfelf to the general
adminiftration of juftice.

Atrocious crimes, fuch as murder, &c. are punifhed by be-
heading or hanging; leffer delinquencies by whipping, hard
labour, and imprifonment : the nobles never fuffer any corporal punifhment; but are liable only to imprifonment and
death.   Torture was abolifhed in 1776, by an edict of the
diet, introduced by the influence of the king ; a regulation as
expreffive of his majefty's judgement as of his benevolence.
It is an infinite fatisfaction to fee the rights of humanity extending themfelves in countries, where they had been but little known ; a circumftance that muft caft a great reflection on
thofe nations which, like France, have attained the higheft
pitch of civilization, and yet retain the ufelefs and barbarous
cuftom of torture *.

The defects of the police in this country are by no circumftances fo ftrongly evinced, as by the frequent impunity of the
moft atrocious crimes : this abufe may be traced from the
following caufes. 1. The greateft criminals find at times little
difficulty in engaging the protection of fome of the principal
nobles, who occafionally affemble their vaffals and retainers
in arms, and drive the officers of juftice from their lands. This
anarchy refembles the ftate of Europe in the 14th century,
during the prevalence of the feudal laws, when every great
baron poffeffed territorial jurifdiction, and was almoft equal in

---

* *La queftion preparatoire*, or the infliction
of torture, for forcing the confeffion of a
crime from an accufed perfon, has indeed been
lately abolifhed in France ; but the torture
ufed for the difcovery of accomplices is ftill
retained.

authority

authority to the king.   2. The law, efteemed by the Polifh gentry the great bulwark of their liberty, which enacts *, that no gentleman can be arrefted for mifdemeanors until he is convicted of them, notwithftanding the ftrongeft degree of prefumptive proof: the offender, of courfe, if likely to be found guilty, takes care to withdraw himfelf before the completion of the procefs.   Murder indeed, and robbery on the highway, and a few other capital crimes, are excluded from this privilege: but even in thofe flagrant enormities no gentleman can be taken into cuftody, unlefs actually apprehended in the commiffion of the offence; and when the crime is thus pofitively afcertained, which in the nature of things can feldom occur, the culprit cannot be fentenced to capital punifhment by any other tribunal than a diet.   3. The right which every town poffeffes of having its own criminal courts of juftice, with judges felected folely from the inhabitants.   Many of thefe towns are at prefent reduced to fuch a low ftate, as fcarcely to deferve the name of villages: in thefe places, of courfe, the judges are neceffarily perfons of the loweft defcription, and totally unqualified for the difcharge of their high office.   Innocence and guilt, by this means, are often not diftinguifhed, and as often wantonly confounded.   Not only the power of levying difcretionary fines, but the infliction of corporal punifhment, and even of death itfelf, is entrufted to thefe contemptible tribunals.   The chancellor Zamoifki has, in the new code of laws which he is preparing for the infpection of the diet, defcribed the abufes of thefe petty courts of juftice in the moft forcible language; and propofes, as the only adequate remedy of the evil, to annihilate this right of penal jurifdiction in all but nine of the principal towns.   4. There are no public officers whofe province it is to profecute the offenders in the king's name.   Hence, even in cafe of

* Neminem captivabimus nifi jure victum.

4

murder,

murder, robbery upon the highway, and the moſt atrocious crimes, the delinquent generally eſcapes, unleſs ſome individual indicts and brings him to trial : this ſeldom happens, as the proceſs is attended with no ſmall ſhare of expence. The juriſdiction of the great marſhal is almoſt the only exception to this flagrant defect of common juſtice. His juriſdiction is in force in the place where the king reſides, and to the diſtance of three Poliſh miles. Within that diſtrict the great marſhal can arreſt and proſecute for crimes of felony without any plaintiff. In caſes alſo of high treaſon, certain officers of the crown, called *inſtigatores*, are impowered of their own motion to cite ſuſpicious perſons before the diet. 5. The power which every plaintiff poſſeſſes of with-drawing his proſecution, even in caſes of the greateſt enormity : this cuſtom ſcreens all but the indigent from the purſuit of juſtice ; as perſons of moderate property are generally able to bribe the neceſſity or avarice of their proſecutor. This practice, founded on a narrow principle, that outrages againſt individuals are merely private, not public offences, is an inſtance of the groſſeſt barbariſm, which all civilized nations have renounced ; for it requires a very ſmall degree of legiſlative improvement to perceive, that private wrongs, when unchaſtized, become highly injurious to the community at large, by affording encouragement to ſimilar offences.

In viſiting the priſons I ſaw the bad effects of this uſage exemplified in a ſtriking inſtance. Two perſons, indicted for the aſſaſſination of a Jew, had been permitted to remain in priſon upwards of a twelvemonth, without being brought to a trial. The widow of the deceaſed, upon whoſe accuſation they were impriſoned, having agreed, on the payment of a ſtipulated ſum, to drop the ſuit and grant them a releaſe, their inability to ſatisfy her demand had been the only reaſon for detaining them ſo long in confinement ; and as when I ſaw
them

them they had juft raifed the money, they were upon the point of obtaining a final difcharge.

From this fketch of the adminiftration of juftice in this country, the expediency of a thorough reformation is very apparent. That able legiflator count Zamoifki, in the new code of laws which I have frequently had occafion to mention, has paid particular attention to the amendment of the criminal laws. But as any innovations in the courts of juftice, calculated to produce any effential benefit, muft materially infringe the privileges of the nobles, and counteract the national prejudices, the moft ufeful code can fcarcely expect to receive the fanction of the diet.

The laws relating to debtors are as follow. The creditor proceeds againft the debtor at his own expence; and, until the trial is finifhed, allows him eight grofchens, or three half-pence, a day for his maintenance; when the debt is proved, the creditor is releafed from the above-mentioned contribution: the debtor continues in prifon, at the difcretion of his creditor, until the debt is difcharged; and, if he has no means of fubfiftence, is obliged to maintain himfelf by working with the other delinquents in cutting wood, fawing ftone, or cleaning the ftreets. In cafe a gentleman contracts a debt, an action lies againft his lands and goods, and not againft his perfon, unlefs he gives a note of hand with a double fignature, one intended as an afcertainment of the debt, the other as a renunciation of his exemption from arrefts; but a perfon of high diftinction, even though he fhould bind himfelf by this engagement, can bid defiance to all danger of imprifonment.

C H A P. VI.

Departure from Warſaw.——Bialliſtock.——*Entertainment at the
counteſs of* Braniſki's *palace.*——*Dutchy of* Lithuania.——*Its
union with* Poland.——*Deſcription of* Grodno.——*Diets.*——*Phy-
ſic garden.*——*General productions of* Lithuania.——*Account of
the Wild-ox.*——*Of the Remiz and its pendent neſt.*——*Manufactures.*——*Entertainments.*——*Hoſpitality of the* Poles.——*Election-
dinner, and ball.*

BOOK II.

BEFORE we quitted Warſaw we received another inſtance
of his majeſty's wonderful condeſcenſion, a letter written
with his own hand to the poſt-maſter at Grodno, ordering that
we ſhould receive every accommodation which could be procured, and that we ſhould be permitted to viſit the manufactures and every object of curioſity.

We quitted the capital on the 10th of Auguſt, croſſed the
Viſtula, and paſſed through the ſuburbs of Praga. About an
Engliſh mile from Warſaw a foreſt begins, and continues, with
little interruption, to the diſtance of eighteen miles. At Wen-
grow we obſerved a fine corps of Ruſſian troops quartered in
the village. Some of the places in our route, though extremely wretched, enjoyed their own police and courts of juſtice : they conſiſted of wooden huts, moſtly thatched, ſome
roofed with wood, and a few with tiles. The country was
chiefly ſandy and level until we arrived at the Bog, which we
croſſed at Gran: the river was broad and ſhallow. We
aſcended from its banks a ſmall riſe, and found a better ſoil, and
the country more diverſified. The road was not unpleaſant,
running through fields ſown with different ſpecies of corn,
hemp, and flax ; but we never loſt ſight of the foreſt, and always

ways faw it fkirting the horizon. In many places I obferved the wood encroaching upon the fields, and young trees fhooting up in great numbers wherever cultivation had been neglected. I was informed that this is the cafe in moft parts of Poland, many traces of former enclofures, and even the veftiges of paved ftreets, being difcernible in the center of the forefts.

The largeft place we paffed through was Bielfk, capital of the palatinate of Podalachia, where the dietine for the diftrict is held : it is little better than a miferable village, though called, in the geographical defcriptions of Poland, a large town. Between Bielfk and Woytfzi, our wheel was nearly taking fire, and while we ftopped at a fmall village to have it greafed, I entered feveral cottages, which I found infinitely worfe even than thofe wretched dwellings which I had before examined in the towns where the inhabitants were more free; in the latter we obferved furniture and fome conveniences; in thefe nothing but the bare walls. The peafants were perfect flaves, and their habitations and appearance correfponded with their miferable fituation : I could fcarcely have figured to myfelf fuch objects of poverty and mifery. The country we traverfed from Warfaw to Bialliftock was in general fandy; but in fome places the foil was very rich. All parts were fit for cultivation, and many fpots had the appearance of great fertility. We remarked, however, that the harveft, even in the moft fruitful tracts, was but indifferent; a circumftance evidently owing to the defect in hufbandry.

We arrived late in the evening at Bialliftock, a very neat and well-built town. The ftreets were broad, and the houfes, which were in general plaftered, ftood detached from each other at uniform diftances. The fuperior neatnefs of Bialliftock is owing to the illuftrious family of Branifki, whofe palace ftands clofe to the town, and who have contributed to ornament their place of refidence. It belongs to the countefs

BOOK
II.
Braniſki, ſiſter of the preſent king, and widow of the late great general Braniſki ; who, notwithſtanding this alliance, warmly proteſted againſt the election of his preſent majeſty.

The morning after our arrival, the counteſs, to whom we had a letter from prince Staniſlaus Poniatowſki, honoured us with a moſt polite invitation to dinner, and ſent her carriage to convey us to the palace.   We were moſt politely received by our noble hoſteſs, and were convinced from her amiable manners, condeſcending behaviour, and lively flow of converſation, that affability and good ſenſe are natural to the family of Poniatowſki.

We found a large company aſſembled at table, whom the counteſs had invited to partake of her hoſpitable board, which was elegantly ſupplied with every delicacy.   Among other topics, the converſation turned upon our mode of travelling through a country ſo poor and wretched, and ſo deficient in comfortable accommodations.   " I ſuppoſe," ſaid a Poliſh gentleman, " you carry your beds with you ;" to which we replied in the negative.   " How do you ſleep then ?"—" Upon " ſtraw, when we can get it ; and, when we are not ſo for- " tunate, upon the floor, upon a bench, or upon a table."— " You take your proviſions," returned the Pole.—" Very ſel- " dom."—" How do you live then ?"—" Upon what we can " procure : one of our ſervants is ſent before, and generally con- " trives to obtain ſome kind of proviſion, which may ſooth, " if not ſatiſfy, the demands of hunger ; but we have travel- " ling appetites, and are not faſtidious."—" You are not, how- " ever, without knives, forks, and ſpoons ; for ſuch conveni- " ences are not known among the peaſants."—" We each of " us carry a claſp-knife ; are now and then ſo fortunate as to " meet with a wooden ſpoon ; and never regret the want of a " fork."   Here our noble hoſteſs made a propoſal to ſupply us with knives, forks, and ſpoons, together with wine and

proviſion :

provifion : upon our declining this offer, fhe pleafantly replied, " Perhaps you are above accepting them; I know the
" Englifh are very haughty ; will you purchafe them ?" We
made anfwer, that we were not afraid of laying ourfelves under any obligations to a perfon of her politenefs and generofity;
but that the object of our travels was to gratify curiofity rather
than appetite; and that we thought ourfelves moft likely to
become acquainted with the domeftic œconomy of the peafants, by partaking of their accommodations, and by relying
on them for the fupply of our wants. Willing, however, not
to appear rude in a rejection of the whole offer, we accepted a
few bottles of wine.

The countefs did us the honour to conduct us herfelf
through the apartments of the palace, which is a large building in the Italian tafte ; and, on account of its grandeur and
magnificence, generally called the Verfailles of Poland. It
was formerly only a royal hunting feat ; John Cafimir gave
it, together with Bialliftock and other eftates, to Czarniefki, a
general highly diftinguifhed by his victories over the Swedes
at the time that Poland was nearly crufhed by her enemies.
Among the curiofities preferved in the palace is a golden cup,
which Czarniefki ufed after the cuftom of thofe times to wear
faftened to his girdle ; and an embroidered fafh which he took
among the fpoils after a defeat of Charles X. and fuppofed to
belong to that monarch. Czarniefki left one daughter, who
married Branifki the father of the late great general, by which
marriage the eftate came into that family. There is one apartment which Auguftus III. ufed to occupy whenever he paffed
this way to the diet of Grodno ; and which, out of refpect to
the memory of their late fovereign, is left in its original ftate.
In another room is a fine portrait of Auguftus in his royal
robes, with his head fhaved in the Polifh fafhion, as he appeared on the day of his coronation. In the afternoon we

drove

drove about the park and grounds, which are very extenfive, and elegantly laid out in the Englifh tafte.

We clofed this agreeable day with a fupper at the palace, and took leave, with regret, of its amiable and noble miftrefs.

Auguft 13. We fat off early from Bialliftock : for fome way we traverfed a continued foreft ; afterwards the country became more open, abounding with corn and pafture ; the towns and villages were long and ftraggling ; all the houfes, and even the churches, of wood; crouds of beggars furrounded our carriage whenever we ftopped ; Jews made their appearance without end. About four we arrived at Grodno ; we firft paffed through fome wretched fuburbs inhabited by Jews, and ferried over the Niemen, which is broad, clear, and fhallow, afcended the rifing banks, and came to the town, which is built upon an eminence overlooking the river.

Though Vilna is the capital, yet Grodno is efteemed the principal town in Lithuania.

Formerly Lithuania was entirely unconnected with Poland, and was governed by its own fovereigns under the title of great-dukes. From that rivalry which ufually fubfifts between contiguous ftates, the two nations were engaged in a feries of perpetual wars until 1386, when the great-duke Ladiflaus Jaghellon, having efpoufed Hedwige and embraced the Chriftian religion, was raifed to the Polifh throne, and reigned over both countries.

Ladiflaus foon became fo fincere a convert to the new religion, which he at firft adopted from interefted views, that he endeavoured to propagate its doctrines among his idolatrous fubjects in Lithuania. In fubferviency to this great work, he ordered the hallowed groves to be cut down, the oracular fhrine to be deftroyed, the facred fire to be extinguifhed, and the ferpents worfhiped as Gods by his fuperftitious fubjects to be flain. A belief univerfally prevailed among the people,

that

that whoever profanely attempted to deſtroy theſe objects of their worſhip, would be ſtruck with inſtantaneous death : when the falſity of this tradition was proved by the impunity of thoſe concerned in the ſuppoſed ſacrilege, the Lithuanians flocked in ſuch crouds to be converted, that the prieſts could only beſtow ſeparate baptiſm on perſons of diſtinction ; but diſtributed the multitude in ranks, and, ſprinkling them with water, gave one chriſtian name to each rank without diſtinction of ſex *. Ladiſlaus, having thus introduced the Chriſtian religion into Lithuania, nominated his brother Caſimir Skirgello governor of that duchy, and returned to Poland ; but a civil war being excited by the ambition of Alexander, ſurnamed Vitoldus, and by the diſcontents of the people, ſtill attached to their Pagan rites, Lithuania was for ſome time a ſcene of tumult and hoſtility. At length, by a compromiſe in 1392, Vitoldus was appointed great-duke, and Ladiſlaus contented himſelf with a reſervation of nominal ſovereignty.

In 1401 the nobles of Lithuania aſſembled at Vilna, and entered upon an offenſive and defenſive alliance with the king and republic of Poland. In 1413 it was ſtipulated, in a diet of Poles and Lithuanians held in the town of Hrodlo, that, upon the demiſe of Vitoldus, the Lithuanians ſhould acknowledge no other great-duke but the perſon who was appointed by the king, and with the agreement of the two nations ; that, in caſe Ladiſlaus died without iſſue, the Poles ſhould elect no king without the conſent of Vitoldus and the Lithuanians ; and that a diet, compoſed of repreſentatives from both nations, ſhould meet whenever it was thought neceſſary, at Lublin or

---

* " Ægrè gens barbara maj: rem ſuorum " religiones relinquebat. Sed cum juſſu regis " ſacer ignis extinctus, templum aráque ejus " diruta & adytum, unde oracula à ſacerdote " edebantur, everſum Vilnæ eſſet, necatique " ſerpentes, & ſucciſi luci nulla cujuſquam " læſione," &c. &c.

" Sed cum immenſi laboris eſſet ſingulos " ſacro fonte tingere, nobilioribus tantum hic " honor habitus : reliquum verò vulgus turmatim diſtributum, aquâ luſtrali ſive ſacrâ " à ſacerdotibus conſperſum eſt, unumque " nomen cuique turmæ tam virorum quàm " mulierum inditum." Cromer, p 368.

Parzow *. From the demife of Vitoldus, who expired in 1439 in the 8oth year of his age, the great-dukes were fometimes, in conformity to this compact, nominated by the kings of Poland ; at other times, in violation of it, by the Lithuanians. At length Sigifmond I. fortunately united in his perfon the two fovereignties, and was fucceeded in both by his fon Sigifmond Auguftus.

Hitherto the connection between the two nations had been more an alliance than an union ; but Sigifmond Auguftus having no children, and being the only furviving male heir of the Jaghellon family, planned the union of Poland and Lithuania, left upon his deceafe the connection fhould be diffolved, and the two nations be again governed by different princes. After fome difficulties, and being once fruftrated in his attempt, he obtained, from a general diet held at Lublin in 1569, that Poland and Lithuania fhould from henceforth be united and confidered as one nation ; that one fovereign fhould be chofen conjointly by both people; that the Lithuanians fhould fend nuntios to the general diet, be admitted into the fenate, and have an equal fhare in the public honours and employments ; that no alliance fhould be made with foreign powers, and no embaffadors difpatched without the confent of both parties ; that the fame money fhould pafs current in both countries; in fhort, that they fhould have no diftinction of privilege or intereft. Upon the ratification of this union, Sigifmond Auguftus renounced all hereditary right to Lithuania. From this period the fame perfon has been uniformly elected king of Poland and great-duke of Lithuania ; and the two nations have been incorporated into one republic †.

Grodno is a large and ftraggling place, but contains no more than 3000 Chriftians, excluding the perfons employed in the manufactures, and 1000 Jews. It has greatly the appearance

* Dlugoffus & Cromer.   † Lengnich, Jus Pub. v. I. p. 30 to 33.

of

of a town in decline; containing a mixture of wretched hovels, falling houfes, and ruined palaces, with magnificent gate-
ways, remains of its ancient fplendour. A few habitations in
good repair make the contraft more ftriking.

The old palace, in which the kings ufed to refide during the
diets, ftood upon an hill of fand rifing abruptly from the river, and forming part of its bank: fome remains of the ancient walls ftill exift. Oppofite to this hill is the new palace,
built, but never inhabited, by Auguftus III. as it was not finiſhed at the time of his death. In this palace are the apartments wherein the diets are held, or rather will be held if
they are ever again fummoned to Grodno. According to the
treaty of Hrodlo, Lublin, or Parzow, or any other more commodious town, was appointed for the meeting of the Polifh
and Lithuanian deputies; but in the articles of union it was
ftipulated, that Warfaw fhould be the place where the reprefentatives of the two nations were to affemble *. In 1673, as
I have already obferved, it was enacted, that every third diet
fhould be held at Grodno; and, in conformity to this law, the
firft national affembly was convened here in 1678 under John
Sobiefki. But when the next turn of Grodno arrived, that
monarch fummoned the diet to Warfaw: the Lithuanians
ftrongly oppofed this infringement of their rights; and their
deputies, inftead of proceeding to Warfaw, where the king,
fenate, and nuntios of Poland were met, repaired to this town,
and formed a feparate diet. In order to prevent a civil war,
which this divifion might occafion, a negotiation took place,
and it was at length fettled, that the diet of 1673 fhould affemble at Warfaw, but be called the diet of Grodno, and that
the marfhal fhould be chofen from the Lithuanian nuntios †.
From that time the diets have been occafionally fummoned to
Grodno; until the reign of his prefent majefty, when they

* Lengnich, Jus Pub. v. II. p. 315, &c.   † Vie de Sobiefki, p. 19.

have

have been uniformly held at Warfaw; and this innovation has been tacitly agreed to by the Lithuanians, on account of the diftance of this town from the royal refidence, as well as in confideration of the troubles which convulfed the country.

We carried a letter of recommendation to Mr. Gillibert, a French naturalift of great learning and abilities, who has the fuperintendence of the college and phyfic garden. The king of Poland has eftablifhed in this place a Royal Academy of Phyfick for Lithuania, in which ten ftudents are inftructed in phyfick, and twenty in furgery. They are all lodged, boarded, and taught at his majefty's expence: an inftitution that reflects the higheft honour upon the king, and which has greatly flourifhed under the royal patronage and protection. The phyfic garden, which did not exift in 1776, made, when I paffed through the town in 1778, a very refpectable appearance; which was entirely owing to Mr. Gillibert's attention and care. It contained 1500 exotics, amongft which were feveral delicate American plants fown in the open air, and which thrived remarkably well in this climate. Mr. Gillibert told me, that he had difcovered 200 fpecies of plants in Lithuania, which were only thought indigenous in Siberia, Tartary, and Sweden; and that in the whole duchy he had obferved 980 fpecies, exclufive of the forts common to moft countries in Europe.

Mr. Gillibert had lately formed a fmall collection, chiefly confifting of the productions of Lithuania; and was employed in arranging materials for a natural hiftory of this duchy: he propofes to begin his publications upon that fubject with a *Flora Lithuanica*; which will be fucceffively followed by an account of the mineralogy, infects, quadrupeds, and birds. Confidering the infant ftate of natural knowledge in this country, the defign will require great length of time and perfeverance before it is completed; but there is nothing which affiduity and attention will not effect.

The

The animals roving in the boundlefs forefts of Lithuania are the bear, the wolf, the elk, the wild-ox, the lynx, the beaver, the glouton, the wild-cat, &c.

At Grodno I had an opportunity of feeing a female of the wild-ox, probably the fame quadruped which is defcribed by Ariftotle under the name of *Bonafus*, ftyled *Urus* in the Commentaries of Cæfar, and called *Bifon* by fome naturalifts. That which fell under my obfervation was not full grown, about the fize of a common Englifh cow, fhaped like a buffalo, but without the protuberance over its fhoulders : its neck was high and thick, and covered with long hair, or mane, which fringed down the throat and breaft, and hung almoft to the ground, fomewhat refembling that of an old lion : the forehead was narrow, with two horns turning inwards *, and the tongue of a bluifh colour. The male, as we were informed, is fometimes fix feet in height, and is more fierce and fhaggy than the female.

Linnæus has claffed the *Bonafus*, the *Urus*, and the *Bifon* (probably the fame animal with different names) under three fpecies ; Buffon reduces them to two, the *Urus* and the *Bifon* ; and Pennant has comprifed them all under one fpecies †. His opinion has been lately adopted by Pallas, in a very curious differtation publifhed in the Acts of the Imperial Academy of Sciences of St. Peterfburgh. That celebrated naturalift informs us, that this fpecies of the wild-ox, which was formerly very common in Europe, exifts no where in that continent, but in thefe Lithuanian forefts, in fome parts of the Carpathian mountains, and perhaps in the Caucafus. He agrees alfo with

---

* Ariftotle defcribes the horns of the *Bonafus* as γαμψα και κικαμμινα προς αλληλα, " *crooked and bending towards each other.*" A circumftance which feems to have puzzled fome naturalifts who have commented upon Ariftotle, who did not confider that the figure of the horns varies exceedingly in the fame fpecies, in a wild or tame ftate, and cannot be admitted as forming a fpecific difference. See Arift. Hift. Anim. L. IX. c. 45. alfo Camus Hift. des Animaux, cited in Maty's Review for April, 1783, p. 313. &c.

† Syftema Naturæ. Buffon's Hift. Nat. Pennant's Hift. of Quad. p. 15.

BOOK
II.

Buffon, in holding the *bifon* or wild-ox of America to be only a variety of the *urus* changed by the climate *.

Lithuania is very rich in ornithology : among the birds of prey the eagle and vulture are very common. The *Remiz* † or little fpecies of titmoufe, called *Parus Pendulinus*, is not unfrequently found in thefe parts. The wondrous ftructure of its pendent neft induced me to give an engraving of both that and the birds themfelves. They are of the fmalleft fpecies of titmice. The head is of a very pale bluifh afh colour ; the forepart of the neck and the breaft tinged with red ; the belly white ; wings black ; back and rump of a yellowifh ruft colour ; quill feathers cinereous, with the exterior fides white ; the tail ruft-coloured. The male is fingularly diftinguifhed from the female by a pair of black-pointed whifkers.

Its neft is in the fhape of a long purfe, which it forms with amazing art, by interweaving down, gofs-a-mer, and minute fibres, in a clofe and compact manner, and then lining the infide with down alone, fo as to make a fnug and warm lodge for its young brood. The entrance is at the fide, fmall and round, with its edge more ftrongly marked than the reft of this curious fabrick : the bird, attentive to the prefervation of its eggs or little ones from noxious animals, fufpends it at the leffer end to the extremity of the flender twigs of a willow, or fome other tree, over a river. Contrary to the cuftom of titmice, it lays only four or five eggs : poffibly Providence hath ordained this fcantinefs of eggs to the *Remiz*, becaufe by the fingular inftinct imparted to it, it is enabled to fecure its young much more effectually from deftruction, than the other fpecies, which are very prolific.

Mr. Gillibert acquainted me that a great quantity of yei-

---

* Sur le Buffle à Queue de cheval in Nov. Act. Pet. 1771. Part II. p. 252, &c. Alfo in his Neue Nord. Beytrage, p. 2.

† I am indebted to that able naturalift, Mr. Tennant, for this defcription of the Remiz, and for the annexed plate.

low

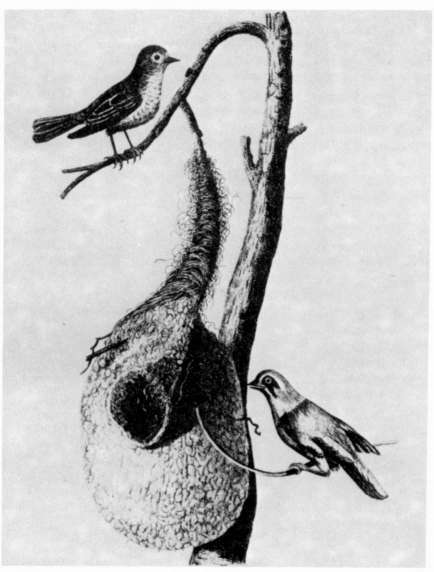

MALE and FEMALE REMIZ; or PENDULINE TITMOUSE.

Published according to Act of Parliament January 1, 1781, by Liddell in the Strand.

low amber is frequently dug up in the Lithuanian forests, sometimes in pieces as large as one's fist, and that it is probably the production of a small refinous pine *. He informed me that the duchy abounds in iron ochre, called by Linnæus *Tophus humofo ochreaceus*, and defcribed by Wallerius † under the article of *Ferrum limofum*, which produces forty pounds of metal in an hundred weight; that it yields alfo feveral fpecies of copper and iron pyrites; black agate, which always bears a refemblance to the roots of pines ‡; detached maffes of red and grey granite; pudding ftones, containing chryftals of white quartz; the *echinus* agatized; a prodigious quantity of falfe precious ftones, particularly amethyfts, topazes, garnets, alfo chalcedonies, cornelians, milky agates, the *oculus catti*, or cat's eye, jafpers, and particularly the red fpecies. He added, that Lithuania was extremely rich in marine petrefactions, and chiefly in thofe which are common in the Baltic: of thefe the madrepores are the moft numerous, and amongft others

---

* Naturalifts have long differed concerning the origin of amber. Some maintain it to be an animal fubftance : others clafs it among the minerals ; fome affert, that it is a vegetable oil united with a mineral acid ; but the moft common opinion feems to be that it is a foffil bitumen. A few, with Mr. Gillibert, hold it to be the refinous juice of a pine hardened by age : this latter opinion was alfo maintained by the antient Romans. Amber is moft ufually found upon the fea-coaft, and though frequently difcovered feveral feet beneath the furface of the ground, yet has been fuppofed to have never been dug up at any confiderable diftance from the fea ; a circumftance which has led feveral naturalifts to conjecture, that it owes, in a great meafure, its production to the fea. But this hypothefis is confuted by the difcovery of thefe large pieces of amber in the heart of the Lithuanian forefts far from any fea. See Plin. Hift. Nat. L. 37. Sec. XI. Tacitus de Mor. Germ. Macquaire's Chymiftry, v. II. p. 206. Bifhop of Landaff's (Dr. Watfon) Effays on Chym. v. III. p. 12. and particularly Walle-

rius Syft. Min. v. II. p. 115—117. where the reader will find a lift of the principal naturalifts, who have written upon Amber.

† Wallerius Syft. Min. v. II. p. 255.

‡ Mr. Gillibert thus defcribes thefe agates in the Acts of the Imperial Academy of Sciences. " Mr. Gillibert dans une lettre à Mr. " le Profeffeur Pallas, parle d'une petrifica- " tion très remarquable, commune dans ce " pays [Lithuania], laquelle eft agathe par " fa nature, mais refemble parfaitement par " fa forme, à des racines de fapins pétrifiées. " Les racines agatifées font bandées de noir " autour de leur axe, et incruftées d'une " écorfe grife ou blanchâtre. On en trouve " à demi petrifiées ; et toutes donnent une " odeur empyreumatique au feu, qui provient " d'un refte de principe bitumeneux. D'Ail- " leurs toutes les petrifications d'origine ma- " rine fe trouvent agatifées dans ce pays cou- " vert d'un fable fin, dont les eaux peuvent " extraire un principe pétrifiant de cette na- " ture." Nov. Act. Acad. Pet. for 1777, p. 45.

the

the *Corallinum Gothlandicum* is not uncommon; which is deſcribed in the firſt volume of the *Amœnitates Academicæ* * as
extremely rare.

The next morning we viſited the manufactures eſtabliſhed
by the king in 1776. They were carrying on in wooden ſheds,
built by Auguſtus III. for ſtables, which had been converted
into temporary working looms, and dwelling houſes for the
accommodation of the manufacturers; the whole eſtabliſhment was expected to be ſoon removed to Loſſona, a village
near Grodno, where convenient buildings, conſtructing at his
majeſty's expence, were nearly finiſhed for that purpoſe. The
principal manufactures are cloth and camlets, linen and cot-
tons, ſilk ſtuffs, embroidery, ſilk ſtockings, hats, lace, fire
arms, needles, cards, bleaching wax, and carriages. The
country furniſhes ſufficient wool, flax, hemp, beavers hair,
and wax for the ſupply of the manufactures which employ
thoſe commodities; but the ſilk, cotton, iron, colours, gold
and ſilver for the embroidery, and fine thread from Bruſſels
for the lace, are imported.

The manufactures employ 3000 perſons, including thoſe
diſperſed in the contiguous villages, who ſpin linen and worſted
thread. There are ſeventy foreigners, who direct the different
branches; the reſt are natives belonging to the king's demeſnes.
The apprentices are boys and girls, all children of Poliſh peaſants, who are clothed and fed, and have beſides a ſmall al-
lowance in money. The directors complain that there is no
emulation among them; and that, although they are better
fed and clothed than the other peaſants, yet they cannot excite
them to induſtry by any other means than force. Nor is this
a matter of wonder; for as they ſtill continue in a ſtate of ſervitude, if they acquire any unuſual profit, and carry it to their
parents, they are apprehenſive leſt it ſhould be taken away; it

* P. 211.

3   having

having frequently happened, that any little pittance, they had gained by their labour, has been wrefted from them, in order to pay the quit-rents which their parents owed to their lords. One of thefe apprentices, more fhrewd than the reft, faid to the director, who was trying to ftimulate her induftry, " What ad- " vantage fhall I obtain if I follow your advice ? let me be- " come ever fo fkilful in my trade, I fhall always continue " fubject to my mafter : the labour will be mine, and the pro- " fits his." To which obfervation no anfwer could be given. Moft of them appeared with fuch a fettled melancholy in their countenances, as made my heart ache to fee them ; and it was eafy to perceive that they worked from compulfion, and not from inclination. As fome remedy to this evil, it has been propofed, after a certain term of years, to give liberty to thofe who particularly excel, and diftinguifh themfelves by any ex- traordinary exertions. But this humane propofal has been rejected, from a notion that fuch perfons, when once made free, would no longer continue to work ; and that by thefe means the manufactures would be deprived of their beft hands. Though this inconvenience, however, might occafionally take place, yet the encouragement of fuch a regulation would beget alacrity and excite induftry, and would therefore create a greater number of artifts than it would emancipate. It would now and then occafion the lofs of a manufacturer ; but would dif- fufe fuch a knowledge of the manufacture, as to render the lofs immaterial.

Thefe manufactures are ftill in their infancy, but their in- ftitution reflects a confiderable luftre upon his majefty's reign ; and more particularly as his attention was not withdrawn from them during the civil convulfions which fo lately fhook his throne.

On the firft evening of our arrival at Grodno, a Polifh no- bleman, to whom we were introduced by Mr. Gillibert, invited us to fupper with fuch franknefs and cordiality, that it would have been rudenefs not to have accepted the invitation. After an hour's converfation, he configned us to the care of his wife, and retired ; nor did he again make his appearance the whole evening. This feeming inattention, fo contrary to the politenefs of the invitation, occafioned at firft fome furprize ; but we afterwards found that good manners equally directed his behaviour in both thefe inftances. Having before our arrival invited fome Polifh gentlemen to fup with him who could not converfe in French, and who drank freely, he thought juftly enough that we fhould pafs a more agreeable evening with the ladies. We had a fmall party at fupper, which was cheerful and agreeable, for the Poles are a very lively people, and the women in general amiable and well-bred.

We dined the following day with count Tyfenhaufen vice-chancellor of Lithuania : it was an election-dinner previous to the dietine, which was to affemble at Grodno, in order to chufe the reprefentatives of this diftrict for the approaching diet. There were eighty nobles at table, all, a few excepted, in their national drefs, and with their heads fhaved in the Polifh fafhion. Before dinner they faluted the count with great refpect, fome kiffing the hem of his garment, others ftooping down and embracing his legs. Two ladies were at table, and, as ftrangers, we had the poft of honour affigned to us, and were feated by them. It was my good fortune to fit next to one who was uncommonly entertaining and agreeable, and never fuffered the converfation to flag. After dinner feveral toafts went round :—the king of Poland—the diet—the ladies who were prefent—a good journey to us, &c. The mafter of the feaft named the toaft, filled a large glafs, drank it, turned it down to fhew that it was empty, and then paffed it to his next neighbour ; from whom it was circulated in fucceffion and with the fame ceremonies through the whole company.

The

The wine was champagne, the glafs large, and the toafts numerous : but there was no obligation, after the firft round, to
fill the glafs ; it was only neceffary to pour in a fmall quantity and pafs the toaft.   As it is efteemed a kind of hofpitality
in Poland to circulate the wine freely among the guefts, my
fair neighbour, when it was my turn to drink her health,
propofed that I fhould fill a bumper.   Though I had already.
drank one in honour of his majefty, and would willingly have
declined another, I could not difobey the orders of an agreeable
woman, and did the fame homage to beauty that I had before
paid to royalty.   The next turn was the health of the other
lady, which my fair neighbour urged me to do juftice to in
the fame manner ; but I excufed myfelf by intimating, that
fhe alone was deferving of fuch a tribute.

In the evening the count gave us a ball concluded by an
elegant fupper.   The ball was lively and agreeable.   The
company amufed themfelves with Polifh and Englifh country-
dances : the former was fimple, but not deficient in grace, and
accompanied by a moft pleafing air ; the company ftood in
pairs ; the firft man led his partner round the room in a kind
of ftep not much unlike that of a minuet, he then quitted
her hand, made a fmall circle, joined hands again, and repeated the fame movements until the conclufion.   The fecond couple began as foon as the firft had advanced a few
fteps, and was quickly followed by the remainder, fo that all
the parties glided after one another at the fame time.   The
Poles are very fond of this dance : although it has little variety, they continued it for half an hour without intermiffion,
and frequently renewed it during the courfe of the evening.
The intervals between this national dance were filled with
Englifh country dances, which they performed with equal
expertnefs, and with no lefs delight.   An elegant fupper, to
which

which only a felect party was invited, agreeably concluded the entertainment of the day.

The count politely preffed us to continue fome time at Grodno, and to take up our abode in his houfe; but as we were defirous of arriving at Peterfburgh before the commencement of the winter, we declined the invitation, which we fhould otherwife have accepted with the greateft pleafure. Some of the company, however, had kindly endeavoured to detain us by the following ftratagem : they privately defired the coach-maker employed in mending our carriage to execute the commiffion in a dilatory manner; and although we had accidentally difcovered this project, yet it was not without the moft urgent remonftrances that we obtained the neceffary repairs. In order to fpare our acquaintance the trouble of making, and ourfelves the pain of rejecting, any further folicitations, we thought it moft expedient to fteal away in the night without apprifing any one of our defign.

It was our intention to have proceeded to Vilna ; but as this was the time of electing nuntios, the poftmafter informed us, that for want of horfes we fhould be delayed upon the road at fome wretched village without a poffibility of proceeding; we therefore, very unwillingly, altered our route, to our great difappointment, as we wifhed much to have vifited the capital of Lithuania,

C H A P. VII.

Continuation of the tour through the duchy of Lithuania.——*Number of* Jews.——*Badnefs of the roads and want of accommodations.—-Clofe of the dietine at* Minfk.——*Poverty and wretchednefs of the natives.——Comparative view of the* Swifs *and* Polifh *peafants.——Remarks on the* Plica Polonica.

IN our route through Lithuania we could not avoid being ftruck with the fwarms of Jews, who, though very numerous in every part of Poland, feem to have fixed their head-quarters in this duchy. If you afk for an interpreter, they bring you a Jew ; if you come to an inn, the landlord is a Jew ; if you want poft-horfes, a Jew procures them, and a Jew drives them ; if you wifh to purchafe, a Jew is your agent : and this perhaps is the only country in Europe where Jews cultivate the ground : in paffing through Lithuania, we frequently faw them engaged in fowing, reaping, mowing, and other works of hufbandry.

The roads in this country are quite neglected, being fcarcely fuperior to by-paths winding through the thick foreft without the leaft degree of artificial direction : they are frequently fo narrow as fcarcely to admit a carriage ; and are continually fo obftructed by ftumps and roots of trees, and in many parts fo exceedingly fandy, that eight fmall horfes could fcarcely drag us along. The poftilions were frequently boys of ten or twelve years of age, hardy lads, who rode pofts of twenty and even thirty Englifh miles without a faddle, and with fcarcely any covering except a fhirt and a pair of linen drawers. The bridges acrofs the rivulets were fo weakly conftructed and fo old, that they feemed ready to crack with the weight

Vol. I.   D d   of

of the carriage, and we thought ourfelves fortunate in getting over them without an accident.

Some travellers have remarked, that the forefts, through which our route lay, are fet on fire by lightning or other natural caufes, and blaze for a confiderable time. At firft we conceived this reprefentation to be well-founded, as we difcovered in many parts evident traces of extenfive conflagrations. Upon inquiry, however, we were informed, that the peafants, being obliged annually to furnifh their landlords with a certain quantity of turpentine, fet fire to the trunks of the pines while ftanding, and catch it as it oozes from the ftems. We could obferve few trees without marks of fire upon them: fome were quite black, and nearly charred to cinder; fome half-burnt; others confiderably fcorched, but continuing to vegetate.

Auguft 15. After twenty hours inceffant travelling we arrived late in the evening at Bielitza, which is diftant about ninety Englifh miles from Grodno; and fet out before the break of day, anxious to reach Minfk on the morning of the 17th, when a dietine for the election of nuntios was to be affembled. We ftopped a fhort time at Novogrodec, which is all built of wood, except two or three ruinous brick-houfes, a convent that belonged to the Jefuits, and fome mouldering ftone-walls furrounding a fmall eminence, upon which are the remains of an old citadel. Near Novogrodec we paffed a large number of barrows, which the peafants call Swedifh burying-places. In this part the country was lefs fandy, of a richer foil, and fomewhat diverfified with hill and dale: the folitary extent of the forefts was more than ufual interfperfed with villages and dotted with fields of pafture, in which we obferved numerous herds of cattle.

Upon our arrival at the fmall village of Mir, we found that our original intention of reaching Minfk by the next morning

7   was

was fcarcely practicable, even if we continued our journey during the night. The diftance was between fixty and feventy miles; the night extremely dark; the roads bad, and, we were informed, that in fome places we fhould be obliged to crofs feveral bridges not very paffable even in the day without the utmoft circumfpection. Our defire therefore of being prefent at the election of nuntios gave way to thefe fuggeftions; and we facrificed the gratification of our curiofity to the confiderations of perfonal fafety. The pleafures of Mir certainly offered no inducement for delay : the poverty of the inhabitants denied a fcanty fupply of the moft ordinary refrefhments; the higheft entertainment which the place afforded being a fufpenfion of the dangers of travelling, and the fum of our comforts an intermiffion of fatigue.

The badnefs of our accommodations at Mir led us to confider Minfk (where we arrived on the evening of the 17th) as the feat of tafte and luxury. We there experienced comforts to which we had lately been ftrangers, a neat white-wafhed room with a brick floor, no fleas or flies, plenty of clean ftraw, good bread, and frefh meat. After a refrefhing night's reft, we fallied forth the next morning to the refectory of the Jefuits monaftery, the place where the nuntios had been chofen the preceding day. We had fome difficulty in gaining admittance ; at length a perfon, who appeared to be a man of confequence, came out and inquired in the German language our country and our bufinefs. Upon our anfwering that we were three Englifh gentlemen, defirous of feeing every thing worthy of obfervation, he expreffed much furprize at the plainnefs of our dreffes, particularly at our want of fwords. " In Po-" land," he faid, " every gentleman wears his fabre as a badge " of his rank, never appearing in public without it; and I " advife you to obferve this cuftom as long as you continue " in this country, if you wifh to be confidered as gentlemen."

Thanking

BOOK
II.

Thanking him for his advice, we accompanied him into the refectory, where we found the majority of the dietine still affembled, though not upon national bufinefs ; in plain Englifh, they were engaged in drinking, a no lefs effential appendage of a Polifh than a Britifh election.   One perfon, whom they feemed to treat with deference, was conftantly employed in' delivering drams to the electors, who were ftanding in different parts of the room : many ceremonies paffed at every circulation of the glafs; they touched their breafts, ftooped towards the ground, and drank the nuntios' and each other's health with great folemnity.   Several of the Polifh gentlemen converfed with me in the Latin tongue : they informed me, that every palatinate is divided into a certain number of diftricts, and that each diftrict chufes two nuntios.   I afked them whether the election of the diftrict of Minfk had been contefted ; they told me, that three candidates had offered themfelves.   I then demanded whether the elected nuntios were of the king's party ; and they anfwered, " We have in this " inftance complied with his majefty's recommendation."— " You have acted," I replied, " with great propriety : is he not " a good prince ?"—" A good prince !" returned the Poles, " yes, the moft excellent that ever filled a throne."

Minfk is a large place : two churches and the monaftery which belonged to the Jefuits are conftructed of brick ; and the remaining buildings, though formed of wood, have a neater look than the generality of dwellings in this country.   On returning to our inn, we received an invitation to dinner from a Polifh count ; but as the weather appeared fine, as our carriage was at the door, and all things prepared for our immediate departure, we determined to give up an opportunity of focial enjoyment to the expediency of purfuing our journey.

August 18. We were confiderably fatigued with our journey from Minfk to Smolewitzo, which, though fcarcely
thirty

thirty miles, employed us, on account of the badnefs of the roads and other unexpected delays, near twelve hours. The weather was cold and rainy, the wind high, the roads worfe than ufual; and the evening, when it fet in, extremely dark. We were almoft beginning to defpair of reaching our deftined ftation, when a noife of folding doors thrown open, and the rattling of our carriage upon a wooden floor, announced our actual arrival. The leathern blinds of our carriage having been clofely faftened down, in order to exclude the wind and rain, we were for a few moments held in fufpenfe into what kind of place we were admitted. Upon alighting, we found ourfelves in the middle of a large barn or fhed, at the further end of which we defcried two large pines, branches and all, in full blaze upon an hearth without a chimney: round it feveral figures, in full black robes and with long beards, were employed in ftirring a large cauldron fufpended over the flame. A belief in witchcraft, or a little fuperftition, might eafily have reprefented this party as a group of magicians engaged in celebrating fome myftic rites; but, upon nearer infpection, we recognized in them our old friends the Jews, preparing their and our evening repaft.

We fet out the next morning before day-break, as was our ufual cuftom, having no inducement to remain any longer than was abfolutely neceflary in thefe hovels, abounding in vermin, and in which filth and wretchednefs are united. Near Borifow we croffed the Berezyna, which has been erroneoufly laid down by fome modern geographers, as forming the new boundary between Ruffia and Poland; and on the other fide of the town paffed a camp of 2000 Ruffian troops, who were marching to Warfaw.

At Borifow the Jews procured us ten horfes, and placed them all in two rows, fix next the carriage, and four in front*.

* The ufual method of harneffing was by placing four a-breaft, and two in the foremoft row.

There

There was indeed much ingenuity in contriving this arrangement, which was effected in the following manner. The two
middle horfes in the hinder row were harneffed as ufual to
the fplinter-bars, their two neareft neighbours were faftened
to the extremities of the axle-tree, which projected confiderably on each fide beyond the boxes of the fore-wheels, and
the two outermoft were tied in the fame manner, by means of
long ropes, to the axle-tree of the hind-wheels : the four
horfes in front were harneffed to the pole and to the fplinter-
bars of the pole. Well affured that horfes, ranged in this
primitive manner, would require more room than the narrow
roads of Poland generally afforded, we endeavoured to perfuade the drivers to place them two by two ; but fuch was
their obftinacy or want of comprehenfion, we could not pre-
vail upon them to make any alteration. We therefore un-
loofed two horfes from the hindermoft row, and for that permiffion were obliged to compound for leaving the remaining
eight in their original pofition. In this manner we proceeded ;
and ftill found great difficulty in forcing our way through the
wildernefs, which was fo overgrown with thick underwood,
as in many parts fcarcely to admit the breadth of an ordinary
carriage. In fome places we were obliged to take off two, in
others four of the horfes ; and not uncommonly alighted, in
order to affift the drivers and fervants in removing fallen trees
which obftructed the way, in directing the horfes through the
winding paths, and in finding a new track along the almoft
impenetrable foreft. We thought ourfelves exceedingly fortunate, that our carriage was not fhaken to pieces, and that
we were not frequently overturned.

In various parts of the foreft, we obferved a circular range
of boards fixed to feveral trees about twelve feet from the
ground, and projecting three in breadth from the trunk.
Upon inquiry we were informed, that upon any great hunting

ing party, ladders were placed againſt theſe ſcaffoldings; and that when any perſon is cloſely preſſed by a bear, he runs up the ladder, and draws it up after him : the bear, although an excellent climber, is ſtopped in his aſcent by the projection of the boards.

We were very happy at length to reach Naitza, although we took up our ſtation in one of the moſt wretched of all the wretched cottages we had yet entered. The only article of furniture it afforded was a ſmall table, and the only utenſil a broken earthen pot, in which our repaſt was prepared, and which ſerved us alſo for diſhes and plates. We ate our meagre fare by the light of a thin lath of deal, about five feet in length, which was ſtuck into a crevice of the wainſcot, and hung over the table : this lath, thanks to the turpentine contained in it, ſerved us inſtead of a candle, of which there was not one to be found in the whole village of Naitza. It is ſurprizing, that the careleſs method of uſing theſe lights is not oftener attended with more dreadful effects; for the cottagers carry them about the houſe with ſuch little caution, that we frequently obſerved ſparks to drop from them upon the ſtraw which was prepared for our beds : nor were we able, by the ſtrongeſt expreſſions of fear, to awaken in them the ſlighteſt degree of circumſpection. For ſome time after coming into this country, we uſed to ſtart up with no ſmall emotion in order to extinguiſh the ſparks; but, ſuch is the irreſiſtible influence of cuſtom, we became at laſt ourſelves perfectly inſenſible to the danger of this practice, and caught all the indifference of the natives. I once even ſo far forgot myſelf as to hold a lighted ſtick for a conſiderable time over an heap of ſtraw, while I was negligently ſearching for ſome trifle. This ſupineneſs, which I ſo eaſily acquired in this particular, convinced me (if I may compare ſmall things with great), that I could live with the inhabitants at the foot of Mount Veſuvius

without

without dread of an eruption ; or fit unconcerned with the natives of Conſtantinople amid the devaſtations of the plague.

It is inconceivable how few are the wants of the Lithuanian peaſants ! Their carts are put together without iron ;
their bridles and traces are generally plaited from the bark of
trees, or compoſed merely of twiſted branches. They have
no other inſtrument but a hatchet, to conſtruct their huts, cut
out their furniture, and make their carts. Their dreſs is a
thick linen ſhirt and drawers, a long coarſe drugget coat, or
a ſheepſkin cloak, a round black felt cap lined with wool,
and ſhoes made from the bark of trees. Their huts are built
of trunks of trees heaped on each other, and look like piles of
wood in wharfs with penthouſe roofs. How very unlike the
Swiſs cottages, though conſtructed of the ſame materials !
Nor are their houſes more diſſimilar than their manners.
The ſtriking difference between the Swiſs and Poliſh peaſants,
in their very air and deportment, ſtrongly marks the contraſt
of their reſpective governments. The Swiſs are open, frank,
rough, but ready to ſerve you ; they nod their heads, or
ſlightly pull off their hats as you paſs by, but expect a return
of civility : they are rouſed by the leaſt rudeneſs, and are not
to be inſulted with impunity. On the contrary, the Poliſh
peaſants are cringing and ſervile in their expreſſions of reſpect ; they bowed down to the ground ; took off their hats
or caps, and held them in their hands till we were out of ſight ;
ſtopped their carts on the firſt glimpſe of our carriage ; in
ſhort, their whole behaviour gave evident ſymptoms of the
abject ſervitude under which they groaned. Yet liberty is
as often the ſubject of encomium in Poland as in Swiſſerland :
how different, however, are its operations in the two countries !
In the one it is equally diffuſed, and ſpreads comfort and happineſs through the whole community : in the other it centers
in a few, and is in reality the worſt ſpecies of deſpotiſm.

Before

3

Before I clofe my account of Poland, I fhall juft curforily mention, that in our progrefs through this country we could not fail obferving feveral perfons with matted or clotted hair, which conftitutes a diforder called *Plica Polonica :* it receives that denomination becaufe it is confidered as peculiar to Poland ; although it is not unfrequent in Hungary, Tartary, and feveral adjacent nations, and inftances of it are occafionally to be found in other countries.

According to the obfervations of Dr. Vicat, an ingenious Swifs phyfician long refident in Poland, and who has publifhed a fatisfactory treatife * upon this fubject; the *Plica Polonica* is fuppofed to proceed from an acrid vifcous humour penetrating into the hair, which is tubular † : it then exudes either from its fides or extremities, and clots the whole together, either in feparate folds, or in one undiftinguifhed mafs. Its fymptoms, more or lefs violent, according to the conftitution of the patient, or malignity of the difeafe, are itchings, fwellings, eruptions, ulcers, intermitting fevers, pains in the head, languor, lownefs of fpirits, rheumatifm, gout, and fometimes even convulfions, palfy, and madnefs. Thefe fymptoms gradually decreafe as the hair becomes affected. If the patient is fhaved in the head, he relapfes into all the dreadful complaints which preceded the eruption of the *Plica* ; and he continues to labour under them, until a frefh growth of hair abforbs the acrid humour. This diforder is thought hereditary ; and is proved to be contagious when in a virulent ftate.

Many phyfical caufes have been fuppofed to concur in rendering the *Plica* more frequent in thefe regions than in other parts : it would be an endlefs work to enumerate the various conjectures with which each perfon has fupported his favourite

---

* Memoire fur la Plique Polonoife.

† The dilatation of the hair is fometimes fo confiderable as to admit fmall globules of blood ; this circumftance, which however very rarely happens, has probably given rife to the notion, that the patient, if his hair is cut off, bleeds to death.

hypo-

BOOK
II. hypothefis : the moft probable are thofe affigned by Dr. Vicat. The firft caufe is the nature of the Polifh air, which is rendered infalubrious by numerous woods and moraffes ; and occafionally derives an uncommon keennefs even in the midft of fummer from the pofition of the Carpathian mountains ; for the fouthern and fouth-eafterly winds, which ufually convey warmth in other regions, are in this chilled in their paffage over their fnowy fummits. The fecond is unwholefome water : for although Poland is not deficient in good fprings, yet the common people ufually drink that which is neareft at hand, taken indifcriminately from rivers, lakes, and even ftagnant pools. The third caufe is the grofs inattention of the natives to cleanlinefs ; for experience fhews, that thofe who are not negligent in their perfons and habitations, are lefs liable to be afflicted with the plica, than others who are deficient in that particular. Thus perfons of higher rank are lefs fubject to this diforder than thofe of inferior ftations : the inhabitants of large towns than thofe of fmall villages ; the free peafants than thofe in an abfolute ftate of vaffalage ; the natives of Poland Proper than thofe of Lithuania. Whatever we may determine as to the poffibility that all, or any of thefe caufes, by themfelves, or in conjunction with others, originally produced the diforder ; we may venture to affert, that they all, and particularly the laft, affift its propagation, inflame its fymptoms, and protract its cure.

In a word, the *Plica Polonica* appears to be a contagious diftemper ; which, like the leprofy, ftill prevails among a people ignorant in medicine, and inattentive to check its progrefs ; but is rarely known in thofe countries, where proper precautions are taken to prevent its fpreading.

5